# ■ Life on the Line ■

**DOUBLEDAY**
NEW YORK   LONDON   TORONTO
SYDNEY   AUCKLAND

# Life on the Line

*One Woman's Tale of
Work, Sweat, and Survival*

**SOLANGE DE SANTIS**

PUBLISHED BY DOUBLEDAY
a division of Random House, Inc.
1540 Broadway, New York, New York 10036

DOUBLEDAY and the portrayal of an anchor
with a dolphin are trademarks of Doubleday,
a division of Random House, Inc.

*Book design by Claire Vaccaro*

Lines from *Black Dog* by Jimmy Page, Robert Plant,
and John Paul Jones © 1972 Superhype Publishing.
All Rights Administered by WB Music Corp.
All Rights Reserved. Used by Permission.

Library of Congress Cataloging-in-Publication Data
De Santis, Solange.
Life on the line : one woman's tale of work, sweat, and
survival / by Solange De Santis.
p.   cm.
1. De Santis, Solange. 2. Women automobile industry
workers—Ontario—Scarborough. 3. General Motors of
Canada—Employees.
I. Title.
HD6073.A82C23   1999
331.4'8292'092—dc21
[b]                98-51974
CIP

To my mother, Florence Stevenson De Santis:
teacher, mentor, scholar, leader.
What fun we had.

# ACKNOWLEDGMENTS

Although this book is dedicated to my mother, my father, Arthur A. De Santis, has had an equally profound effect upon my life. From my father, I learned that a man can truly love and admire a strong woman and never lose any of his own power. I saw—and continue to see—a life grounded in common sense, lived with eloquence and style.

My brother, Arthur L. De Santis, has been a source of support and friendship. His adventurous spirit is a constant inspiration. My husband, Camille G. Peters, raised an eyebrow when he realized he was going to appear in a book. I hope the results do not embarrass him too much and thank him for his graceful forbearance. My daughter, Florence De Santis Peters, showed excellent timing. Her arrival allowed me to combine maternity leave with book writing.

This book would still be a vague thought were it not for Jan Whitford of Westwood Creative Artists, who inexplicably stayed with this project for years and whose counsel I value. Peternelle van Arsdale of Doubleday in New York, with patience and wisdom, guided the material into its final form. I am grateful also to John Pearce and Pamela Murray of Doubleday Canada for their support.

Many people at General Motors shared their lives, experiences, and opinions with me. Names and identifying details have been changed, but I wish to express special thanks to: Bill Skinner, Dan Aleksich, Darlene Bond, Eric Dowling, and Gayle Hurmuses.

# CONTENTS

# ▪ Life on the Line ▪

# Through a Windshield, Darkly

It's late Friday night at the end of a long, hot summer week. Many of the good citizens of Toronto are settling in to watch the eleven-o'clock news, or climbing into bed, or leaving a bar. In the Trim 2 department of General Motors Corporation's Scarborough Van Plant, it's very quiet on the 5 P.M. to 1 A.M. shift, a purely relative concept considering the robotic racket from the body shop. But the rhythms seem muted tonight, muffled by air hanging heavy as a steel curtain.

The line hasn't gone down once—automatically the high point of any shift. Boxy vans glide through the plant, dragged by the squeaky assembly-line chain, inexorable as death. We've seen our supervisor, Lance, just once, at the beginning of the evening. No union reps, no fights, no company bulletins, no nothing—just us and our jobs.

After a week of stifling days, every single piece of machinery in the plant seems to radiate heat. Some folks space out, daydreaming, while literally going through the motions, waiting for the shift to end, waiting to be released into the cooler night. A big yellow floor fan near my workstation is whirring, trying to be helpful. As I finish a van, I step up to it, close my eyes, and let the warm breeze cool my flushed face a little. Thank God for this fan. I love this fan. It is the most important object in the world right now.

I'm installing windows on the passenger side of the vans—both the big window that you, Mr. or Ms. Van Passenger, roll down and the smaller window that you push outward. As they crawl by, painted but only half assembled, I pick up a triangular small-window assembly in my left hand and the main window in my right. They weigh a couple of pounds apiece. I walk around the van's open door and rest the small window, called a c.v. for some reason, against the steel skeleton of what will be the dashboard.

I slide the larger window down into the door and jam its bottom bracket onto the regulator, the X-shaped device that raises and lowers the window. Then I fit a black rubber window liner into the c.v. bracket and shove the c.v. into place next to the main window. I push the rest of the black liner around the main window frame. If you're short, like me, you shove it with your arms over your head. You do this two hundred times a day.

As I push on the liner, feeling my neck and shoulders ache, my heat-soggy dreaminess is interrupted. I spot one of the trainers in our department, Barry Harvey, and his buddy, forklift driver Monty Allen, tiptoeing behind the parts racks across the aisle with a Y-shaped piece of wood and a bag of water balloons.

They have constructed a truly magnificent weapon, a slingshot made of wood and rubber tubing that's so big one man holds the ends above his head and the other pulls back the cradle. Had Barry and Monty been medieval arms merchants, they would have had offers from every lord in Europe.

They have checked the aisle. Not a supervisor in sight. They are loading the siege engine. Monty is kneeling in the aisle, arms up, holding the ends. Barry is pulling back the rubber. They are aiming directly at me.

"Now, wait a minute, you guys!" I yell. "Yipes!" I duck behind the door of a van as a water balloon explodes off the window-subassembly machine next to the line, spray flying. "Ha! Missed me!" Another van is up to my station, so I have to abandon my cover and move into the open to heft the glass.

The saboteurs, who have had a liquid lunch in the parking lot, slink down the aisle, so I have to install the windows facing down the line, yet I glance nervously over my shoulder every few seconds. From roughly forty feet away, the balloons become flying bombs.

I look away from the ballistics crew to pay attention to my windows and—*whongggg!*—I hear the sound of a launch. *Blonk!* A loud clunk from behind me, but no spray. What the hey . . . I check the next van, a nifty dark-blue number, and notice a distinct dent in the lower passenger-side door. Upon further search, the water balloon, which is not broken, is found under a garbage bin.

"Holy shit." We gather around the dented truck, moving along in its stately procession on the line. "Look at that. You guys dented the truck." It's the sort of bend that can, and will, easily be hammered out in Final Repair, but we're in awe of the Iron Water Balloon. Looking at each other guiltily, we start giggling. I know I should be outraged at this wanton, childish vandalism, this utter flouting of the Quality Process, but at 11 P.M. on a Friday, at about the 150th window, this kind of behavior makes complete sense.

Someone farther down the line will find the dent; someone will fix it. Someone will buy this dark-blue van and never know (let's hope) that it was hit with a water balloon fired by human beings who had to do something to break up the heat, the noise, the dirt, the monotony.

The Iron Water Balloon makes my week worthwhile. Barry and Monty have no personal vendetta against me; in fact, I think they like me (mostly), and I like them (ditto). Right now I love them for their utterly juvenile piece of antiauthoritarian theater, a prank that jolted a few people out of contemplating their lot.

Not so long ago I was a boss and would have been considerably less amused. Now, picking up the 151st window, I watch with delight as they fire off another water balloon and it travels a good seventy-five feet down the aisle, splattering on the painted concrete floor. I am a prisoner of the line, and I am completely free, free of anyone's expectations beyond the correct installation of this window.

■

Another part of this person, the reporter, is looking at this from a vantage point far away, an out-of-coveralls experience. The worker jams in another window, fits another liner to the frame. The reporter, a visitor on this blue-collar planet, thinks, Yes, this is perfect. This is why I am here. This will make a terrific story.

# INTRODUCTION

Two things drew me toward General Motors' doomed Scarborough Van Plant: a rare chance, for a journalist, to live a news story and a chance to step over the line between white collar and blue collar.

The line is widening. As the industrial age enters its third century and the technology revolution its second, more of us work in carpeted, cubicled veal pens, staring at glowing screens, many times removed from the human labor that hides in dirty, dangerous places. There are 12.9 million production jobs now in the United States, compared to 14.1 million in 1980. Who made your computer keyboard? The one I'm using right now was made in Thailand. This trend will only pick up speed in the developed world as technology continues to advance and manufacturing jobs move offshore. The pervasive image of work, the one to which we are told we should all aspire, is more than ever the office.

Consider how dominant that image is already. Let's look at a selection of articles in some women's magazines: "Exercises You Can Do at Your Desk," "Find the Job That Best Suits You: Let the Stars Be Your Guide" (none of the jobs listed were blue collar, with the possible exception of gardener), "Cosmo's Guide to Hot-Weather Office Wear." Another article tells women how to beat stress at an all-female spa retreat. No tips on how to beat stress or exercise appropriately when you're on your feet eight hours a day. A city magazine's recent annual survey of "Who Earns What" listed compensation for people in eighty-two jobs. Of those, six were blue collar: exterminator, streetcar driver, prison worker, bike courier, car mechanic, and truck-company operations manager. Seventeen were presidents of companies or organizations—this, in a story that purported to show a wide range of occupations.

Make a list of popular television shows that have been set in a working-class environment: *Roseanne, Grace Under Fire, All in the Family, Sanford and Son, Married with Children, The Honeymooners.* Make another list of shows featuring doctors, detectives, lawyers, judges, executives, yuppies, even just plain rich folks (*Dallas, Dynasty,* et al.). Make allowances for the fact that everyone's a sucker for glamour, and you will still realize that we see far more of J. R. Ewing's level of society than of Ralph Kramden's.

My life on the line began in a bar, in the person of an autoworker who inadvertently jogged my curiosity about a world of work that had so far been nearly hidden to me. As I became friends with him and saw, through his eyes, how hard such a life can be, I wondered why I knew so little about what it's like to work in a factory. News stories mostly covered blue-collar people if there was a plant closing, a strike, or a disaster such as a fire or explosion. I and my office-dwelling friends drove cars, lived in houses, used all manner of appliances that someone else had put together. Occasionally someone would make a remark that indicated "we" despised the beer-bellied jerks who made our Cadillacs. We didn't value those jobs, and yet we couldn't live our comfortable modern lives without them.

I wondered why the work performed by "professionals" was often regarded as intrinsically more interesting and valuable to society than the manual laborer's. High-school teachers complain they can't find enough kids who want to learn a trade—perfectly respectable, well-paid, satisfying careers. The kids equate white-collar living with money, power, drama, excitement; blue-collar with losers.

When I had these thoughts, I had been a journalist for fifteen years, twelve as a business reporter. I had seen, most of the time, just one side of a story in all those years covering business. Perhaps if I'd reported on crime or the arts, with daily human dramas writ large, I wouldn't have been so restless. Although business certainly had its share of drama, far too much of my business writing—especially when I left local news—involved strategy and numbers.

The news story I saw a chance to inhabit had been rumored, dismissed, and feared for several years. After a few back-and-forth dances with the union in the late 1980s, GM announced the closing of a plant in suburban Toronto that made full-size cargo vans, workplace for some twenty-seven hundred people. It was part of a huge restructuring for the world's largest automaker—seventy-two thousand jobs cut, twenty-one plants closed.

At the time I was a freelance writer; I did not contact any publication concerning a story about the van plant, nor was I working for one. I didn't "presell" the idea; I just thought working in an auto-assembly plant that was scheduled to close, next to people facing a job crisis typical of the early 1990s, would be an experience worth recording. The very biggest names in corporate America—IBM, AT&T, General Motors—were laying off thousands of people due to the recession. The numbers were so big that the headlines blurred: thirteen thousand jobs here, ten thousand jobs there. Who were all those people? Each one of those numbers had a face. I needed to meet some of those faces. I needed to know what was happening inside them.

White collar and blue collar were both losing jobs, but I knew white collar. I lived in the genteel world of desks, air-conditioning, computers, telephones, and Post-it notes, where people wore nice clothes and, mostly, spoke in polite tones. White collar got out its résumé and pressed its suit. What did blue collar do? How was a woman who worked on an assembly line different from the receptionists, or publicists, or executives, or reporters I'd known?

As I considered it, I found I was excited, rather than appalled, at the idea of performing physical work, although few could have started from a more sedentary base. The prospect of performing hard labor would take me into a world that was the domain of men possessing physical power, a clan that had always fascinated me. The business world was dominated by men, too, but their power came from brains, personality, or money. Women had those things also, and if it weren't for job discrimination, they'd be equally paid and represented in business. But muscles ... I had assumed as a kid that women didn't and never would have those. When I read the classic adventure stories, I was Jim in *Treasure Island,* Huck Finn, King Arthur, Captain Nemo, until I faced the fact, in my early teens, that I was a girl. My fantasy life also embraced such active types as Jo in *Little Women* and Dorothy in *The Wizard of Oz,* but men rode horses, brandished swords, were thrown in dungeons, shouted heroic things. They had all the fun! Something was wrong. I was Peter Pan, not Wendy. As I came to terms with growing up as a girl, I still wondered what it was like to be a man, with all that easy strength.

At the same time I was feeling more trapped than inspired by my education and career. Working at the van plant was the first time in my life that I would do the unexpected, and because no one in my world knew anything about a factory, it was the first time nothing was expected of me. Always I had fulfilled the hopes of my parents and fit nicely into the round holes of my social class: earned a bachelor's degree and a master's degree from Ivy League schools and made a good living working for sizable news organizations: NBC Radio, the Associated Press, *The Palm Beach* (Fla.) *Post,* Reuters, *The* (Toronto) *Globe and Mail.* Although my parents, and several of my friends—both blue collar and white collar—thought what I was doing was ridiculous, I felt free.

The kind of journalism I'd fallen into—mostly routine stories on business and finance—no longer jounced my imagination. I was so bored at the last job I held before the van plant—bond-market reporter at *The Globe and Mail*—that, a couple of times, goaded by a trader, I had inserted hidden baseball references into my daily market story. One day the first letters of the first seven sentences spelled out BASE HIT. Another time I got the name of a ballplayer into each of the first few sentences: Bonds, Rose, Key, etc.

In the dozen years that I'd been writing business news, I nearly always covered companies from the top. The exception was during my time at *The Palm Beach Post,* where I detailed the effect of the shutdown of a Piper Aircraft plant on the town of Vero Beach and wrote a continuing series profiling the small businesses in one local strip mall. I liked making direct contact with readers, for good or ill. But my work at the AP and Reuters mostly involved covering markets or major corporations, not people. To create a little variety in my life, I would write arts features on the side, but it wasn't enough. I estimate I've covered more than three hundred annual shareholder meetings. I've listened to dozens of chief executive officers explain the carefully measured reasoning behind this or that cost-cutting move. The closure of this office, that facility, this plant was absolutely necessary to ensure the company's survival. Sales slump, tough competition, slow markets, low productivity, outmoded equipment, sinking prices—whatever the reason, layoffs were unfortunate but unavoidable. Perhaps it's just human nature not to admit mistakes, but I never heard an executive say, "We in management really ran this company into the ground."

It all seemed so easy, sitting in those comfortable hotel meeting rooms, staring at pie charts and graphs, emotion drained from every decision. I can't think of a single corporate officer who looked forward with glee to firing hundreds or thousands of people (with the possible exception of Al Dunlap), but their jobs kept them focused on numbers, not names. Besides, even if an executive deeply regretted tossing people out of jobs, he or she could hardly afford to be emotionally crippled by it, since the primary responsibility was to keep the company running. Nevertheless, the bottom line was that the suit I was interviewing still had a job. When the numbers didn't fall into line, sometimes they got the heave, too, along with a goodly pile of cash, but the jobs at the top were a great deal safer than the ones near the bottom.

There were times I utterly despised the slick, tie-wearing jerk in front of me, such as the corporate president who pompously declared how the company's most valuable resource was "its people." Those were often the same companies that ran pictures of employees in the annual report without mentioning their names.

As I thought about working at the van plant, I considered the possibility that the experience might never see its way into print and wondered whether that might render the whole exercise useless. I decided it wouldn't. I was just so damn tired of the office. I wanted to stand on the bridge of a ship, in the cab of a trolley car, in the middle of a logging camp, in a wheat field at harvest time—something more active than paper shuffling and typing on a screen, with the phone grafted to my ear. More important, I felt I needed the experience to be able to appreciate fully the life I was charting. The experience alone would be worth it, I decided. Trying to understand the world of manual labor would enrich a working life that was beginning to pall.

Outside of work, my life, up to that time, had nearly defined comfortable. I had never known real hardship. My parents had always made a good living, although we were not wealthy. I grew up in a house in a nice neighborhood with a backyard and plenty of food on the table. My father was an executive with a trade organization, and my mother's job as fashion and beauty columnist provided an extra measure of luxury— clothes at a discount or free, a steady stream of cosmetics samples, sponsored press trips. Nobody I knew came home from work with bruises. Our only employment crisis blew up when it looked as if Dad might lose his job over a power struggle at work, but he won. We traveled, attended ballet, opera, and theater and generally lived the good middle-class life of New York City.

Everything seemed to come easily to me—I was accepted by an Ivy League college, got my first job at NBC Radio before I graduated from Columbia, always seemed to be able to make a good living, was tapped for promotion at Reuters without asking. As my view of the world began to form, during teenage years, I naturally was curious about lifestyles that were not familiar to me. So I was less interested in those at the top than in those who didn't grow up in a stimulating household with bright, educated parents and lots of books and music, those who had to struggle

on painful journeys. Not only were we comfortable, but my highly educated mother and European-raised father possessed a distinct sense of
social superiority, an attitude I both enjoyed and wanted to rebel against.
I knew very well what life was like for those who had it easy, and as I
approached forty years of age, I did not believe it was good for my
character to sail along on the plush carpet life had woven for me without
stepping off and walking barefoot on the gravel. I could see myself
growing old, plump, and complacent, never understanding a vital part of
our world. Working at the van plant would be a character test: my Ever-
est, my Zen monastery.

I didn't have any political motives. I came to know a young woman
of strong leftist persuasion who'd gone to work at the van plant partly to
radicalize the workers, a project that had had mixed results. As my
mother said during the 1968 presidential election, "The AFL-CIO can
endorse McGovern all it wants, but half the membership is going to vote
for George Wallace anyway." Although I believe that unions are absolutely essential, I have seen union politics cause as much distress as any
macho management. I went to work at the plant not to transform them
but because I was interested in the people on the factory floor—who
they were, how they got there, how they felt about their work, and how
their work—and the loss of it—affected their lives.

Though my interest wasn't political in nature, politics, of course,
from the macro level in Washington and Ottawa to the micro level of
Canadian Auto Workers Local 303, affected the citizens of GM's little
industrial city in Scarborough. Unable to prevent the shutdown, the
union used the closing to bolster its anti-free-trade position and support
of leftist politicians. General Motors, faced with a small, aging facility in
Canada, moved twenty-seven hundred jobs to Michigan, a gesture
aimed at pleasing politicians and union leaders in its home base, a state
wounded by auto-industry cuts.

I found that my reporting methods changed. As a co-worker, I
couldn't sit down and interview people as I might while wearing the
mantle of journalist. I was also working seven hours a day trying to

■

survive tough, physical labor and then have the brains left to write about it in my journal. I carried a pad in my work bag and would take notes with taped fingers on breaks or in the washroom so as not to arouse suspicion. Working on the line, I had no access to the public-relations department or upper management. All I knew was what I saw and heard on the factory floor.

Finally, a photograph helped crystallize my desire to get into the heart of the factory: a postcard reproduction of one of Lewis Hine's Empire State Building photographs, a series taken in 1930–31 during the construction of what would for many years be the world's tallest building. The photo shows a worker, a young man, sitting on a beam high above Manhattan—the then-new Chrysler Building and New York General Building above Grand Central Station visible behind him. A bandanna is tied around his head; he leans against a larger beam with several holes in it. It is a hot summer day, and he's taken off his shirt; his body is lean and muscled. He straddles the beam, his arms crossed gracefully in front of him, his right forearm resting on the left and his right hand holding a cigarette. The picture is titled *A Break from Work*. But it's the look on his face that made me buy the photograph. He is wearing the hard, fixed stare of a soldier in the trenches. His smooth shoulders sag a little against the beam. This man is bone-tired and trapped, and his thoughts are miles away. He wears no tool belt, so it's impossible to identify his job. What is his name? The picture isn't titled *Jim O'Flaherty's Break from Work*. When more beams are riveted to the one he's sitting on and leaning against, and the skyscraper acquires its stone skin and electrical and water veins and arteries, he will cease to exist. The tough expression on his face, his weary posture—they seem to know that. To me, he is the Empire State Building.

Maybe, I thought, if I write about the people of the van plant, they won't dissolve like shadows into the pounded sheet metal, the taillights, the power door locks. If I could get past the hard part—getting in—I would just let it all unfold around me and write it down. I knew that my life up to then had drawn me no map for this strange land I was entering, but I did not fathom how long and complex my journey would be, how my story would unfold beside those whose tales I had assigned myself. I thought I had it all figured out. I would shake a finger at my world and point to the workers—Look, see how these people suffer!— while virtuously mouthing, There but for the grace of God go I. That was before I saw suffering in hundreds of shades, like paint at the hardware store. As I fell into step with my cast of characters, large and small lessons were written every day. Among them: Never take anything good in your life for granted. I amended my pious musings to, There . . . go I.

Here, then, is a tale of a woman who invaded a world of men, who sought to understand rough work, who asked to be transformed, and here are the people whose stories she set out to tell.

# B E G I N N I N G S

I was rock-solid positive my parents had not raised me to be an autoworker.

When I announced I would be working in a dying van factory, my mother took the news best, possibly because she, too, was a writer. "Well," she said over the phone from New York, "anything that broadens your experience of life is worthwhile." Since a great deal of psychic energy in my life had gone toward trying to please Mother, I mentally fell at her feet in relief and gratitude at her apparent acceptance of this wild notion.

My father, who always had misgivings about anything that didn't appear to be well planned, well thought out, and on the middle class straight and narrow, was less sanguine. He hated the idea. Thirty years in Europe had given Father a sense of social class that most definitely did not include a vision of his only daughter in grimy coveralls. Why had he paid for the Barnard College B.A. and the Columbia University master's degree in journalism—the sorts of things that are supposed to keep people off of the assembly line, not draw them thither?

I tried to explain. "Dad, I'm a journalist. I'm supposed to experience things, not just sit in an office writing about corporations and doing interviews over the phone." Problem was, my dad thought that wearing a suit, sporting a title, and working in an office was just fine. Factories were for the *cafone,* Italian for peasants, or the *stupidos,* to use my mother's bald term. After all, hadn't he put on a suit and tie and gone to work at the Italy-America Chamber of Commerce in Manhattan for thirty-five years? Hadn't he achieved the highest salaried position at the chamber, executive secretary, and built the organization into a respected voice in Italo-American trade? What was so terrible about that kind of work?

When I was Canada news editor with Reuters, both Mom and Dad, though they were accomplished people themselves, would ask me for a few of my business cards so they could proudly show them to friends. What were they to make of my proposed flirtation with manual labor? ("So, is your daughter still a bright light at Reuters, Arthur?" "Well, no, not quite.")

Car factories—indeed, factories of any kind—seldom entered my consciousness as I grew up in the comfortable neighborhood of Bayside, in the New York City borough of Queens. Our two-story white stucco house stood out on the street like a castle, being one of three built several years earlier than the flatter post–World War II bungalows, all set close to the sunken whoosh of the Long Island Expressway. My world embraced houses, stores, schools—a typical residential community.

By the time I was old enough to travel alone into Manhattan, I saw the major industrial area of Queens only from the elevated subway line. At those times I glided through Long Island City like a bird, gazing at the windows of the various plants. So dark, those windows, set in blocklong buildings whose design always seemed to be Early Dickens, no matter what decade they'd been erected.

In summer some of the windows were angled open, and that meant no air-conditioning. I wondered about the lives lived in those buildings, so different from mine. My romantic imagination saw men and women, bent to some brutal, tedious task, yearning for escape, cool air, and light. I saw handsome faces clouded with anger over their lot in life. I thought of a flushed forehead resting briefly on a graceful hand. I saw old men and women, dragging their bodies to work because lives depended upon them.

The train's wheels would scream round the curve toward the East River tunnel, and in my mind the dissonant notes of Long Island City rose to a harmonic crescendo. Before me, laid out like a huge painting that never failed to thrill my heart, were the yearning towers of Manhattan as the Flushing Line ran directly parallel to the East River for a few seconds. Behind me I felt the spirits of all those workers looking toward the beauty and promise of those spires, as prisoners in Alcatraz knew the exquisite torture of gazing upon San Francisco.

You'd have had to go back a couple of generations in our family to find someone who worked with his hands. My father's father, Luigi Menotti De Santis, who immigrated to New York in 1910 from Puglie, in southern Italy, was a cabinetmaker. My father's mother would probably qualify also. Concettina Bonforti headed for the streets of gold from Sicily in 1911 and worked as a passementerie seamstress, specializing in trimmings: beads on dresses or tassels on curtains.

They both possessed a limited education, but Luigi turned a nimble, restless mind to a series of pursuits: guitarmaker, piano repairer, cosmetics/perfume distributor, cake decorator. He married Concettina, a woman of sober and gentle dignity, and was training as a barber in The Bronx (yet another skill) when my father was born in their living quarters behind the shop. Luigi's next profession occurred by chance.

Dad told me that one Christmas his father had decorated the mirrors of the barber shop and one of his customers, "a German fellow," admired the decorations and asked who did them. Luigi didn't want him to think that the barber did them, so he told the man that he'd paid a man a dollar to do them. The German pestered him some more, and Luigi owned up. "Oh, Luigi," his customer exclaimed, "you have a real talent there; you should learn engraving." And the man came to the shop after hours and taught Luigi engraving.

That led to his last, and best, career, as a jeweler. He opened a jewelry salon in The Bronx, working in diamonds and gold, designing and making his own pieces, and was an enormous success in the post–World War I era of prosperity.

But what had become a chronic pain in his back was bothering him more and more, and his friends suggested consulting specialists in Italy.

"I also heard him say he wanted to give me an Italian education," my father said.

And so in 1924, with a remarkable fifty thousand dollars in savings, the Italian-immigrants-made-good returned to the old country, to live on an elegant, leafy street in Rome near the Colosseum. Luigi set up a jewelry business there, and life was sweet for the little family. Photographs taken in the twenties and early thirties show the three of them on summer vacations in the Alps, or at the Côte d'Azur. What style they had! Luigi's deep-set dark eyes, perched above a hawklike nose, are usually looking directly at the camera. His chin is slightly raised, a fedora set on his head just so, his hand resting on a walking stick. On a stocky frame, he is wearing a beautifully cut suit—tweed for the mountains, gray in the city—his shoulders square, his bearing proud and erect. In Italian they say such a man cuts *una bella figura.*

Concettina didn't have quite as much flash to her personality as Luigi, but she is always seen wearing well-made, though never flamboyant, dresses and hats. She had calm eyes, a Roman nose, and a smile like the Mona Lisa. Only a few of their pictures show them smiling or laughing with abandon. They were not sad or unpleasant people by any means, but their sense of reserve did not allow them to make a spectacle of themselves just because someone was pointing a camera their way.

Luigi's financial success allowed him to send his son to good schools, where he met Italian kids from families with more refined backgrounds than those of Puglie and Sicily. As converts often take religion more seriously than those raised in the faith, Luigi, aware of his rise in society, impressed upon his son the importance of behaving well, dressing properly, maintaining appearances. Dad felt it was an important part of his father's character, this striving to fit into the class above him. Though he keenly felt his lack of education, Luigi also possessed a healthy measure of self-confidence, a sense that he could tackle anything if he put his mind to it.

When my father was in his early twenties, he went to live in the great diamond center of Antwerp, where he was a buyer for Luigi's jewelry business. Several years earlier, Luigi, who always seemed to have useful friendships, had worked his connections with a sympathetic Italian police chief to get Dad out of Italy and away from Mussolini's military draft. In my mind the police chief is always played by Claude Rains, in his *Casablanca* role.

Luigi, meanwhile, did consult the local medical specialists about his recurrent back pain, and they discovered it stemmed from a duodenal ulcer. He was put on a bland diet and underwent a couple of operations. When he was in the hospital for the second time, Concettina called Dad and told him to come down from Antwerp. Modern medicine probably would have saved him, but in 1939 the ulcer killed Luigi at the age of fifty-four.

Concettina joined Dad in Antwerp, where World War II caught up with him. In 1943 the Germans were arresting enemy civilians. Since he was born in New York, he had an American passport. Concettina, who had an Italian passport, was spared since she was nominally an ally of the Führer. Dad was interned in Germany for eighteen months with British, Australian, and American civilians guarded by bored German soldiers too old for the front.

It always seemed to me that there were three formative experiences of Dad's early life, and they colored his view of my leap into the blue-collar world. One was the move to Italy at age eleven. Not only was he uprooted from his friends in The Bronx, but he was put with younger kids in his first Italian school because he had to learn the language. "Here was this little dummy trying to keep up with the lessons," he would say. The second was the death of his father when Dad was twenty-six. The third was his arrest by the Nazis.

My father concluded from these experiences that life is a shaky thing and it's best to have security. It can all be snatched away at any time—the familiar place you live, your loving protector and teacher, your freedom. Aim for stability and exhibit a certain class: those were his guiding principles. My brother and I, children of the sixties, sought more adventure out of life, and it made Dad nervous. He didn't understand why I would want to quit Reuters, after six years, to try my wings as an entrepreneur and start a magazine. The project didn't fly, but it was an invaluable learning experience. Throughout the two-year process, Dad would ask, lightly but pointedly, "Do you still hear from anyone at Reuters?" Or he would remark, "You had it good there at Reuters."

After the war Dad and his mother decided to return to New York. Dad went alone on a scouting expedition, and it was on a transatlantic steamer that he met my mother, returning home to Brooklyn from a job in Europe.

Not only was Florence Catharine Stevenson's heritage white collar, it was a seventeenth-century lace collar at that. She was descended through her mother, Florence Marie Paddock, from an Englishman named William Brewster, who caught passage in 1620 on a little ship named the *Mayflower*. Mother believed she belonged to a special kind of American aristocracy, legitimized by time and strength of character rather than by mere money. "My New England ancestors would be aghast," was how she would criticize some tasteless excess of modern life. Her family fought for the North, of course, during the Civil War, and we have the stiffly posed photographs to prove it. We could have belonged to the Daughters of the American Revolution if we'd wanted, but my mother, though proud of her lineage, was not much of a club joiner, and dismissed the venerable Daughters as a bunch of gossiping hens. There were thirty-second-degree Masons on that side of the family, and members of the Eastern Star, the Masons' women's auxiliary.

The Paddock side of the family was so steeped in its White Anglo-Saxon Protestant sense of noblesse (without much "oblige") that when my grandmother proposed to marry a man of German descent, my great-grandmother responded, "Are you really thinking of bringing a foreigner into the family?" She certainly was, and she did. By the time my mother decided to marry a man of (gasp) Italian descent, the times had mellowed to the point where my great-grandmother hardly remarked upon it.

My grandfather, George Horton Stevenson, was that man of German descent, and his family hadn't been lounging on these shores as long as the Paddocks. He had just an eighth-grade education and he worked with his hands, but he was no ordinary manual laborer. He was a pianist of such talent that, it was said, he could have had a concert career had he received the proper training. But he was the product of uneducated parents and he never did attend conservatory. "It was all right for Georgie to play at home for friends, but not to go away to school," my mother related. He turned to another kind of theater for his performances. As Mary Pickford, Rudolph Valentino, or Colleen Moore flickered across the screens of the ornate RKO Keith and Paramount theaters in Manhattan and Brooklyn, his muscular hands played Chopin and Rachmaninoff on the five-manual Wurlitzer organs. On Sunday he volunteered at the organ behind the church choir. In 1929 he had an experience not many have: He watched a movie and saw his career evaporate. The film was *The Jazz Singer*.

The Depression would have thrown the Stevensons (my mother's sister, Marjorie, had also arrived by that time) onto welfare were it not for my grandmother's career. She taught in New York City's "600" high schools, so named because they were all numbered in the 600s and were where girls were sent who were delinquent and/or had emotional problems.

Like many bright young women of the thirties, Mother was determined to shuck conventional attitudes toward domesticity and education for women. Her sterling academic career was the stuff of legend in our household. With her mother as role model and encouragement from both parents, she was ranked top of the class in Brooklyn's Girls High School. At age seventeen, she beat 375,000 other New York State high-school students in a statewide essay contest, writing, without notes, on the topic "Why I Am Being Given an Education." She was named to the national honor society, Phi Beta Kappa, in her junior year at Hunter College in New York City. She earned her bachelor's degree magna cum laude in English literature and acquired a master's degree in English literature at Columbia University.

From an early age I was pressured to excel in academics and achieve in life, most intensely by my brilliant, leonine mother. When I was a child, my mother seemed to own everything that mattered in my world. In the beginning, she gave me the words, from alphabet blocks through Dr. Seuss and *Winnie-the-Pooh*. Nothing was more important than the words. I never went anywhere without a book. What was the use of an idle moment if not to read a page or two of *Captain Horatio Hornblower* or *Michael Strogoff, the Courier of the Czar?* My New York suburban existence embraced King Arthur's court, Alice's rabbit hole, Tom Sawyer's cavern.

The childhood classics were all given to me by Mom: *The Secret Garden, Mary Poppins, Peter Pan, The Wizard of Oz,* and on and on. I discovered *The Count of Monte Cristo* and *The Man in the Iron Mask* at the age of twelve. Mother read Conan Doyle, Charles Dickens, Jules Verne to my brother and me before bed, with accents and dramatic intonations. She was the high priestess of the Book, gatekeeper to the worlds where I lost myself.

Mom had migrated from schoolteaching to a highly glamorous job. If she'd been a university professor, lecturing endlessly on the novels of Henry James, or a lawyer trying tort cases, maybe I wouldn't have felt so intimidated. No, even then, Florence De Santis would have been one of the best-known professors on campus or the most colorful tort lawyer. Instead she toiled in the vineyards of fashion and beauty, writing a weekly package of stories for United Feature Syndicate, which it then sold to newspapers in the United States and Canada. I practically grew up playing under runways as models pranced overhead. At age five I walked down one myself, holding a doll, to end a fashion show and hear middle-aged editor ladies emit a collective "ohhh."

She wasn't a drab, skinny little thing either, always slinking around in black. Her favorite color was purple in all its hues, with pink not far behind. Photographs taken in the thirties, forties, and fifties showed she had style, but the sixties were her time to shine. Blue and green eye makeup, a halo of hair dyed blond from its natural brown, wild Pucci prints, shoes matching handbags, pink-, yellow-, and turquoise-colored Sobranie cigarettes with gold paper filters. Twice a year Mother would put away two seasons' worth of hats and bring out the next two seasons'—the white leather fedora, the orange mohair turban, the red velvet one shaped like a cardinal's miter.

She knew all the great American design names of the age—Blass, de la Renta, Gernreich, Beene, Norell. I would tag along to fashion shows on Seventh Avenue and lunches at the Broadway restaurant Sardi's while she interviewed Kim Novak or Angela Lansbury about their wardrobes. It could take fifteen minutes to get to her table at Sardi's as she said hello to everyone, although she always was given an excellent table near the front. I swam in her generous wake, at once thrilled and struggling to keep my head above water.

I loved my childhood, but I felt that the pressure was relentless. In my dance classes I won the best-in-class prize for a couple of years, but Mom wanted to know why I hadn't won the top prize. At the end of each year's dance recital, Mrs. Sullivan read out the names of the top prizewinning students. My heart thumped each year, hoping my name would be called, but it never was. I had let Mom down again. How could I ever be as smart and knowledgeable as my mother, as debonair as my father? What could I possibly do to contribute to this family, so rich in experience?

Education was a given in my family. The question was not whether I was going to college, just which one. Mom recommended I follow her trail at the Ivy League, but she was less impressed by the fact that I just didn't have the relentless drive to make Phi Beta Kappa or get one of the "laudes" attached to my diploma. I got my degrees, but I also had a social life and wrote for the Columbia newspaper. I became theater editor at the *Spectator* and had a wonderful time reviewing Broadway shows, with some campus theater mixed in.

Mom gave me my first job in journalism. I worked as her office assistant in the summer when her secretary was on vacation and, as a teenager, began writing some brief items, under my name, for her fashion and beauty package. She began to trust me with larger articles, and that's how, in 1972, I found myself on a Florida press junket interviewing Robert Redford about the costumes in his new film, *The Candidate,* and how I got my first news clipping, from the old *Montreal Star,* at the age of eighteen.

Once I graduated from university, I started my career with a bang, and there was no disappointing Florence De Santis then. Three months before graduation, through one of her contacts, I got an audition at NBC Radio, which was one year into a new concept: a nationwide all-news radio network. I went down to Rockefeller Center, was asked to write a five-minute newscast from the front page of *The Washington Post,* then was asked if I wanted a job as a newswriter after I graduated. I said I most certainly did. I was told the starting salary was four hundred dollars a week. This was in 1976. My rent was a hundred dollars a month.

Getting the job also meant I had proven Mom wrong, for what seemed the first time in my life. Throughout my year in journalism school she'd said, "You'll have to go out of town for your first job. You won't get a job starting out in New York." I was also practicing a type of writing she'd never done; she couldn't overwhelm me with help as she had in high school and in my early days at college.

And so I was launched upon the waters of professional journalism, boiling down wire-service stories into bite-size chunks of news to be read on the air by such well-known radio voices as John Cameron, son of John Cameron Swayze. Despite the good money and the fact that I was working for one of the Big Three of American broadcast journalism, I felt I was on a detour from my intended path. I was meant to be a theater critic, or, if I couldn't do that right away, a newspaper reporter, talking to people, telling tales that shed light on the human condition, not regurgitating stories someone else had written.

Apparently someone at NBC decided that all I needed was a little push, because after two years the network decided it was losing too much money on the News and Information Service in those presatellite days and shut it down. So I went looking for newspaper jobs, firing off application letters to newspapers across the country and following up with a job-interview drive across America.

I was ready to begin an enduring affair with newspapers; I just needed one to ask me to the dance. I am the classic newspaper romantic. I love the characters, the crumple of paper, the stink of ink, the grumble of presses, the history and legends of newspapers. When I began to apply to newspapers for a job, I had a pretty good opinion of my professional experience. Newspaper editors did not share my opinion. They wanted to see newspaper clips, not printouts of radio scripts. I had done some original reporting, usually by phone, but it wasn't what they were used to seeing. So I trudged back to New York, having failed to land a job as what I called a "real" reporter in the colorful places I had chosen: New Orleans; Austin, Texas; Memphis; and Nashville.

I went across the street from NBC to the Associated Press and got a job writing news summaries for the radio broadcast wire. Back up in the skyscraper. Almost the same job as at NBC, except I never saw who read my stories on the air; they sped down the wire to hundreds of radio stations across the country. After a couple of years I landed the business-writer's position. I went down to the New York Stock Exchange and saw prices put up by hand at wooden trading posts, but computers were coming, I was told, and the old posts would be museum pieces. The 1970s had seen recession and oil shortage. Now we were seeing the beginnings of the merger boom that would characterize the 1980s and the throes of rampant inflation with interest rates heading toward 20 percent.

Still, I didn't figure business would be my calling for the long term, much less that the job would make me a prisoner of my résumé. As always, I wanted to write about the arts, so I also started a popular-music column for the radio wire. Funny how the busywork of a job can distract us from a long-term career goal. After a year or so I was getting the hang of broadcast writing, and I was making a very fine living with a major news organization. The jaws of the velvet trap were slowly closing, until I got involved with a man who wanted to move to Florida and I resurrected my desire to write for a newspaper.

The business editor at *The Palm Beach Post* didn't have any problem with my radio experience, and the next year and a half were the happiest in my career. The business editor and I broke stories that led the front page or were major features in the business section—land-development deals, the inside story of a bank takeover, the bankruptcy of a high-society social club, the travails of small businesses. I was also on the radio every Friday, talking about the week in business.

At last I could write stories about people and their communities. I had ventured out of New York City to discover the rest of America, and I had landed in a town of about a hundred thousand (small for a New Yorker), but my influence was far more deeply felt. My work for NBC and the AP had anonymously reached millions of people, but my stories in West Palm Beach directly reflected my existence and the fact that I had talked, one-on-one, to another human being.

The *Post* wasn't a large enough newspaper to stay at for very long, unless one were interested in moving up the editorial hierarchy and within the Atlanta-based Cox newspaper chain. I like running around and writing too much. Being shackled to a desk and sending other people out reporting didn't interest me at all.

A former AP acquaintance, now with Reuters in New York, told me of a job opening in Los Angeles as senior financial correspondent. On the belief that it is always better to apply than not to apply, I sent my résumé and clips to New York, and, of course, Reuters complicated my life by offering me the job, which involved supervising one other reporter. I decided, after much agonizing, that the positives of a promotion and a new environment outweighed the negatives of continuing to write business news and returning to the wire services.

We moved to the West Coast. My three years there, ending in 1986, were remarkably tranquil, considering the news events to come in Los Angeles after my stay there: O.J. trial, earthquake, riot. I began my term there in a tiny office off Wilshire Boulevard near the shabbily genteel Ambassador Hotel, site of the first Academy Awards ceremony and now in a section of town that was long out of fashion. I was covering much larger companies—Lockheed, Bank of America, Occidental Petroleum—than I had in Florida, and my work was seen by many more people, mostly on the financial news service, which appeared on dedicated printers and computer screens.

My colleague and I were expected to cover so many companies based on the West Coast that we spent most of our time in the office, doing phone interviews and talking to analysts. You couldn't beat the variety—banks, oil companies, industrials, defense contractors, aerospace manufacturers—but once again I felt the office prison closing in. I used to envy the *Wall Street Journal* reporters who seemed to have the time to write long, in-depth stories while I was chasing a company's outlook for its second-quarter earnings per share.

Our bureau chief had the general news beat, but he couldn't be everywhere, so I would propose features for the newspaper wire. I covered fencing at the 1984 Olympics. I covered the Oscars two years in a row, doing sidebars from the ceremony while the bureau chief sent out bulletins and wrap-ups from the television broadcast. I interviewed Jacques Cousteau and film director Robert Altman. But while the general-news editors in New York were always glad to see another feature, my first priority was to file those stories on takeovers, dividend cuts, corporate strategy, and annual meetings to the business desk.

After about three years I thought I had built up a decent portfolio and the business writing grind was wearing me down, so I tried to get back into newspapers, but *The Wall Street Journal* and *The Los Angeles*

*Times* didn't hold their doors open for me. The trade-off I'd made with my career was beginning to look like a bargain with the devil.

Three years after I arrived in L.A., Reuters complicated my life further by offering me a promotion—news editor of Canada in Toronto, supervising two reporters in Toronto, two in Ottawa, and one in Montreal. I was itching to get out of the wire-service environment, but how could I turn that down? I received assurances from my editors that I could still continue to write, so off I went. My steady had moved to New Orleans, where there were more opportunities in the commercial diving work he loved to do, and we maintained a commuting relationship.

I always wore a suit to the office, figuring a jacket projected an air of authority and professionalism. My office was an enclosure off the newsroom, featuring a big desk and a large, executive-type swivel chair, into which I felt I melted. I guess my first inkling that my life was changing came in L.A., when someone from Toronto called and asked, "What color do you want your office painted?" The second ego-booster came the first time a secretary from accounting brought me some papers and said, "I need your signature on these."

The lifestyle of a manager wasn't too hard to take. I flew business class and relaxed in first-class hotels. I remember walking out of my apartment house early one morning, in my suit and high heels, carrying my briefcase, and folding myself into the waiting limousine for the trip to the airport, feeling important and excited.

The flip side of all that spending came after the great stock-market crash in October 1987. I had been authorized to hire an additional reporter just nine months before, and now I was told I had to let her go. I asked whether we couldn't make some cuts elsewhere—my private parking space, for one—but was turned down. I had a lot of trouble with that one. The young woman I'd hired was bright and energetic and didn't deserve that. I was no stranger to the realities of budgets, but I saw a lot of spending going on (the art we rented for the walls, the flowers we bought every week for the reception desk) that I would have cut first before taking away someone's job.

My managers in New York were hinting that I should move up in management, take some training courses for the next step. It was so flattering, so seductive, but one night in my living room I made a conscious decision to turn off that road. Can you work at a desk job that doesn't involve writing? Is writing too important for you to give up? I asked myself. No and yes were the answers. But what about the money? You could be making more than a hundred thousand dollars a year fairly soon. I looked around at my stuff and asked myself, How much more do I want to buy? Not that much, was the answer.

As I continued to cover takeovers, corporate earnings, etc., etc., the kind of journalism I was practicing ceased to be much of a challenge. Often my gaze was drawn away from the computer terminal, the Reuters screen, the phone, the desk papers, drawn out the window of my ninth-floor office. Perhaps I was editing a particularly eye-glazing story—the one from that tedious stringer on the genetic engineering of canola plants. Maybe I was writing a story of my own and the subject—say, the expected third-quarter earnings of the five major Canadian banks—was less than scintillating. Maybe I was just daydreaming. I stared down at the city's Lake Ontario waterfront, a gray industrial landscape of railroad tracks, concrete grain elevators, docks, and ships, just a few vessels since the heyday of Great Lakes shipping had passed. As usual my gaze focused on the huge Redpath logo, mounted on the side of that company's sugar plant, and I began to wonder.

Who works there? What do they do? Do they walk on catwalks above huge mounds of raw sugar, in danger of falling through the heavy, sweet air onto a hill hard as wet sand? Do they shovel the brown granules, like coal stokers in the *Titanic*'s boiler room, into a greedy processor maw that churns, clanks, and spits neat little white cubes out of its nether region? Can sugar dust suffocate a man?

It wasn't until later, until I met someone who worked in that kind of place, that I really ached to explore working lives so unlike my own. But every so often I'd stare at an industrial setting and wonder. On summer drives to the Shakespeare Festival in Stratford, I daydreamed about the

Fag Bearings factory, a long, low building just a mile or so from Macbeth, Hamlet, and Juliet. I tried to remember what bearings were and fathom how an entire building could be dedicated to making them. Wheels. Bearings are used in wheels. Somehow. Ball bearings. What else needs a bearing? "Give that flange a stiff bearing, Jim." Is working there past all bearing?

On the way to ski trips in Collingwood I wondered what it was like to work at the Consumers Glass plant. Sand is used to make glass, I thought. I imagined huge chutes pouring sand into massive hoppers, melting and mixing it with whatever else is used to make glass. Probably a hot place to work. Giant molds cranking out windshields and windows.

I wondered about that world. If only I could toss the quiet, clean, soft confines of the office for a little while to visit that land of bang, smash, yell, and heave. I was getting tired of middle-class life, of sitting on my butt all day, with a lunchtime visit to the health club for exercise. I knew what life was like among the smooth-skinned, the clear-eyed, the educated, the comfortable. I longed to push back my chair from the captain's table and go below to eat with the seamen. I yearned for a little downward mobility, but knew the concept was as far-fetched as a steelworker's stepping into my job at Reuters. I couldn't just toss my upbringing and step off a prosperous path in life to work in a cement plant.

# FOR MANY APPLY, BUT FEW ARE CHOSEN

I had no idea what to do with these inchoate desires, and in the meantime an opportunity had arisen to step outside the corporate world and take a flier as an entrepreneur. I and a fellow journalist had been struck with what we thought was a great idea for a magazine, and so, in 1989, I decided to leave Reuters. The working title was *North America: The Continental Business Magazine,* and the two of us—me, the American, and my friend, the Canadian—would direct business coverage from a genuinely binational point of view. We sought to raise financing over the next two years, and if I had a nickel for every time I heard "Wow, that's a great idea for a magazine," I'd have a magazine by now. However, I truly learned what the phrase "to put your money where your mouth is" means, because, great idea that it supposedly was, no one wanted to open a checkbook for it.

While my friend and I were performing our soft-shoe routine in front of anyone we thought might invest in our idea, I embarked on a freelance career. When I toted up my receipts to file my taxes after the first year, I nearly gasped to discover I'd made less than half of my Reuters salary. But I didn't indulge in expensive habits, so I wasn't facing imminent eviction, and the intoxicating freedom of directing my own time just about made up for the mini-paychecks.

As a freelance writer I began to revive that interest in working lives that were different from mine. Some of the dirtiest, most dangerous occupations interested me: steelmaking, which looked like a job lived in the very mouth of hell and which was losing thousands of workers under withering competition from abroad; anything done aboard a ship that didn't sport a swimming pool; working on an offshore oil rig; and the auto industry, one of the great engines of the North American economy, a tangible gauge of our standard of living, its products a reflection of our individual selves.

As it so happened, once I was on my own, assignments on the auto industry—a major part of the economy of southern Ontario—were the first to come calling: how the auto facilities in and around London, Ontario, were adapting to global investment and competition, what automakers were doing to lessen pollution. These assignments were all well and good, but they weren't getting me any closer to the factory floor.

My formless curiosity was sharpened when I happened to meet an autoworker. A Canadian journalist I knew urged me to join a group of men and women who played a casual game of hockey every Thursday evening, although, after three years in Los Angeles and one and a half in West Palm Beach, I skated about as well as I flew a 747.

I said I would check out the players first and met my journalist friend, Don Angus, at a bar called Links in a run-down neighborhood called Parkdale. Don introduced me around to the five or six people at the bar, including a man named Billy Davis.

"Billy works at General Motors," Don said, indicating a man of medium height with a day's growth of beard, wearing a green Oakland A's baseball cap. "No kidding! Where is it that you work? What do you do there?" I asked. Reaching toward the bar with a well-muscled arm, he picked up a Molson Export and regarded me with amused blue eyes. "In Scarborough. I'm a welder." A welder! A real assembly-line worker! I felt as if I'd captured an auk, and I peppered him with questions more intensely than if I'd been interviewing the CEO of General Motors.

"So, what do you weld?"

"Side frames. Body panels. Wheel wells."

"Is it hard?"

"It can be brutal."

"So why do you do it?"

"Why does anybody do it? For the money."

"Well, how good is the money?"

"Twenty dollars an hour."

"That's pretty good, I guess."

"It is for unskilled labor. Before I went to work at General Motors, I was laying carpet. My first check from GM, they took out more in taxes than I was taking home from the other job."

"But don't you have to do the same thing every day? How do you stand it?"

"I don't. I'm an AR now—absentee relief. I know all the jobs in the department, so I fill in for people who are off or need a break."

"You must have worked there for a while."

"Six years. The first day I reported in the body shop, I stood in the supervisor's office and looked around. Sparks flying everywhere, guys with dirty faces. You knew you were in hell."

I was intrigued, and charmed a little, by his offhand, macho pose and the way he seemed to recognize and accept, with grace and humor, that hard labor was part of his place in the world. He said he'd tried to work in an office once, but came home and ripped off the tie and never went back. It wasn't for him, he said. I liked him right off and wanted to get to know him better, so I asked him out for a beer or two or, in his case, three.

Billy was on a weekend bowling team, played softball and hockey, was a dedicated sports fan, with baseball and the Oakland A's taking pride of place, and his idea of a great night out was getting loaded with his buddies in a strip club. His education had stopped at high school, but he had a knack for getting to the heart of a situation in a few words. In his mid-thirties, he was single and seemed to be a tad lonely. There was a sweet, sensitive side to his personality, and as an only child, he was intensely loyal to his parents, although their relationship with each other and with him had had its rocky moments.

After that initial meeting at Links I wondered how he'd stuck it out, through the burns, the cuts, the noise? How the hell did people do this, all day, day after day? What kind of physical and mental strength does a person have to summon up to do this kind of work?

I had to get closer. I decided to see where Billy worked, so I phoned GM and asked for a tour of the plant, explaining that I was a freelance writer who often wrote about the auto industry. I wasn't quite sure what to wear, so I opted for a gray plaid business suit, once one of my Reuters-editor costumes, and high-heeled boots. On a chill, drizzly February morning, I headed for the Scarborough Van Plant on Eglinton Avenue, a wide, busy boulevard in a suburb that is to Toronto what chopped liver is to caviar. The factory stretched out, gray and squat, behind two stories of office space and the big blue GM sign that was its face to the world. I stepped through the freezing slush in the parking lot and checked in at the guard booth.

The building had started life in 1952 as a Frigidaire plant, churning out refrigerators, stoves, washing machines, and other appliances, in the days when General Motors equipped your kitchen as well as your garage. It anchored a section of Eglinton Avenue that was pushing east from Toronto in an upheaval of postwar transition from farms and houses to commercial development. An aerial photo of the time shows huge empty lots surrounding the newly finished plant and some houses to the north of it. A local politician decided that this stretch of road needed a catchy name that would reflect its future prosperity, so the remarkably honest caption to the photo reads, "This will be the famous 'Golden Mile'—of industry, thereby putting Scarborough into the forefront of development and bringing in lots of tax money."

In 1970 GM converted the plant to production of its Delco-brand radio components and in 1974 expanded the facility to manufacture vans. Next to the plant, the Golden Mile Chev-Olds dealership set up shop, drawing much of its clientele from the plant workers. Over the years, Eglinton Avenue was extended and widened, and the empty lots were filled in—a shopping mall at a major intersection, a Sears warehouse next to the plant, a spice plant down the road, various smaller outposts of industry and solid residential development north and south of the boulevard.

My guide, Bob, was a genial, officious GM retiree. Apparently playing tour guide was a part-time gig for retired guys who wanted some extra money and activity. As we pushed open the swinging doors leading to the factory from the office hallway, my ears were assaulted by the sounds of an auto plant in full cry, with Led Zeppelin—"Hey, hey mama, say the way you move/Gonna make you sweat, gonna make you groove"—driving the beat. It was like trying to listen to the radio in the shower while someone beats the plumbing with a tire iron.

Dozens of people were attaching things in, on, through, over, and under naked metal boxes that moved through the plant on carriers dragged by a chain. "This is the drag-chain assembly line," shouted my guide. The drag chain. That sounded awful, like some ball-and-shackle equipment used on the job. I was scared and thrilled—there's no other word for it—at being inside the heart of this mechanical giant. To some, probably those who are trying to escape its clutches, a factory is a malevolent, depressing hunk of metal and cement. To me it was exciting, at once ugly and beautiful.

Bob and I stopped at an area called Respot [pronounced REE-spot] 2 and watched workers on a platform guide a hoist carrying a roof toward a van on the assembly line. They grabbed big welding guns—half the size of a man's body—and moved the tips into position to weld the edges of the roof to the body of the van. As they pulled triggers, sparks flew, hitting their heads and bodies. I was horrified.

I heard a voice behind me. "Hey, looking good!" It was Billy, in blue coveralls, heading down the aisle with a friend. I smiled and waved, but he looked as if he was in a hurry to get where he was going.

My guide and I strolled through a confusing maze of aisles, machinery, rumbling forklifts, cables, tools, and moving lines. It seemed like barely organized chaos. I looked at the people—women, men, large, small, fat, thin—and I still didn't understand how they did this every day. The people were the machines. The machines were the people.

■

We stopped at the area where the tires were installed on the van and stared at a man grunting as he lifted tires off a conveyor belt and brought them over to the vans, now moving along six feet off the ground. Bob had been filling me with facts about General Motors, van-plant production, the good wages and benefits people here earn. But right now we stood silently watching this poor guy hump a tire every two minutes. "The thing about the line is, it never ends," said Bob, a little sadly.

I asked to see the body shop and mentioned that I knew someone there. We walked over, and it seemed that this area of the plant was even darker than the rest. We found Billy welding wheel wells. He had a toothpick tucked in the corner of his mouth and was wearing tinted safety glasses as he banged out his welds—twenty-six wheel wells per hour welded to the side panels. He saw us, finished the job, and walked over.

"Hi, there. Well, what do you think?"

"This looks dangerous," I replied. "Be careful!" He smiled and winked and strolled back as the next job came along.

The shrinking North American auto industry had marked Scarborough for extinction, but in early 1990 the fat lady was merely humming, in Billy's phrase. GM chairman Roger Smith had announced in 1989 that van production would be consolidated in 1992 in Flint, Michigan, from Scarborough and Lordstown, Ohio. When I walked through the plant, a GM–Canadian Auto Workers union committee was looking for another product for the facility, amid hopes that something could be found to keep it open.

My commuting relationship, wonderful though it was, was showing signs of strain under the long separations and over the next few months my friendship with Billy cartwheeled into an on-again, off-again affair with lovely highs and shattering lows. During the good times I met his closest friends among the van-plant workers. He played softball with Chuck and Sharon. Chuck was a bit of a grouch. Sharon was such a good pitcher that she played on the men's teams at the van plant and years before had even been offered an athletic scholarship to a U.S. college, but turned it down because she was in love with a guy in Ontario. Dave was a tall, dark-haired man with an attractive wife and cute little boy who invited us to his house in Oshawa one New Year's Eve. They were wonderful hosts, and it was one of those evenings when everyone glows with just the right amount of alcohol and camaraderie. Dave and I hit it off especially well, as I entertained him with stories of interviewing B. B. King and Billy Idol. "This lady has had quite a career," he exclaimed.

But Billy fell into a black mood as we left the party, something that happened a little too frequently for my taste. He was often ambivalent about the relationship. He met my journalism friends and was comfortable with some, uncomfortable with others. I wanted things to work out, but was often impatient with him when he wanted to have one of those nights out with the fellas.

A few months after I toured Billy's workplace in Scarborough, I saw quite a different world. I received an assignment on how auto companies were adopting—and adapting to—automation. I went to one of the most advanced GM facilities on the continent: the so-called Autoplex in Oshawa, about thirty miles east of Toronto, which made Buick Regals, Chevrolet and GMC pickup trucks, and Chevrolet Luminas.

A manufacturing operation of any size makes a human being feel small. As I drove toward the Autoplex, where a warren of huge, faceless buildings was spread over more than six hundred acres, employing ten thousand people, I felt like a speck. I located the gate I'd been told to find (there were dozens), parked, and was signed in by my guide, the superintendent of manufacturing, engineering, and maintenance.

Compared to Scarborough, this was another planet. My first impression was: larger, brighter, cleaner, quieter. Robots handled the welding. There were only about a dozen robots in the entire Scarborough plant. In Oshawa, AGVs, or automatic guided vehicles, carried the car carcasses on computerized tracks in the floor. The AGVs were a great improve-

■

ment over the old drag-chain line, said my guide. The old way, if the line went down, everything stopped. This way the AGVs carried cars into several job stations, so if a problem developed at one, the vehicles were automatically routed to the others. Oh, I see, I thought, so the line truly never stops.

I asked how AGVs affected the workers. They had advantages over the old line, he said, because the X-lift on the AGVs automatically raised or lowered the body shell to the right height for the job. Before, the worker had to bend or stretch to do the job, increasing the possibility of injury or strain.

As he spoke, I looked at the vehicles, but I also looked beyond them to the people. They waited for the AGV to advance to their job station, then went at their tasks with parts and tools, then stood back as one person pushed a large button and sent the AGV off to its next appointment. I wanted to talk to the people waltzing with automation, but they were pretty busy, and I had to get most of my story's material from management standing next to me.

I got a chance when we stopped at one area with a large robot on which someone had painted NO GO JOE. I mustered up the courage to lean over and ask a man next to the robot, "What does that mean?" "Joe used to do that job," he answered, then laughed and moved off. Later a senior engineer told me that the graffiti referred to the problems encountered in programming the robot to do the job as well as Joe. "What happened to Joe?" I asked. No one could tell me.

After seeing Oshawa, I said to Billy, "Scarborough's dead. It's way behind the times. What are you going to do if it closes?" "Too soon to worry about that," he replied, but he seemed to be whistling past the graveyard. Gradually the idea of applying for a job in Scarborough occurred to me. The writer George Plimpton, who wrote about sports by getting into the ring with boxers and venturing on football and baseball fields with big-name players, had always been one of my heroes. Another hero was a man named Dr. John R. Coleman, who was the president of

Haverford College in the seventies and took a sabbatical to work as a garbageman, ditchdigger, and short-order cook. If I wanted to get inside the story of a plant closing, I had to get inside the plant. If I wanted to enlarge my experience of life, I had to plunge in. Money wouldn't be a problem, since I'd make twice what I did the first year freelancing. Maybe, too, I would understand what made Billy tick. He thought it was the dumbest idea since Boston had traded Babe Ruth. "Why don't you stick with what you know?" he asked. "I'm bored with what I know, Billy," I answered, "I need to do something new." He shook his head.

I applied to work in the plant in September 1990. Iraq had invaded Kuwait, and rising gasoline prices added to the woes of an auto industry that had suffered sluggish sales for months. GM continued to trail Ford and Chrysler in efficiency, amid pitched battles with the UAW. Nobody thought the giant automaker would ever again see the days when it commanded 50 percent of the North American vehicle market and employed half a million people. Market share was sliding below 40 percent, employment was at two thirds of that peak, and the analysts said GM still needed to cut costs.

In the midst of all this dismal news I arrived at the provincial government employment office that was processing applications for GM and sat down with a form. I eliminated any mention of my university education and of my former employers. I said I'd worked for the fellow writer with whom I'd tried to start a magazine. He'd agreed to recommend me. I figured I needed something else in the world of tools, so I said I'd worked in a hardware store that, conveniently, had gone out of business. I wasn't particularly proud of making up an entry on the application form, but I felt it was the only way I could get in and live the life of an autoworker.

Two months later GM called me to be "assessed," a process that involved three days at the GM training center in Oshawa. Apparently GM had taken to heart the lessons of the 1970s, when Japanese quality kicked American automotive ass. Where workers in Osaka lined up in neat uniforms for calisthenics every morning, Americans supposedly slouched to the job hungover, sporting bad attitude. By 1990 gone were the days when walking and breathing were pretty much the only prerequisites for a job on the line. Later I knew a man who in the early 1980s had won his job in an all-night poker game. A friend who was a supervisor in the van plant lost one too many hands and offered to get the man a job at GM as payment. They discussed seafood at the job interview.

To get a shot at repetitive labor I went through a more rigorous, longer evaluation process than any I'd known. For most of my journalism career a writing test and an interview were about it. I was told to report at 7 A.M. The training area consisted of a classroom or two and a large space holding a mini-assembly line and two work areas.

About a dozen people walked into the classroom on the first day—a diverse group of men and women of various races and work experiences. A nicely dressed woman who looked to be in her mid-thirties told me she was originally from Kuwait. Since we were not paid for the three days and there was no guarantee this process would lead to a job, those already employed had to scramble to attend. Desiree, who worked at an insurance company for seven dollars per hour, said she was calling in sick for three days.

The first day we were shown videos on safety and the importance of quality and of showing up on time for the job. Attendance was important, it was stressed, because when you didn't show up, someone else had to do your job and quality could suffer. Why did they have to show us this? Obviously, I thought, this company has a problem with absenteeism, even though people seem to be lining up at the doors to get in. What happens once they're in there?

We were broken up into teams of four or five each, given a Lego set, and told to build a car. We were told this was a team-building exercise, and the importance of teamwork at GM was stressed. Next we were each given a sheet of paper headlined HOW EFFECTIVE IS 100% INSPECTION? There were nine columns of numbers on the sheet and an introductory paragraph beginning, "Industry has been laboring under the impression that 100% inspection gives complete assurance that lots submitted for inspection will be effectively sorted." I liked the cynical tilt of that sentence, as if the person writing it thought this whole exercise was a lot of hooey. The columns consisted of 405 random three-digit numbers. "Assume that numbers in the range 851 through 900 inclusive are defectives. Go through this 'lot' once only and see how effectively you can sort out the defectives by circling each one you find." We were given three minutes to do this.

We were taken out into the work area and given cards reading "Oshawa Plant 1 & 2, Paint Inspect." A van was sitting in the area, and we were told to go over the paint and mark down problem areas on the card, which had drawings of the back, front, and sides of a car. This was a practice quality audit. We found scratches on the bumper, rough paint on the hood, chips in the roof paint, dings, an unpainted screw, and bubbles in the paint on the doors.

That afternoon we got our first taste of the assembly line. The mini-line held about a dozen car bumpers with parts bins at the top. We were assigned spots and told we were to put on or remove bolts in a certain order with an air gun and fasten some metal parts to the bumpers. If the bolts were on, we were to take them off. If they were off, put them on. Our instructor, a very grumpy old man, showed us where to put our hands when using the air gun to tighten down the bolts. Otherwise, he said, the gun would torque out of our hands and possibly cause injury. Each of us was in a yellow-bordered work area, and we were not to step out of it. A dropped bolt was to stay dropped.

We were not given gloves, and our hands quickly became greasy and dirty. I was excited and scared about handling a power tool for the first time, and sure enough, it got away from me once, inflicting a small cut. It wasn't too bad, and I didn't mention it. Mr. Grouch was right about the hand placement. The mini-line ran for an hour; then we were told to go wash up. The washroom had a huge round sink in the middle of the

■

floor, with fountainlike water action. God, I thought, you could wash a cow in there.

We were called in for individual interviews. I was asked why I wanted to work at GM, a question that momentarily nonplussed me. I mentioned good wages and benefits and that I thought it would be interesting to build cars. I was asked what were my goals in life. Now, no one in my world of journalism had ever indicated an interest in this subject, either officially or otherwise, and I was touched that the spiritual descendants of Henry Ford were concerned with the very essence of my time on this planet. Again this question stumped me for a second. How did they propose to use this inquiry to weed out the good from the bad and the ugly? Would I be rejected if I answered something like "To avenge by the bloody sword all male violence upon oppressed womanhood"? I said my goals were to make a good living and have a family.

Two new jobs followed. Working in teams, we put parts on and took them off on mock auto underbodies, marching back and forth to a workbench where the parts sat. The next job took place at workbenches and involved putting hose, clamps, and valves together in a certain order to build a larger part. We were timed on this task.

On the third day Desiree didn't come back for more. One of the other women commented, not unpleasantly, "She didn't look like the type." We were given manual-dexterity tests—putting pins into holes within a certain time—and reading-comprehension and math and spatial-orientation tests on paper. Most of us felt as if we were back at school, which could mean terror, depending upon our educational experiences.

We also did all three assembly-line jobs. Back at the bumpers, and tired on the third day, I started to feel the rising fear of not being able to keep up. The screws and bolts had thin coatings of grease, and the more slippery my hands became, the harder it was to keep the bolts on my fingertips and twirl them on the screws. The air gun got slippery, too, and I had to be extra careful to keep a good grip on it so it wouldn't fly out of my hands once it tightened down the bolt. I tried to settle into a rhythm and not dwell on the fact that we were building nothing, simply taking bolts on and off in a merry-go-round of futility.

After the three-day peek at the world of automotive labor, General Motors fell silent. Months passed with no clue as to whether I was to be invited to become a tiny cog in the giant GM wheel. Meanwhile the company-union new-product committee in Scarborough failed in its mission, and in July 1991 GM announced that the Scarborough plant would close in the summer of 1993.

About a year after I applied, I was invited to the party. It was the last job available right now, said Gigi of the personnel office. She said I had to report Thursday at 7 A.M. for "women's" training. Hmm, I thought, they give special training to women? This, ladies, is a wrench. This is a welding gun. Okay, I said, I'll be there for "women's" training. "No, no," she said, laughing, "it's 'wimmas' training. You don't get to be with the women." I suddenly realized she thought I was a man, which often happened on the phone, since I have a low voice. She explained what she was pronouncing was WHMIS, which stands for Workplace Hazardous Materials Information System.

The next day I woke at five from nervous anticipation, though I had set the alarm for five forty-five. I tried to get back to sleep, but no use. I left at six, after a couple of mugs of coffee. Sunrise was just blooming as I headed east on Eglinton Avenue, past IBM, the Ontario Science Centre, auto dealerships, Eglinton Square mall, and finally, the skinny stacks of the plant. I spotted them before I glimpsed the GM sign out front. There were a couple dozen of them, a malevolent, stiff forest of metal sticking out of the roof like bullets. You don't see them on any other kind of building. They are the sentinels that announce, "This is a factory. This is where the hard, dirty work goes on that lets you have your toys. Sometimes we break people here. Will you be one of those about whom we can say, 'Abandon hope, all ye who enter here'?"

The butterflies in my stomach were wearing welding masks and pounding rivets. I imagined walking in the door of the factory. Dozens of muscular, grimy men turn and stare. "Hey!" comes an echoing shout,

■

"what's *she* doing here? She's not an autoworker! She's a *writer!* Get out!" They start to bang wrenches on machines and chant. "OUT! OUT! OUT! OUT!"

I shook my head. Gotta stop this. You're overdramatizing once again. Nobody cares. This is a huge place to work. Nearly three thousand people get lost in the shuffle here every day. You will hardly be noticed. You are a number, a warm body. This is not the soft, cuddly white-collar world, where people pay attention to you, nurture your career, and solicit your opinions. The object here is to churn out big, boxy machines on wheels. You will be one little tooth in the enormous gears of General Motors, one of twenty-eight thousand GM Canada employees, one of seven hundred fifty thousand employees of the General Motors Corporation of Detroit, Michigan, the world's largest vehicle manufacturer.

I turned in at the plant and drove past the salaried workers' parking lot to the hourly workers' lot. It was a chilling, blocklong hike to the main security gate.

Half a dozen men sat or stood in a small waiting room just inside the door, across from the security desk. Nobody talked. Nobody read a newspaper. A couple smoked. We looked as if we were nervously awaiting passage across the River Styx. We'd made it thus far—filled out the applications, sat through the videos on attendance and quality, worked the going-nowhere mini–assembly line in Oshawa, apparently mouthed the right answers at the interview—but what lay behind the swinging doors just down the hall from the security guards?

At seven o'clock we were ushered down the hall, past the double doors that led to the factory floor, and into a classroom near the body shop. As we took seats around three tables pushed into a U shape, I noticed that there were nine other members of the class and two instructors. I also noticed that none of them were women.

Our two instructors introduced themselves. Alan Andrews was about fifty-five, pleasant, open face, cardigan and jeans, with an accent that sounded faintly Scottish but hailed from Manchester, England. He'd been with GM five years and was an electrician on the line. The other was Ian Grayson, a tall, dark-haired man, about thirty-five, nice-looking, wearing gray Docker slacks and blue-green casual shirt. He'd been with GM fifteen years and was an absentee-relief man. "We're all union men here," said Alan, telling us not to be nervous as this course was for our benefit and there would be no tests or grades. Throughout the rest of the day our group would be addressed or referred to as "men" or "fellas." Well, I'd always wanted to be one of the guys.

We were asked to write our first names on pieces of cardboard and prop them in front of us. I wrote "Sal," which I decided was easier than "Solange," and would be my *nom d'usine de voiture*. Alan then asked us to introduce ourselves. He started with me, since I was the first person seated at the end of the table to his right, as he faced us. Yikes. What do I say? "Well, fellas, I was recently news editor of Canada with Reuters—that's an international news service—for which they paid me sixty-five thousand dollars per year. But I decided I'd had enough of the wire-service grind, so I left that company to start a magazine. What I know about power tools, welding, and machines, you could put in a thimble and rattle it. I'm here to do something completely different because I'm weirdly drawn to blue-collar life. I'm seeking to prove something to myself, but I'm not even sure what that is. How about you guys?"

What I actually said was, "My name is Sal. I've been working in offices. I applied for this job a year ago and finally got called this week." As Alan went around the table, the others picked up this cue and all mentioned how long they'd been waiting to be called. Next to me, Chris had commuted from Lindsey, about an hour away, because construction work dried up in the recession. Ben, who looked Hispanic and wore a Midas cap, said he was laid off at Midas Muffler. Derek, a young, slim guy with shaggy blond hair and blond mustache, had driven in from Port Parry, also about an hour away, also because of no construction work. Most had applied a year ago or more, except for Dwayne, who had a tattoo on his left forearm and one on each slightly pudgy upper arm. He wore a T-shirt, sleeves rolled up, which bore three saluting, bikini-clad babes superimposed on the American (!) flag and the words TRUE COLORS.

When Dwayne's turn came, he said a bit sheepishly, "My parents work at General Motors, and I waited a month." A couple of knowing looks were passed among the rest of us.

We received a book explaining various types of hazardous materials, physical problems that can result from using certain chemicals, our right to information about hazardous substances, and provincial law covering the subject. All I could think of was the line from *The Wizard of Oz*: "Toto, I don't think we're in Kansas anymore."

At break I listened to the talk. Derek chatted with Stan, a big man with graying hair, forty-five-ish, with a pronounced Eastern European accent and a ready smile. Again, both had driven from towns at least an hour away to get there that morning. Both had had construction businesses that sank under the weight of recession. "There's no work out there in construction," said Derek, and Stan nodded.

Marlon, a young, slim black man with a modified high-top haircut who never removed his snazzy black leather jacket, worked in a can factory north of Toronto. He had been laid off last year. He was exhausted—up all night at a hospital with his goddaughter, who cut her eye. Jim, a tall, bony young guy, wore a high-school letter jacket and mentioned he'd gone to Guelph University for two years but now was taking some time off. He told me he'd been putting himself through school, studying phys. ed., but didn't work over the summer. Basically, he needed money. "I don't know if I'll want to go back," he said, meaning university.

We got an hour for lunch. That would be the last time. The usual line lunch break was half an hour. At lunch Ben discussed various welding techniques with another fellow, Tino. I had absolutely no idea what they were talking about. I was five feet four inches tall and I weighed about 130 pounds. I wondered how many of these men thought, She doesn't belong here. What will they have me do here? Can I handle it?

One of the handouts we were given concerned carpal tunnel syndrome, a condition that can develop when the hand and wrist are put under constant strain. Nerves in the wrist are compressed, and you gradually lose the use of your hand. The paper said, "Wrist flexion is required, for instance, to position a pistol-shaped nut runner on a horizontal surface." What in the living Sam Hill was a pistol-shaped nut runner?

These men know machines. They know tools. I know computer keyboards, words, and desks, I thought.

Alan and Ian took turns reading aloud from the WHMIS book we were each given. This took a remarkably long time and was quite tedious. Eyes glazed. Marlon's head drooped. Then it was video time again, and we were shown three films on workplace safety. One thing stuck in my head: Ian said the Scarborough plant uses six hundred to seven hundred chemicals.

After lunch we were led on a tour of the plant, starting with the body shop, a jungle of cables, spark-shooting welding guns, crashing metal—Satan's private playground. Deep in the heart of the body shop sat a large welding booth, as big as a living room, with a door at one end. The door swung open briefly, and I glimpsed the white-hot light of mig welding and two men in dark coveralls and welding masks bending over a frame. As the door swung shut again, I saw that someone had scrawled in black paint HELL—MAIN OFFICE.

Even the guys in our group looked a little green. I was scared senseless, but tried not to show it. It was break time, and the line workers looked at our group with amusement. "Don't come to work here!" "New hires!" they shouted. Some took no notice of us at all. Dressed in dark-blue coveralls and big white welding gloves, they sat on benches, staring at the floor. When we got back to the classroom, Derek apprehensively said to me, "Didn't see many happy faces out there." Didn't see all that many women either.

On the breaks several of the group gathered around Ian and Alan. "How much will we be making?" asked Ben. "Sixteen dollars an hour to start, plus one dollar and six cents per hour cost-of-living allowance. Then, for the two weeks on nights, there's ten-percent night-shift premium," Ian said. Smiles broke out. Beats unemployment. Beats mini-mum wage by a country mile. Beats ten-dollars-an-hour nonunion la-bour.

"There'll be a lot of overtime," said Ian. Saturdays were time and a half—$25.59 an hour, $204.72 for an eight-hour day!

The only catch to all this happiness is that the ten of us were clutching a rotting life preserver. It was not known yet exactly when in 1993 the plant would be going down, but these men had been so beaten and bashed by the recession that, right at this moment, the horizon was golden. The mortgage was paid, the car was saved, the wife got a Christ-mas present, the kids kept their hockey lessons.

At the end of the day a young woman with gold-rimmed glasses and short dark hair, who introduced herself as Tracy, arrived from the per-sonnel department and gave us our department and shift assignments. Stan was sent to the "ladder" area. There were groans from a couple of those shipped to the body shop. "That paper doesn't mention anything about 'the pit,' does it?" said Brian, a young man wearing a Desert Storm T-shirt and grimacing. Tracy looked over her spectacles sympathetically. "No." God knew what "the pit" was.

I was assigned to Trim 2, B shift, reporting to work the next day at 5 P.M. Hmmm, trim department. I'd heard that women were often as-signed to the trim departments, where the workload was less arduous than in the heavy-lifting areas, like the body shop and chassis line. So this is going to be pretty easy, right? I jog, I work out in the gym, I'm in shape, no problem, right? Hey, in my career I've questioned Margaret Thatcher and covered the Pope—I should be able to handle the foreman (-woman?) of Trim 2, no? What's the worst that can happen? I could fall under a van and get killed? Nah. Sure, it'll be tedious and might take a little getting used to, but nothing all that bad is gonna happen, right?

I was scared.

The next day, late-afternoon traffic on Eglinton Avenue was heavier than I'd expected, but I arrived, feeling a bit frazzled at the possibility of being late, at ten minutes to five, recalling the video we were shown in Oshawa last year on the importance of punctuality and attendance.

"You are paid from the start of your shift, but that does not mean that you walk in the door at seven A.M. or at five P.M.," our elderly instructor sternly told us. "And it does not mean that you arrive at your workstation at that time. It means that's when the line starts, and you should be at your station and ready to work."

So I arrived, out of breath from the jog from the parking lot, to find half our class—Stan, Jim, Derek—stuffed into the little waiting room near the main security gate. Five o'clock came and went with no appreciable change in our status.

At about a quarter after, a man stuck his head in the door, called out three names, and off they went. A few minutes later a couple more were taken, until, by six o'clock, I was the only one left. I was beginning to wish I'd brought a book. A rugged-looking blond man appeared at the door. "Are you De Santis?" I nodded. "Nobody told me I was supposed to get someone today." Ah, bureaucracy.

"I'm Lorne O'Halloran," he said as we walked down the hall. We pushed open the large swinging doors and were greeted—blam!—by the sounds of an auto plant in full cry. We entered by Respot 1, 2, and 3. Music was blaring, machinery crashing, tools whanging, fans humming, men shouting. I glanced up to a platform about six feet off the floor and recognized the roof-securing operation that had so appalled me on my first visit. Since we didn't stop there, I guessed I wouldn't have to do that. We skirted the Respot line and walked for what seemed like miles. Lorne's office was a small box nestled next to the Trim 2 line—in fact, if he were to fall out his office door, he would land in a van.

He took a look at some papers and dispatched somebody who stopped by with a question. "Let's get a coffee," he said, and we walked back through the plant up to the main cafeteria. A year and a half ago I had walked through those swinging doors in a business suit as a visitor. Now, in jeans, I was a worker. I was excited, apprehensive, my senses

wide open. I liked Lorne right away. He had an amused, sardonic manner, and he regarded me with curiosity.

Hmmm, I wondered, when am I actually going to do some work?
Don't rush it, I thought; it'll be time soon enough. We settled in at a
table. Lorne asked where I'd been working, and I gave him what would
become my standard answer: "in offices." Not wanting to answer too
many questions, I asked him the same question. He was not a GM lifer;
he'd been at Scarborough only about a year.

"I worked for a steel company for thirteen years. They went through
a restructuring, and one day I was called in to the main office and I was
out. I worked nights, and the next day I was getting ready to go to work
at about eleven P.M. and my wife said, 'Um, you don't have to do that
anymore.' That's when it hit me. I just got in my car and drove around
for a couple of hours."

With his severance package Lorne was able to take the summer off
and spend it with his family. He applied to GM after seeing a want ad
for production supervisors and got the job. But he was at Scarborough
on what the company called a "per diem" basis: When the plant goes, he
goes. As the factory wound down toward closing, the company was moving experienced foremen to other facilities and hiring people like Lorne
on a contract basis.

We passed an hour in the cafeteria, smoking and chatting, and as we
walked back to his office, Lorne asked, "Well, what do you think of the
job?"

"Hey, piece of cake, so far," I answered, laughing.

"Are you right-handed or left-handed?" Lorne asked.

"Right-handed."

"Are you allergic to anything?" he wanted to know.

"Just cats and pollen sometimes."

"Well, we don't have any cats here. Some real dogs, though."

He led me to a workstation along the line, column D22. Each column in the plant was numbered. Letters ran from east to west, numbers

from north to south. At D22 there stood a battered dark-green metal worktable, two bins filled with pieces of some stiff material, yellow on one side, silver on the other, and some boxes full of black plastic molded items that looked a bit like squarish funnels. Lorne introduced me to Caitlin, who presided over this particular work area. She was a slim young woman with long, wavy brown hair, a sharp, prominent nose, and dancing, amused eyes.

"Caitlin, this is Sally. I want you to train her on insulation."

# E V E R Y B O D Y    C R I E S

Hi, Sally! Okay, Lorne." It seemed I had become Sally. I liked that; it sounded jaunty. Rosie the Riveter, meet Sally the Autoworker. A Frenchwoman once told me that my name, in France, was considered "BCBG," a colloquial acronym meaning "bon chic, bon genre," loosely translated as "quite stylish, quite fashionable," with a connotation of being a bit upper-middle-class snooty. But that wasn't Sally, no, sir. Sally was a calmly efficient factory worker, who probably bounced around in a ponytail or wore a long braid down her back. She certainly wasn't this awkward thirty-six-year-old journalist who kept her dark-brown hair in a short, wash-and-run cut, an introvert by nature with a tendency to gain weight, who would be happy to spend all her life reading books.

Caitlin suggested I watch her for a while, then do a few myself. I sat cross-legged on a pile of boxes next to the worktable as she carried two panels of the stiff material, which was fiberglass insulation for the engine compartment, over to a van moving slowly down the line. She bent over the front, whisked one piece in, then the other, and secured them with a big black clip. Caitlin then grabbed one of the black molded pieces—which she told me was an air vent that went in what will be the dashboard—leaned into the van on the driver's side, and secured it with a clip and a screw. She then changed bits on the drill gun and affixed three screws that secured a piece of plastic to the metal of the engine compartment. The job looked impossibly complicated.

As she went to the next van, I surveyed the scene. Robots banged away behind me, across the aisle in the body shop. The rising, panicked sounds of what seemed to be giant dental drills were everywhere, each singing a different note. At the workstation before mine, two women installed the big, square taillights. Their guns made a drawn-out sound—*screeeeeeee*—as they slid in the three-inch screws, four to a taillight.

At the workstation after mine, a woman installed some small pieces in the driver's-side door, plus a long black rubbery thing that hung out of the window opening after she put it in. She used three small, stubby screws to do something, and her gun made short—*ungh, ungh*—sounds. There was a wild, discordant rhythm to all this, and I thought, Well, here I am. At last. After eighteen months of waiting, I am about to find out what it is like to work in a factory.

After she finished a job, Caitlin motioned me over. I walked to the bins and took one piece of insulation in my left hand, another in my right. I managed to snag a large black clip with an outstretched finger. I walked over to a white van just entering the work area and laid the pieces down on the carrier tongue protruding from the front of the van. I wrestled with the left-side piece, slowly stepping backward as the van moved forward on the line. Then the right-side piece. Then the clip. I was sweating with the exertion; I'd reached the end of the work area and I hadn't even done the vent yet. Caitlin finished up in what seemed to be two seconds.

We decided that I'd do insulation only for the next ten vans (everybody called them trucks, I soon learned), while she took care of the vent-screw combination. Caitlin waltzed along, zapping vents in trucks, strolling back to the worktable to read the *Sun*. I never stopped. As soon as I finished wrestling with one set of insulation/clip, it was time to go to the bins for the next.

I was stiff and clumsy and completely out of my element. I fantasized that at any moment a couple of General Motors officials would materialize. "There she is." "Yup, that's her, all right." "Okay, we found you, the jig's up. Come with us." Other workers would gather, forgetting their jobs. An official would turn to them. "Impostor. White-collar worker. Third one this week." A buzz of conversation would go up from the line workers, a couple nodding, as if something had been confirmed that they'd already guessed.

We were out at 1 A.M., and I slept soundly that night. The weekend was filled with lunches and dinners out, a film, a volleyball game, watching a friend in a kendo tournament. My roommate, a fellow journalist, knew where I'd started working, but most of my friends didn't, and I felt partly detached all weekend, involved in activities that would normally be part of my old life but thinking of my new life at the van plant. Keeping such an immense secret felt as if I were carrying a stone on my chest. I decided not to tell most journalists I knew, since they would blab or, worse, possibly want to write about what I was doing, and GM would fire me. It wasn't that hard to conceal what I was doing for forty hours a week, since I told most people whom I knew socially that I was freelancing. Curbing my natural journalist's tendency to spin a good yarn was the hardest part, but I kept telling myself, The only way to keep a secret is not to tell anybody. A terrible thought occurred to me. What if GM reversed its decision and kept the plant open? Result: twenty-seven hundred relieved autoworkers, one dismayed writer.

I tried to get to sleep early Sunday night, because B shift rotated onto two weeks of days on Monday, which meant starting at 7 A.M., which meant rising at 5:15 A.M., but it was useless. It is a known fact that nervously anticipating an early rising leads to sleeplessness the night before, so I got maybe four hours of rest.

My second day with Caitlin went much like the first. I still found it hard to keep up. I discovered that fiberglass was a bitch to handle. It stung; the glass fibers were stuck on my hands; they snuck up my nose. My jeans and sweatshirt were covered with fibers at the end of the day. I hated to put on my jacket, because that would press the fibers into my skin as I sat in the car. I couldn't wait to get home and strip off the filthy garments. Caitlin said, "Don't wash your work clothes with your other clothes," and she was right. Even after a washing I could see the glint of glass fibers in the fabric.

I could have brought a change of clothing to work each day, but there was no women's locker room at the plant; in fact, there was no men's locker room. Banks of lockers were located in each department next to the line, and most men had absolutely no compunction about changing at their lockers. I never came across a naked guy, but it was not unusual to go to my locker and find, a few feet away, a man in his underwear shrugging into his coveralls. In order to change with privacy, I would have had to retrieve new clothes from my locker, go up the stairs to the women's washroom, which also held a shower, and change there. Too much effort for end of shift, when I just wanted to get the hell out into the fresh air.

I'd been told that you got three days of training on a new job; if you couldn't do the job after that, you were out. I was hoping that, on the third day with Caitlin, my body and hands might retain some muscle memory, like being able to play a piece on the piano after much practice, without thinking of every single note.

No such luck. They took Caitlin away. I arrived about fifteen minutes early and got a pair of the rough-weave white cotton gloves that made us look as if we were auditioning for an industrial minstrel show or perhaps a stint at Disneyland as Mickey Mouse.

I grabbed the silver screw gun that weighed about a pound. I asked the trainer, whose name I had forgotten, to hook it up to the long hose at my workstation, because I had absolutely no idea how to do it. I put my jacket, lunch bag, and purse under my battered green metal worktable and reached for the five-pocket dark-blue apron filled with screws and clips. As I tied it around my waist, I looked at the big metal bins holding the insulation panels, yellow pressed fiberglass on one side, silver foil on the other. Welcome to my nightmare, I thought.

The body shop had started a half hour before us, at 6:30 A.M. Across the aisle, the thirteen huge welding robots swung into action. *Bang! Bam-boom-chukka-bang-boom! Bang! Bam-boom-chukka-bang-boom!* It's got a beat, you can dance to it. Sparks flew as the robots, like giant praying mantises, bobbed and weaved in jerky patterns. The aisle, and my workstation, were protected from flying sparks by long strips of heavy plastic that resembled a heavy-duty shower curtain hanging next to the robots.

Occasionally a particularly energetic spray of sparks shot up and across the aisle. Bending over my purse for a second, I felt a slight tap on the top of my head, followed immediately by a tiny burning sensation. "Hey, what the—" I jerked up and grabbed the top of my head, only to see the rest of the sparks burn out on the floor.

Slightly dazed by the bashing rhythms of the General Motors Body Shop Steel Band at this hour of the morning, I stared farther down the aisle. Two men in navy-blue coveralls wearing dark safety glasses and thick white gloves were welding the front part of the floor pan to the back part. I couldn't make out their features; my tired mind saw dusky ghosts.

They walked over to a rack and pulled out a big metal rectangle with a U-shaped opening cut in one end—the front part of the floor. They swung it up and—*blam!*—banged it down on the jig where the back part was sitting already. They pulled down the big welding guns, slung them into position, and started pulling the triggers. *Thunk! Thunk! Thunk!* Sparks flew at each *thunk* as the tips of the guns met metal—sparks that landed on heads, faces, chests, arms—sparks that bounced into coveralls and boots and burned unmentionable body parts.

Our section of the line started, and the vans began their stately procession. I peered into the empty engine compartment of the first one and saw silvery insulation. Ah, the first one was done. Thank you, unknown A-shift person. A minute later the next one was at the start of my job station, and the engine compartment was bare. I picked up the left insulation panel with my left hand, then a large black clip, then the right panel with my right hand.

I walked up to the front of the van, gradually moving toward me, and laid the right piece and the clip down on the protruding tongue of the carrier. I leaned over the front of the truck and wrestled the left piece into the "doghouse," the curved area where the engine would rest. Stepping slowly backward as I did this, I picked up the right piece, flopped myself over the front again, and jerked it into place. Still walking backward as the truck bore down on me, I leaned over again, felt for a small bracket, and pushed the black clip into place at the top of the doghouse, securing the panels.

The van was about halfway through my station. I walked over to the stack of boxes and picked up a black plastic vent, walked to the driver's side of the van, leaned in, and shoved it into the plastic base of what would become the dashboard.

I reached into my apron, grabbed a little clip, and placed it on a protruding bit of plastic, got the gun and took a screw out of the apron. *Zap,* I secured the vent. Then I changed bits on the gun and fumbled for three screws in the apron. Placed a screw on the gun bit, leaned in, and screwed it into a hole in the plastic that went through the body metal. One, two, three. Oops, the third one was tough. I used both hands to push it in and heard the grinding sound that meant it'd gone through the metal. One job done.

The van was at the end of my job station. Time for the next one. Insulation, clip. Vent, clip, screw. Screw, screw, screw. Insulation, clip. Vent, clip, screw. Screw, screw, screw. I struggled with each part of the job, always keeping my eye on the pillar marked D22—the end of my job station. I was supposed to get the job done between D21 and D22, which had a parts list affixed to it with funereal black tape.

Shit! The panels wouldn't fit in the next one. Something seemed stuck. I was draped over the front of the truck, stepping backward, trying to get this itchy fiberglass thing into position and it *just wouldn't go.* Damn, damn, damn, the Pillar of Doom was looming. I was breaking out in panic sweat. I would just have to leave the edge sticking out like that. I supposed somebody would see it and fix it, if our repairman missed it. I hustled around to the side, grabbed a vent, and dropped a screw. Oh, jeez, almost up to the pillar. Changed the bit, now the three screws. I grabbed five, dropped a couple. None of them went in easily, and I had to use two hands on all. I was a step or two past the pillar, and the next job was more than halfway through my job station.

Jesus, it was hot. I kept falling behind. The insulation was awkward, I missed the big-clip bracket and lost precious seconds feeling for it, dropped screws, dropped the little clips. The more perspiration ran down my face, the more nasty yellow fiberglass wisps stuck to me. They were embedded in my gloves, jeans, and T-shirt.

I noticed a tag on the bin and read "CAUTION: Based largely upon studies of laboratory animals in which glass fibers were surgically implanted in the chest cavity, the International Agency for Research on Cancer classified glass fibers as a possible carcinogen. The release of glass fibers during normal handling can cause irritation to the skin, eyes, a stuffy nose or scratchiness in the throat." Well, thank you very much; I may come away from this with more than a story. I shall hunt down a mask tomorrow, I thought.

First break. The line stopped. It was 9 A.M.—two hours, sixty jobs. When I worked in an office, I would be just sitting down with a cup of coffee at my desk at this time. Here, I got my first chance to sit down in two hours. There was no seat at my workstation, just the pile of boxes holding the big clips. Someone had folded a box flat and placed it on the other boxes, and I gratefully sank down on the makeshift seat. Coffee. Really needed coffee. The closest cafeteria was half a minute's walk down the aisle, and I plodded over there to get a large cuppa with triple cream, no sugar, and a muffin. Back to my seat, a couple of sips and— Holy cow, the line's starting again. Nine twenty-three already?

Insulation, clip. I saw an LL4 designation on the next truck's manifest, which was affixed to the open driver's-side door with a bit of masking tape. That meant a diesel engine, and it took thicker insulation panels from a different bin. Wow, these were heavy. I dragged a left and a right out of the bin and over to the moving van. They were tougher to maneuver, and once again I fell behind.

The three screws were still giving me problems, and I was using both hands on just about every other job. Caitlin appeared on the other side of the van as I was grunting over the screws.

"Gee, you're having a tough time with that," she said cheerfully.

"Yeah. Maybe the holes aren't lined up," I panted. Yes, that was it, of course! That must have been why it was so difficult. The screws had to go through a hole in the plastic, then one in a quarter-inch-thick fabric layer, then one in the metal.

Balthasar, our genial Hispanic repairman, came along to find out why so many of my screws were loose when they arrived at his workstation, midway through the Trim 2 department.

"Hey, sweetheart, what's the matter here? You don' like doing the screws?"

"No, well, I don't know, Balthasar, maybe the holes aren't lined up."

"Uh-huh. Hey, George." He motioned to a fellow who didn't seem to have anything to do. "Help Sally with these screws. She's not strong enough."

Oh. But that couldn't be it. Nobody could be strong enough to push those things through metal. Next truck was a diesel, and I dragged the panels over to the line. George grabbed a vent and the gun, secured it, and then started the three screws. Crunch, crunch, crunch, in they went. I didn't believe it. What was the secret?

Eleven o'clock and the thirty-minute lunch hour. Caitlin bounced past. "Come on over. Sit with us." I took my sandwich and can of soda to the next workstation up the line, where an alcove contained a picnic table, large bulletin board, and a locked tool cabinet. Marilyn, another member of our department, had the cards out and was shuffling as Keenan, a visitor from Trim 1, sat down with his lunch next to Clyde, Caitlin's brother. "Marilyn, you dizzy bitch, hurry up," Keenan snipped.

At first I thought he was gay, but he pulled out a photograph and said, "We're losing our baby." The picture was of a black child, about ten months old, with huge, liquid, dark eyes, dressed in a pretty pale-blue outfit with matching lacy bonnet. Keenan wasn't exactly pale—he had swarthy skin that looked as if it tanned easily—but he was definitely not black. "What do you mean?" I asked, with the worst possibilities running through my mind.

The little one, he explained, was a foster child. Keenan and his wife, although they had a couple of kids of their own, had taken in a foster child, and they were losing this one after several months to another placement. "She's such a darling," he said mournfully.

A euchre game got rolling. I'd never seen the game before, but it seemed like a simple version of bridge. The players kept it fast-moving, not that there was much choice with just thirty minutes to play, punctured by piercing whoops of excitement from Marilyn and Caitlin. I observed the game, but felt a bit intimidated by these people who were all so at ease with each other, so I didn't say much. "Well," Keenan observed, after a bawdy description of his play from Caitlin, "It's nice to sit next to a woman who's not always *flapping her gums.*" Much laughter, but since it was eleven twenty-five already, I said so long in order to visit the washroom before sluggin'-it-out time started again.

This was the hump—two hours until second break. It seemed like an eternity. For the first two hours of the day I was relatively fresh, but this one was a bastard. My arms were sore, my chest bone was bruised, and my legs felt like wobbly plant stems. George didn't come back after lunch. Tightening those screws was such an effort that I was grunting with nearly each one. Sweating like a pig again, too, even with the fan on. Insulation, clip. Vent, clip, screw. Screw, screw, screw.

I was laboring over the Three Blind Screws when Chris, an Austrian lady who installed taillights across the line from me, gave me a worried look. "Sally, are you all right? You can ask for help."

"No, no, it's okay. I'm fine," I panted. Help? Yikes, what was she talking about? Ask whom? Where? And then what? Get fired because I couldn't do the job? New hires were put on ninety days' probation, during which, I was told, GM could cashier your ass for any reason whatsoever. The union couldn't help you because you were not a member until the ninety days were up. However, they did take union dues out of your check in that period. Hmmmm.

■

I was determined not to get help. It was embarrassing enough having to grunt and struggle over nearly every job while everyone else seemed so competent. I was going to gut this thing out myself. I knew it would end at 3:30 P.M. I just had to keep going, going. But God, I wanted to sit down so badly, and there was just no letup. The line kept bearing down on me, moving, moving, world without end, amen. I tried to bargain with it. "C'mon, line, one little stop, okay? How about it? Just stop. Stop, please stop. One minute, all right? I just need a minute to sit down. Stop, for Christ's sake, stop."

Sometimes, as I was bending over the front of the van and facing the floor, trying to shove the insulation pieces into the doghouse, I hallucinated for a second that the drag chain had stopped. The carriers were pulled along the floor by a filth-encrusted chain set in a raised track. Since the drag chain was one long line, it did indeed stop for a second if a glitch developed farther along. It was a cruel second.

I had taken off my watch and put it on the worktable. For one thing, the glass fibers worked themselves under the watchband and stung like crazy. For another, I just didn't want the temptation of looking at it every two minutes. I snuck a peek at the watch only to discover, to my horror, that it was just twelve-thirty. I plunged into the slough of despond. Obviously three-thirty would never come and I would simply trudge through this treadmill existence until death's welcome release.

Gotta keep going, gotta keep going. My arms and chest were so sore now that sometimes my eyes filled with tears when I was bent over the front of the van. But I figured it was okay, nobody could see, since I had my head under the hood. Jim, a blond American who did some job across the line, passed by and asked, "How's it going?"

"Okay," I gasped, "but the line seems to go so fast, doesn't it?"

"Oh, sometimes it'll go down." My heart leapt. "For as much as fifteen minutes." My heart sank. Fifteen minutes. Was that all?

I kept checking my watch. One o'clock. One-fifteen. One-twenty. Only five more jobs. One-thirty. I was behind, as usual, so I was still working when the line stopped for second break. I finished the job and dragged over to my throne of boxes. I did not look at a newspaper or book. I just sat. I never thought just sitting could feel so good. Larry, the supervisor, swung past, saw me, and stopped.

"Are you going to be okay?" I was leaning my head back against the box pile, and I didn't even feel like straightening up. "Sure. Fine," I replied, attempting a pleasant smile. "Hmm," he commented and walked off.

No sooner had I sat down than the line started again—that's how fast the twenty-three minutes seemed to fly. My feet still ached, and I was making my body move by sheer willpower. "Running on fumes" took on a whole new meaning. Everything hurt, but I picked up insulation panels, affixed clips, and struggled with the demon screws. My mind and body seemed to be in another country, a different existence. My eyes glazed. I couldn't talk, I couldn't think. I could only will myself to move.

Around two-fifteen activity picked up. People were walking through my work area, carrying boxes of small parts and lugging big parts. What the heck was going on? I plodded through my routine, but by three o'clock I was the only one there. Since the body shop started a half hour before us, it stopped at three. Suddenly it was quiet. Our line was still rolling, but everybody in my department also had disappeared. Where had they gone? How could they leave before the line stopped? The silence was punctuated only by an eerie, metallic *screek* every few minutes. Somewhere, something needed oiling. Every so often there was a faraway thump. Something, somewhere, was gently bumping into something else.

Final half hour. Just thirty minutes, fifteen jobs to go. Come on, come on, just keep doing it. I worked away, alone, determined to get through this. At last the line stopped. I finished the last job half a minute or so past three-thirty, and that was it. I stripped off the fiberglass-encrusted gloves and dropped them in the garbage. The trainer came along, detached the gun from the hose, put it away in the B-shift metal cabinet, and locked up. I retrieved my jacket and purse and headed for the exit.

My aching legs were definitely not attached to my body; they were stomping through the plant by some other motor. I walked through the back gate and found my brown Tempo. I unlocked the door and creakily lowered myself into the driver's seat, shaking with fatigue. I could barely grip the steering wheel. Shifting gears was painful. As I pulled onto the Don Valley Parkway, I sobbed from exhaustion. "I don't know how I can do this; it's just too hard," I wept.

At home I took inventory. My left elbow was black and blue from leaning against the metal to push in the screws. My chest was bruised from hitting the front of two hundred vans. That night sleep was difficult. My hands went numb and tingly as I lay in bed. I dreamed of the line. I was trying to drive a truck down the line, but it wasn't fully assembled. It was the shell I saw in my area. But I was kneeling on the driver's side, pounding the floor in panic. "How do I steer this thing? There's no steering wheel, no pedals!"

Next morning I crossed the parking lot at 6:40 A.M., unwilling to believe I was going to submit again to this torture. A woman I vaguely recognized said hi and asked how I was doing.

"Well, yesterday was my first day alone on a job, and it was pretty rough. I was so beat I burst into tears on the way home," I admitted sheepishly.

"Oh, are you kidding?" she exclaimed. "My husband cried after his first day. Don't worry, everybody cries."

# FOUR

■

# B SHIFT

My second day alone. Back to the stinging fiberglass, the savage jungle rhythms of the body-shop robots, the evil screws.

Okay, Solange, yesterday you worked hard. Today you work smart.

I vowed this as I entered the plant, stumping past the stairs to the cafeteria, past the chassis department, where the vans were suspended on huge carriers six feet in the air. I noticed that as I came in through the entrance nearest the hourly workers' parking lot, I heard a far-off, two-beat squeak (*oo-eek . . . oo-eek*), every couple of seconds. Even when the line was down, something was moving somewhere. It was my bird of greeting, my chirpy little evil robin signaling the start of another eight hours.

My hands were sore from unaccustomed gripping and squeezing, but I could pace myself a little better than the day before. So I did two things. First, I twice called for help from the trainer, a short, pleasant man whose name was Tony and who could often be found at the lunch table near my workstation. The first time was for a bathroom break ten minutes before lunch, which gave me a forty-minute lunch. He didn't seem too happy about that, and I was sure this was a major no-no, but I didn't care. I needed that forty minutes. I called him again when I was falling behind and had trouble shoving in the thicker insulation panels on a diesel model. The other thing I did was not try to tighten all the screws that resisted. I left them for Balthasar to finish. I told him that I

■

wasn't strong enough yet to do all of them, but that I would be. I just couldn't get some of them. It was straining at those nasty, stubborn ones that had nearly killed me yesterday. This time, if one wouldn't go in, I left it loose. I wondered if a vehicle owner, cursing a loose part or washer, ever thought that the assembly-line worker was just in too much pain to tighten it down. It never would have occurred to me before.

During lunch I decided to collect some material from the bulletin boards. The first couple of notices I read caused me to sit down abruptly, momentarily overcome by dismay. The first read, "Due to recent start up difficulties during the month of September, we find ouselves [sic] with a serious shortfall of units to the required Corporate schedules for our Vans." It went on to say that management had decided to schedule Saturday-night overtime in order to build the required number of units. "However, in response to feedback from the workforce relative to these plans" the Saturday-night overtime had been dropped in favor of an additional 1.1 hours of overtime Monday through Thursday on the night shift.

The second notice went on to say that management had not been able to get enough people to work the 1.1 hours at night (which would have meant staying until 2:10 A.M.) and had, after all, scheduled Saturday overtime until Christmas—mostly days and one Saturday night per shift. Under the union contract the company couldn't force us to work overtime at the end of our regular shifts, but could schedule mandatory overtime on a sixth day. Oh, my God, I thought, there really is no rest for the weary. How am I going to survive six straight days of this?

I had thought things were getting better, but by the time second break rolled around, I was just as strung out as the day before. I cancelled an invitation to *Swan Lake* that evening. Because of my arts features, I was still on the media list at the National Ballet of Canada, but, much as I wanted to go, my eyes burned with fatigue, my stomach felt slightly queasy, and all I could think of was rest. What in the world had led me to think I could get up at 5:30 A.M., work at manual labor all day, then go out for the evening? Sleep was difficult again that night. My hands still tingled and went numb when I lay down, no matter how I positioned my arms. You would think that such profound exhaustion would have produced deep sleep, but it seemed that the opposite was true, that my body was so shaken out of its normal existence, it couldn't settle into normal sleep cycles.

What was ironic was that I'd gone into this thinking I was in pretty good shape. When I was an overweight, book-loving teenager, I was intimately acquainted with the phrase "you get her" when sides were being chosen up for school sports. In young adulthood I would make the occasional stab at going to a health club, then lose interest. (In this, I was my mother's child. She hated strenuous physical activity and claimed she got enough exercise gardening, while my father, who is, as I write this, eighty-five years old, continues to work out religiously at the fencing club and the gym.) Everything changed the day I arrived in Southern California. Call it something in the water, the sun, or the air, but I started exercising in my hotel room that first day. By the time I hit Scarborough, I'd lost the excess weight and was jogging a couple of miles and doing a calisthenics routine regularly. Not only that, but under Billy's influence I'd slowly learned how to play softball and ice hockey and was finally enjoying recreational team sports.

I had figured assembly-line work would be hard, but a small piece of my yuppie mind had conceived it as sort of an extended session at the health club, kind of an industrial version of working out. The only other experience I could compare it to was the time I'd gone on an overnight hike and pushed myself way too far. I didn't know about fiberglass. I didn't know about jamming in screws while bent over. I didn't know what it's like to be on your feet for seven hours. I didn't know I'd be sporting brownish bruises along the length of my arms from leaning into the vehicle and bruises on my shins from banging into it as it moved and hit my legs.

On my third day alone, as I got into the car at 6 A.M., I fumbled tiredly with the seat belt, missing a couple of times as I jabbed the tongue at the receiver. In animallike frustration, I screamed at the

buckle, "Uhnuh, uhnuh, uhnuh!" Where did that come from, I wondered? I drove past a man jogging, as I used to do, and he looked effete
and lucky. What world was that, again, where exercise was performed
for fun? My hands hurt so badly, I tried to steer with my wrists. I had
squeezed the air gun four times per van, some eight hundred times. I
thought I was accustomed to using my hands—after all, I typed a lot. I
had no conception of what it really meant to work with your hands.

When I got to work, it occurred to me that maybe I was having a
tougher time than most because of my soft background, but when I
mentioned how I was feeling, Balthasar said he understood. He said that
when he started, he was in the body shop, pulling the trigger on the
heavy welding guns. He made claws with his fingers, held up his hands,
and said that when he got home after the first day, he couldn't straighten
his fingers. Chris understood, too. She said your hands get so sore "it's
like they don't belong to you anymore." Chris said she'd wondered if she
should quit during the first week.

I discovered that the reason I was alone at the end of the shift
yesterday was that, from the end of last break, people participated in the
Sacred Ritual of Working Ahead. At two minutes per job, if you worked
ten trucks up the line from your job station, you could leave twenty
minutes early. It wasn't as easy as it might sound, because not only did
you have to work faster, you had to carry parts up the line and stay out of
your co-workers' way. While I was laboriously installing the dashboard
vent in the shift's last hour, three people were waiting for me to finish so
they could do the various parts of the window assembly and move on.
People customized boxes, cans, all kinds of containers, with wire, duct
tape, and bits of cardboard in order to carry parts and found ingenious
places to stash parts in the aisles and near other people's workstations.
In the last ninety minutes of the shift, there was little banter; everyone
concentrated, working feverishly. People I hadn't seen all day trucked by
me, loaded down with tubing, windows, rods. I couldn't believe it; if the
company had sped up the line this way, the union would be screaming.

On my fourth day alone, the fifth straight day of work, I brought in my hockey elbow pad. As I used the gun to tighten down the Screw Trio, I was bracing my left elbow against the metal, and it was very tender. The hockey equipment helped enormously, and no one really looked twice at it. A variety of materials were used to protect body parts. There were different kinds of gloves—the white cloth ones, dark-blue leather ones, big heavy white welding ones—for different jobs. Green mesh tape was wound around fingers. Pads were strapped around knees. Safety glasses were supposed to be mandatory, but enforcement was lax, and almost no one used them in Trim, with the result that Jim, the American, cut his eye when a thin, whippy tool he was using to pull a wire slipped and hit him in the face. In the body shop, of course, they were used, along with the welding masks and smoked-glass spectacles, but they were hot and fogged up and no one wanted to use them.

That day was the lowest point of the week. "Guts, guts," I kept muttering to myself. "Keep going, keep going, just keep going. Find the reserves. Dig down. Come on, dig down." Arms screamed, shoulders screamed, legs cried, "Stop! Just stop! Just for one second, please! If only it would stop. We could do this more easily if it would just stay still." My fingers felt as if they'd been broken and reassembled. A thermos of coffee in the morning had no effect. My eyeballs were being tugged by reins of fire. I'd weighed myself this morning and discovered I'd lost three pounds this week. The GM Exercise and Diet Plan—work on the line, eat anything you want, lose weight.

As I sat on a pile of boxes near my workbench, staring at the floor, Lorne stopped by again. "Still alive?" he asked.

I cocked my head, managed a half smile and replied, "Sure. Barely."

The closest women's washroom to our department was perched atop two flights of filthy metal stairs, right over the body shop. Suspended over the area where the floors were welded together was a message box wired, I assumed, to the office. Every couple of minutes it displayed a message in red letters in the exotic lingo of the body shop: CARTRAC

■

ACCUMULATOR FULL—STN 4 JOY PLUG—STN 5 JOY PLUG. The joy plug sounded
a bit risqué. At other times it would display little inspirational messages.
That day it read, between CARTRAC messages, "It's not the hours you put
in, it's what you put in the hours." I looked down, sadly, at the men
beating metal to their will and thought, It's not what you put in the
hours, but what the hours take out of you.

On my way home I found myself driving behind one of our vans. I
saw the taillights and imagined Elsie, a rangy woman from the Caribbean, on the left and Chris on the right, both stepping up to the truck,
turning into it in their industrial ballet, sitting on the back to fasten the
lights. Through the van's back windows I saw a dome light and pictured
Jim bending over and twisting his neck up to connect the wires. I saw a
dashboard, and there was Marilyn reaching across to connect speaker
wires. Fatigue unhinged my emotions, and tears of pity and rage—pity
that they had to work that hard, rage that they were invisible—rolled
down my face.

Saturday—sixth straight day at work. Fifth day alone. When I
dragged myself out of bed at 5:30 A.M., I thought, I don't know how I can
do another day. My hands hurt so much I could hardly pull on my socks.
I broke the day into four pieces: 7 to 9:12 A.M. (first break), 9:35 to 11:00
A.M. (lunch), 11:30 A.M. to 1:42 P.M. (second break), 2:05 to 3:30 P.M.
(quitting time). The most gut-it-out part was after lunch—more than
two straight hours. Sixty vans. Do you know how many sixty vans is? It is
a huge number, a number too desperate to contemplate. It is 120 insulation panels, a left and a right, 60 big clips, 60 air vents, 60 small clips,
240 screws, 240 shots with the air gun, 60 changes of the bit on the tip of
the air gun. Sixty times leaning over the engine compartment, gasping as
the van moves forward, your weight on your chest bone, struggling to
reach into the engine well and insert the insulation panels and the big
clip. I saw myself passing out, my body carried along the line, draped
over the frame, a casualty of the auto industry. Sixty times leaning into
the driver's side, taking small steps as the vehicle moves, shoving in

the screws, bracing left elbow, pulling on the trigger. Changing the bit, thumb sore, placing screw washer on bit, placing air vent with right hand, clipping on plastic frame, lining up gun and screw, pressing trigger.

The line went down for nine whole minutes in the morning. Time to talk to a co-worker without constantly moving, bending, working. Time to sit, just to sit, feeling legs and feet breathe gratitude. Nine minutes was forever. A long draft from the plastic gallon water jug. Take off the cotton gloves coated with fiberglass, eat a bit of a cookie. Can't touch food with gloves on. You can't touch your face with your hand or your sleeve either, since it's all got fiberglass on it.

That week was the worst, but I turned a corner that Saturday. After work, for the first time, I didn't feel like closing my eyes and passing out. I seemed to catch a second wind. I went out for a beer with a friend. I was awake and alive, not the sleepwalking dead. Even at 10 P.M. I wasn't really that tired, though I'd been up a long time. I'd done it! Dear God, I'd done it. I'd passed a test, the test I set myself, a test of whether I could summon up buried physical and mental reserves. Athletes talk of reaching deep, of finding something extra. I'd done that, and I was proud. No one really knew what I'd done, even my co-workers, though they could sympathize from their experiences. No one knew the realm of pain I'd dwelled in this week, nor how I'd moved through it, played with it, cheated it, denied it, beat it into a corner, and refused to let it defeat or humiliate me.

I called Billy to tell him of my triumph, gain his empathy and approval, but the conversation took an entirely unexpected turn. He snapped at me. "Why do you think a lot of people drink at the plant? Why do you think I exercise? To stay in shape for work. Why do you think people go out at lunch and drink four beers in the parking lot? Because by the end of the day they are totally gassed."

I was a bit taken aback at first, not getting the expected praise, then chagrined that I'd been so foolish as to expect it. I had lent a sympathetic ear to his tales of the routine horrors of the factory, but when I experienced them myself, he was almost angry. Despite my week at the end of a fiberglass rope, I had barely begun to fathom his existence and that of the thousands engaged in such labor. For me it was drama. For him it was life. I was ready to spike the ball and declare victory after that endless week, but Billy's words showed me just how long that path would be.

Sunday's day off passed like one of our breaks—in a heartbeat—but the body felt better. Arms and shoulders ached less. Thumbs were slightly swollen and sore, but a little less so than earlier in the week. Hands were still tender. One day of rest, just one day for healing. For that blessed day I didn't feel like a brute animal. I went to brunch, shot pool with several buddies from softball who didn't know where I was working, and went to a Greek restaurant for dinner.

I was rooming with my Canadian journalist friend, Don Angus, who, of course, knew what I was up to. Don regarded my adventure with a mixture of interest and bemusement. One day that first week, after I'd dragged myself in the door at 4 P.M., I was telling him about some of my new acquaintances. He said, "They must sense you're not just an ordinary laborer." Thinking of Caitlin and the other lively characters I'd met in just a few days, I responded, "Don, I don't think there are any ordinary laborers." Six-day wonder that I was, I felt instantly defensive about my new acquaintances. I wanted to reject the idea that I was in some way better than my co-workers, reject the thought that they might be gray clones pounding out a living on the rubble heap of society.

I called Mom and Dad and told them I'd started working at the van plant and it was pretty strenuous going at first, but I didn't go into too many details, feeling the universal desire not to worry the folks. "But don't you find it demeaning?" asked Dad. Annoyed at his obtuseness, I replied, "No, I don't. It's not like I'm robbing gas stations or something." Then, ashamed that I had fallen in his estimation, I hurried to assure him that I hadn't planned a permanent change in social standing. "Dad, I told you, I'm not going to make a career of this. I'm going to write about it when the plant closes." Mom told me to be careful and take notes.

Those first few days my social initiation into the Trim 2 fold was surprisingly easy, as Caitlin, Keenan, Marilyn, Balthasar, and several others included me in their group, and I made tentative steps toward discovering how these particular people had fetched up in this department, in this factory. My first impressions were scattered, since no one was inclined to pour out a life history over a thirty-minute euchre game. As the new person, it was natural that I would ask questions, but I kept them to a minimum so my curiosity would be taken as friendliness, not an inquisition.

Caitlin, of the beaky nose and laughing eyes, had followed the well-worn path to the smokestacks of Ontario from Newfoundland, a province whose unemployment rate had been stuck in the double digits for years due to its remote location off Canada's east coast and the seasonal nature of its fishing industry. Her brother, Clyde, also worked in Scarborough. Their last name was Barrow, and Clyde was sometimes teased that he bore the same name as the notorious bank robber of the thirties.

One afternoon I caught rowdy Marilyn, Caitlin's co-conspirator at the card table, singing as she scrambled into the vans installing dome lights (the interior light on the ceiling) and dashboard wiring. She had a fine voice, and I wondered if she'd ever performed.

Another member of the crowd was Bernie, twenty-five and an Ottawa native. He was an AR, meaning absentee-relief worker. He moved around from job to job, depending upon who was out on any particular day. He was humming selections from *South Pacific* as he worked building taillights on a subassembly job, which piqued my interest immediately, my being an intense Broadway fan. Musical entertainment along the line was more likely to run toward Guns N' Roses than Rodgers and Hammerstein. He told me he went to Trent University in Ontario, as an English major. He was able to quote William Blake. His father was a

GM vice president. I said, "Wow, surely he could have gotten you a cushier job than this." But Bernie said Dad didn't believe in using influence that way. "No, I'll probably be here for life," he joked.

I smiled, but my instant, visceral thought was, Oh no, Bernie, I really hope you're kidding, because you're much too bright to be building taillights the rest of your life. I saw dignity and worth in these jobs and the people who performed them, but I couldn't deny the mentally and physically wearing nature of the work. I hoped that if Bernie had a chance at a better deal in life, he'd take it.

I also talked a little to the two women who installed taillights just before I came along with the insulation. Chris had been born in Austria. Her husband and son also worked in Scarborough, Gerhard in the paint shop and Kurt in Trim 2 on the A shift. Chris was a perfect lady. Even on the day shift, when we had to report at 7 A.M., her petite figure was dressed in clean shirt and slacks, her hair was neatly coiffed in a short, curly style, and she wore small pearl stud earrings. I was lucky if my hair was combed at all, not sticking up straight from bed. The only attribute that made her different from other women I knew who looked like her was that she had biceps. Ladylike biceps.

Elsie put in taillights on the other side, my side of the line. She was given to bursts of temper—during this week she went on at high volume about how someone had moved her electric kettle a couple of feet—and I kept well shy of her at first.

After my workstation, Doreeta, who was also from the Caribbean, but a calm eye to Elsie's hurricane, installed a black window sash strip and a doohickey that connected to the handle used to roll up the window. Balthasar was from South America, a stocky, good-natured guy. I once revealed, in response to a question, that I was from the States. When asked how I came to Canada, I just laughed and replied, "It's a long story," at which people asked, "Are you still with the guy?"

Keenan, the man with the black foster baby, was married eighteen years and worked just up the line from Chris and Elsie, but was a member of the Caitlin/Bernie/Marilyn/Clyde group and came down to our department at lunch for the card games.

I also met, for the first time, a man who was ashamed of being an autoworker. I'd noticed a tall, slim fellow with cheekbones to die for and a mane of long, dark, curly hair working across the aisle. He looked like a rock star who had found himself in the body shop after his last tour went sour. I worked up the nerve to say hello to him in the cafeteria, and he proved to be quite friendly. Over coffee he said his name was Chas, and sure enough he was a musician.

"Do people understand," I wondered aloud, "if you can't make a gig because you work shifts?"

"Not a lot of people know what I do. I've got a lot of things going on besides here," he replied. His expression told me clearly that the coveralls he was wearing, the grimy cafeteria he was sitting in, and the steel he banged eight hours a day—this was not him, and he was not about to communicate this life to the life where he felt he really belonged.

# D A N C E   O F   A

# T H O U S A N D   C U T S

Much as I liked my new acquaintances, I had a problem. From the first day I'd been crushed that I hadn't been assigned to the same shift as Billy and his friends. I wanted to see them, especially Billy, though our relationship was in a dormant phase. I wanted to hang out with them, ask them questions about the plant. They all worked in the body shop, which stretched out next to the trim departments, and I looked for them a few times between shifts. (There was an hour between shifts, but many arrived early, and because I was so slow, I usually left late.) I didn't see them and realized how difficult it was to find somebody in a plant that employed twenty-seven hundred people.

So I told Lorne I wanted to transfer to the A shift. He balked a little at the extra paperwork and teased me about whether romance was involved, but he put it through. A couple of days later he came up to me and told me I'd be going to the other shift shortly, but that I'd have to train my replacement. Gladly, oh gladly! An end in sight to fiberglass and screw-jamming! I don't know which made me happier, getting on the A shift or getting off the fiberglass job, but I also feared a worse job awaited me.

Those first few weeks, working six days a week, it seemed as if I staggered through a fog of fatigue. I got up at 5:30 A.M., spent seven hours on my feet, got home by 4 P.M., showered, stayed awake or slept a couple of hours, had dinner, watched TV or went out, tried to get to bed by 10 P.M., but usually fell asleep at 11 P.M. or midnight, then got up at 5:30 A.M. next day and did it all over again. Many people who work in offices get up that early and put in similar schedules, but when you work at manual labor all day, sometimes you can't think of anything but sitting down. Sometimes you can't think of anything, period, and that frightened me. Not only were my hands too sore to type more than a little; sometimes I would just sit and blink at my laptop screen, hearing my own breathing, then close my journal file, thinking, I'll come back to this later. Right now I think I'll just lie down for a bit.

Nearly every day, generally at the very beginning of the shift or at the very end, I comforted myself with the idea that I could always quit and go back to freelance writing—sitting at my desk, talking on the phone, tippy-tapping on my computer, taking a break for a jog along Lake Ontario. But while I embraced that vision of relief, I always, in the end, rejected it. After all, I wasn't dying, and the whole purpose of this test was to stretch my limits. Exhausting though it was, there was something exciting about it, too. I was feeling emotions I couldn't have felt unless I'd gotten out from behind my desk. Besides, every day the work got a little better, a little smoother, a little easier.

Despite the warning tag on the insulation bin, I'd been too busy, or addled, to ask for a mask, but in the second week the tag floated by my face as a forklift driver delivered a new bin of insulation, and I remembered that I was working with hazardous material. If it weren't for the tag, I wouldn't have known. No one had warned me that fiberglass was a possible carcinogen. If I worked with fiberglass for the next year and a half, how much did my chance of getting lung cancer increase? I asked to see the WHMIS book in Lorne's office, but it didn't have much more information than the tag. I requested a mask. Lorne looked at me as if I'd asked for a four-course dinner to be delivered at break, but he came up with a box of disposable ones. I fished a pair of earplugs out of a box in the tool locker, in order to counteract the robot pounding. We were given plastic safety glasses the first day, so I put on the whole regalia as I grabbed the panels, laid 'em down, shoved 'em in. But the glasses quickly fogged up from sweat, the earplugs meant I couldn't hear if someone addressed me from ten feet away, and no one could understand me through the mask. Swell, I thought, the job has finally made me deaf, dumb, and blind.

So, like most people, I used the uncomfortable safety equipment sporadically. I put a mask on every other day. Caitlin advised me to rub a little Vaseline around the inside of my nostrils so the fibers wouldn't go up my nose. I also discovered that wearing foundation makeup on my face formed a barrier between my skin and the fibers, cutting down on itchiness. Sometimes I wore the earplugs, sometimes not. But I always used gloves, and Tony got me some leather ones that were less permeable than the white cotton ones.

As I slogged through the second week, Keenan informed me that GM would give me some coveralls because I had a dirty job. I checked with Lorne, and he put in a request. Ye gods, I couldn't believe it—something else my supervisor had never mentioned. What if I'd never found out? "What else am I entitled to?" I asked my co-workers. Prescription safety glasses, for one thing, they said, and safety shoes. Cripes, I'd been ripping up the soles of my running shoes on the track in which the drag chain is laid. The metal was perforated, and the perforations faced up, like the openings of a cheese grater. As I fitted in the left insulation panel, I needed to turn my right foot slightly. The soles of two pairs of shoes were nearly worn through.

On Wednesday the safety-shoe truck parked in front of the plant, and Lorne told me to go over after lunch—an awesomely sweet extra half hour off the line. I picked out a nifty pair of black shoes that looked like Reeboks, but whose toes packed a steel punch. They were practically a weapon, and I was to discover that the soles refused to wear out.

In the same week Lorne came along one afternoon with Tony, who started doing my job. As he put on the apron, transforming himself from a free-and-easy trainer, lord of the department, into a line slave, I thought, Well, that's it. I've been fired.

■

"Come on," said Lorne, "we're going to get you some coveralls." Another day with some time off the line! This couldn't be happening. Thank you, God of autoworkers' answered prayers.

We walked past the body shop (*bang! pound! slam!*) to the north end of the plant, where the offices were.

"So what do you think of it now?" Lorne asked with a sidelong glance at me.

"Lorne, did I look like grim death last week?" I had been hoping that I'd managed to carry it off, that I'd been able to disguise my embarrassing struggle, that I hadn't looked as bad as I felt.

"You looked like you were suffering," he replied.

I nodded. I'd figured as much; I just hadn't known how apparent it was. "But I got stronger. It's like boot camp."

"We tear 'em down and build 'em back up," he agreed, smiling.

We arrived at "the store," the supply-depot area, and ordered three pairs of long-sleeved, small-medium dark-blue coveralls. I wore a pair back to work, where Keenan and Caitlin were on break. I modeled my new outfit as the "latest from Saks Fifth Avenue," and they laughed and applauded. I wondered if I looked a little more as if I belonged here, in my work shoes and coveralls. I felt as if I fit in better anyway, that my outward transformation to blue-collar worker was complete with—surprise—the addition of an actual blue collar. (Why blue? Why not, say, black or magenta?) I felt I could walk about in my steel-toed shoes with a bit of a swagger.

Modes of dress varied throughout the plant. In the body shop coveralls were nearly the universal uniform, because the work was so dirty and sparks from the guns would burn little holes in clothing, although I saw people who regularly wore jeans, even shorts (!) to work in the body shop. Those with relatively clean jobs, in Trim, for instance, wore street clothes, but the state varied widely, from Chris's neat-as-a-pin outfits to tattered T-shirts and sweatpants. Some women spurned coveralls as unfeminine. I never saw working in a factory as a social event, but some women came to work with full makeup, earrings, hair done, ready to do battle with the animalistic male musk of the place. Only one other woman in Trim 2, Madeleine, who was there temporarily from the Ste. Thérèse plant in Quebec, regularly wore coveralls. I saw it as a practical way to save my clothes.

Some men saved their clothing by not wearing much. Toward the end of the shift, one young man who wore his long black hair in a ponytail would work ahead carrying a duct-tape-wrapped box of parts, jumping in and out of the vans, wearing only a pair of shorts, socks, and running shoes. It was a sight to perk up tired eyes at the end of the day. I was also mesmerized one time by the sight of a man working bare-chested in the body shop. What a fool or daredevil, or both. He wasn't on a welding job, but he wasn't far away from one either.

That week the Message God who posted the notes above the body shop was a vicious little soul. Patience is the best remedy for every trouble, he wrote. How in the hell did he (she? it?) have the nerve to preach patience to people who were driven to slug out a task every two minutes? How about: Murdering your supervisor is the best chance of escape? This all smacked of some dweeb in an office with a little book of sayings in his (her? its?) desk, hoping to buck up the workers. The effect on the other end, of course, was that some malevolent wizard was laughing at us grimy morons who'd had the bad luck to find ourselves trapped in the bowels of industry.

My transfer to A shift had not officially come through, but in the third week my replacement on fiberglass arrived. Jean was fortyish, blond, balding, wearing gold wire-rimmed glasses and royal-blue coveralls, a Quebecer who spoke very little English. The Ste. Thérèse plant, near Montreal, was down for retooling to build Pontiac Firebirds and Chevrolet Camaros, and several dozen workers on layoff had been temporarily transferred to Scarborough. I had taken three years of French in high school and, more recently, persuaded Reuters to pay for a Berlitz course. But, being the lazy human being I am, I hadn't practiced the language, even with my father or my godmother, Solange de Romree, who lived in Belgium. So I groped to communicate with Jean.

■

*"Bonjour, Jean. Bienvenue à Scarborough. Je m'appelle Solange,"* I began.

He answered with a stream of French in the rough accent of a man from rural Quebec.

We started off splitting the job, just as Caitlin had done with me. Jean began with the insulation panels. He was taller than me, about five-ten, and I realized that the job was even harder for a taller person. He wasn't particularly graceful, kind of lanky, and he had to bend down farther than I did to get the fiberglass panels into the doghouse. Meanwhile I nonchalantly popped in a vent and three screws every two minutes. In only the third week things were easier. I found that my gloved fingertips could roll three screws out of my apron pocket—not four, not five—and not drop a one. My feet automatically took the right position to lean into the driver's side for the vent-screw do-si-do.

All the same, I was still tired, and on my way out of the plant I passed a work area in Trim 5 decorated with a tattered bikini-clad pinup from the tabloid *Toronto Sun*. I passed it every day, but that day something snapped. I had put in my hours, same as any man, and worked as hard as any man. That day I'd been told that two men hadn't been able to cope with the same fiberglass job I did and had complained about it until they were transferred to other jobs. I wasn't complaining. I was sticking it out. Ordinarily I would have found most pinups—especially one as unpornographic as a woman in a bikini—relatively innocuous. I don't know what got into me that day, but it struck me that this picture trivialized me and my effort, and in a rage I stormed over, ripped it off the wall, and threw it in the trash.

Next day Jean did the vents and screws for a while. Again, because he was taller, he had to bend farther into the driver's-side door to secure them. I snapped in the insulation panels, thinking that his lower back must be aching something fierce. My chest bone didn't hurt anymore, and I didn't need to feel around for the hole that received the little tongue of the big black clip; I just pushed the tongue to the right spot without searching.

On break I tried to make conversation with Jean, ask him if he had a family. *("As-tu une famille?").* In reply, he pulled out his wallet and showed me a small photograph. "My son," he said, and I smiled and made appropriate admiring noises. He had something else he wanted to say. "Me . . ." he began, "AA. Twelve years." Ah. He was beating an alcohol addiction. I was very touched and groped for the words. I wanted to tell him he should be very proud. *"Fier . . ."* I remembered the word for proud. *"Tu est très fier. Très bon."* I knew this was awkward French, that I was telling him he was proud, but I didn't know the verb construction for "should." I thought I got my point across, because he nodded.

After lunch I picked up the gun, but Jean, putting on the apron, waved me off.

"No. I do it."

I understood. He wanted to do the whole job as soon as possible, break into it, in case I was taken away early. So I sat on the battered dark-green worktable, glancing at a newspaper, keeping an eye on Jean and the jobs he was doing, hopping down to straighten an insulation panel here and there. He was struggling. It took him more than a minute to push the insulation panels into the doghouse and affix the black clip, then another minute to pick up the vent, secure that, change drill bits, and push in the maniacal screws. He was almost in Doreeta's work area when he finished the jobs, and he was trying desperately to work faster. Sweat was pouring off his face, though the big fan was on, and he was panting. I jumped off the worktable to do a few for him and allow him to catch a breath, but he waved me away again. "No. I do it."

My God, I thought, that's what I had looked like in the midst of full-fledged autoworker panic. His hair was blown into a demented coiffure by the fan, but he didn't have a spare second to brush his forehead. His cheeks flushed, his glasses slipped down his sweaty nose. He blinked as his glazed eyes teared up from fatigue. Don't worry Jean, I thought, it'll get better. Although it'll get worse before it gets better.

I remembered Billy had told me once of a new hire who was assigned to the body shop. "They stuck him in the pit. He looked so lost,"

Billy said, with a short laugh. The man was looking mournfully at the cruel, confusing machinery, the tangled cables. Just before that, he'd owned a bar, which had gone out of business. "The hardest thing I've had to do in the past few years is open a beer bottle," he said.

Lorne came by for several minutes. I assured him Jean was doing fine, and Lorne stayed to chat. The trainer from Trim 1, a young guy with a spider-web tattoo on his elbow, whose name I didn't catch, also drifted by. We got to talking about women working in the van plant. Spiderman, to my surprise, criticized his fellow guys, saying that the men are bigger complainers than the women and the women often try harder because they don't want to seem weak. "At GM the men become women and the women become men."

I asked Lorne if he would rather supervise men or women.

"Men," he answered, somewhat to my surprise, since he impressed me as being the kind of man who really liked women.

"Why?"

"Because I have respect for women. If you see a woman doing a job and she's just dying, you want to help her," he replied. Hmm, I thought, a little machismo there, but kindly meant.

"You can't talk to the women like you talk to the men," he added, "like, 'You fucking asshole, that was a shitty job.' " Times change slowly in the factory, I thought. Lorne, a relatively young man, was having to adjust to a mixed workforce.

At the end of the day I walked past the work area that had held the pinup I tore down the day before. I was less tired and felt a little bad about taking it down, although officially pinups were against the rules. Maybe looking at the photo was the high point of some guy's day, I thought. Still, I didn't feel what I'd done was wrong.

Jean was right to worry. Two days after he arrived in Fiberglass Alley, I was taken away. Young Bernie came along and led me up the line to install sidemarkers—small lights on the side of the van, yellow in front, red in the rear. I had to pop little metal clips on each side of a small rectangular opening, feel for a previously installed wire and bulb holder, push a small bulb into the holder, grab a yellow (or red) plastic lens, place the bulb holder in the lens, and affix it to the rectangular opening with two screws. A bit of subassembly was attached to this job: I also had to roll bits of black putty into little balls and place them on the screw holes in the lens, this to prevent rain leaking into the truck.

A new job brought new awkwardness. Shoving the tiny lightbulb into its holder four hundred times a night (two per van) and pushing in eight hundred clips (four per van) per night hurt my thumb and forefinger. These trim jobs waste your hands, I thought. Clumsy, clumsy again. Dropping screws. There was a Wild West aspect to this job: The cordless Makita gun went into a holster I wore around my waist. Lorne, out in the aisle. Draw. Dance, tenderfoot supervisor. Some of the familiar tiredness returned. Once again I was falling behind on a job, working into the repairman's area, where he was supposed to inspect the Trim 2 jobs, not that Balthasar cared. At least there was no toxic substance on sidemarkers, but I needed a couple more days to get the muscles in the groove. I was so slow that I was using my few short breaks to put putty in the lenses.

The line went down for a few minutes, and I sat on the stool attached to the job station, next to my table full of red and yellow lenses, ropes of black putty, boxes of screws and lightbulbs. Maybe it was because I had a few minutes to think, maybe it was the sensory overload of the past few weeks, but for the first time an abrupt, raw hatred of the place rose in my craw, a loathing of the noise, the dirt. All the people are stupid, I thought. The work is meaningless and exhausting. There is no privacy. The line never stops. This last was a bit irrational, since I was thinking this during the instant that the line had stopped.

The intensity of my feelings scared me, but I didn't think of quitting, not then. I thought that perhaps I was starting to understand. I looked across at the pounding body shop, which was still running, and saw two men yelling at each other, arms waving, really exercised about something, across the welding guns. A work screwup? Indigestion from a bad sandwich in the cafeteria? An affair gone south? Or maybe the hatred I'd just felt was finding a convenient place to explode.

A new notice appeared on the bulletin board to inform us that a union-company Scarborough Van Plant adjustment committee had been formed to help workers "transition" to "other opportunities outside General Motors." The first step in the adjustment process, it said, was "to conduct a needs assessment survey to determine the existing skills, training requirements and future career interests of our workforce." The notice said that YMCA counselors who "are extremely knowledgeable about the industrial adjustment process" would conduct the interviews.

A sheet of paper with sample survey questions was also posted, asking about skills, whether we would be interested in relocating to find another job, whether we needed information on résumé writing, financial planning, vocational guidance. The committee would put together the results of the survey "to provide the necessary assistance so that our people will be better prepared for future opportunities."

A couple of nights later Bernie came to tell me I was to go to Lorne's office. I didn't even try to fathom what it might be for. A red-haired lady from the YMCA, wearing a print dress with a lace collar and a name tag reading "Penny" was sitting at Lorne's desk. She had the questionnaire that was supposed to help all of us adjust to the plant closing. Despite my minuscule seniority, I would be receiving this benefit along with everyone else in the department. I answered her questions—maintaining my fiction of a high-school-only education—and said I was interested in retraining in restaurant ownership or carpentry, two fields that actually did interest me.

After the questionnaire was completed, we chatted and I asked her some questions. She was a genuinely nice, earnest person, quite willing to talk about the "adjustment" process. There would be YMCA counselors throughout the plant for quite a while. She said it was to show the workers that GM cared. At this place, I said, some workers feel that the company is out to screw them, while the company feels that the workers are out to screw it. "Isn't that because of the union?" she asked. No, I pointed out, the corporate structure fostered this attitude, the semimilitaristic division of white collar from blue collar. In only three weeks as a line worker I felt I was constantly reminded of my lowly status. Why the separate parking lots, one at the front of the building for salaried, one way at the back for hourly? Why the terms anyway—"hourly" and "salaried"?

I had asked a supervisor in another department if GM offered direct deposit of our paychecks. He looked at me warily, as if I were about to lunge for his throat, and replied, "Direct deposit is only for salaried workers." Treat people like animals and they'll live up to your expectations, I thought.

Penny talked about her job counseling with the Y and, rather pointedly, I thought, mentioned she had a bachelor's degree in social work and other qualifications. I nodded in an "oh, really?" manner and thought that if we wanted to play degree poker, I could see her one bachelor's and raise her a master's. She complained mildly that the office got hot while she was there, interviewing people and filling out questionnaires. That's right, I recalled, people who work in offices do complain every so often about the heating or the air-conditioning. I sat there in my coveralls, my fingers taped, holding a pair of dirty gloves, a newly minted autoworker. How quickly my costume disguised my real self and drew a line, a divide, between this nice, clean lady and myself. A couple of years before, if Penny had decided to look for a job in journalism, she could have been in my office, answering my questions.

So far, the dumb-brute stereotype of assembly-line workers was proving to be just that among the people I'd met, although I'd seen a couple of guys in passing who looked as if they might fit the bill. It seemed that many bright people worked on the line. The fact that we were there, performing repetitive labor, did not automatically mean we were too stupid to do anything else. There were bright people who were not particularly restless and were content to be well paid for a job that often didn't require much thought. They turned their intelligence elsewhere, to their lives outside the plant. There were bright people who didn't get along all that well with the rest of humanity. For them the assembly line was perfect.

I had a chat with Billy once in which we got to discussing the difference between the line jobs and office jobs. "Look," he said, his eyes darkening, "they go to work in their suits and ties and Gucci loafers and they look down on us as factory trash. And we make more money than they do."

When I said I'd told a few white-collar friends that I was working on the line, he quickly interjected, "And they look down on you?"

"Oh, something like that," I responded.

I was too embarrassed to tell him that the opposite was true. Of the few office types who knew, one was puzzled, one scoffed ("Let me get this right. You're going to discover that working on an assembly line is hard."), but several treated it as a great adventure, a voyage to an exotic land. I couldn't tell Billy that without sounding frivolous or condescending. So I continued, "And my blue-collar friends . . ."

He finished, "Wonder what you're doing there." I began to wonder if crossing the line was going to be awfully lonely.

News of my shift change came through at last. Lorne stopped by my sidemarker station to tell me I'd be starting on A shift on Monday. Then he gave me a penetrating look and asked, "What are you doing here? You're too smart to be working here."

My God, I thought, he knows. Somehow, he knows. But I shrugged and made light of it. "Same thing you're doing here," I said, and he laughed and went off. I thought I'd been so careful. I thought I was fitting in. What had prompted him to say that? I hadn't exactly been initiating discussions on Victorian poetry or capitalism versus Communism.

By the time I'd been on sidemarkers a week, muscle memory kicked in, my taped fingers were less sore, and I could work ahead. I went up the line like a latter-day Eliza Doolittle, not with a basket of flowers but a box of plastic sidelight lenses, secured by silver duct tape with a makeshift handle of package strapping. I twirled my Makita gun like an outlaw. That night I was done by 1:15 A.M.—my best time ever. I was on the Don Valley Parkway at one-thirty when the line stopped for good that night.

My last B shift was Saturday-night overtime. Balthasar said at the beginning of the shift that he figured there'd be bad jobs coming down the line, that people would get loaded at the dinner break. Since I remembered from my broadcast days that Saturday-night shifts always feature a looser atmosphere, mainly because people have had an entire weekend day to hang out, I told Balthasar, "I think they'll be loaded when they come in," and he smiled. On my last day on sidemarkers, I finished twenty minutes early—new league record. Since we got off work at 1 A.M. and bar-closing time in Ontario was 1 A.M., my B-shift pals threw me an illegal good-bye party in Balthasar's luxurious van in the plant's parking lot. Not only were we breaking GM rules, which, need-less to say, did not allow us to use the parking lot as a party area, but the local cops probably could have nabbed us for drinking in public. Seven of us, including Caitlin, Bernie, and Keenan, piled into Balthasar's cus-tomized, upholstered mobile fun machine and broke out the Molson and Labatt, colder and tastier when tinged with illicit thrill. A couple of skinny joints made the rounds, but I stayed with my longneck, having lost the taste for weed years before. We told jokes, swapped rock-concert stories from the seventies, slandered supervisors and co-workers. I counted myself lucky to have fallen in with this warm, lively crowd, whose members had invited me to their lunch table and stopped by to talk on breaks or between jobs. I certainly hadn't done anything to de-serve such friendly treatment. Although I desperately wanted to see Billy and my friends on the other shift, I was sorry to leave these folks.

■

# A  SHIFT

I started A shift on days. After working until 1 A.M., then socializing
in the parking lot until 3 A.M. on Sunday, five-thirty Monday morning arrived awfully fast. Each shift worked two weeks on days and
two weeks on afternoons. I was joining A shift in the middle of the two
weeks on days. The transition from night shift to day shift was rougher
than the other way around, I was discovering. You just got used to staying up until 2 A.M., and then you had to set the alarm for 5:30 A.M. and try
to get to sleep at 10 P.M. It was a bleary-eyed crew on the first day of
days.

I reported to the office, where a supervisor named Warner Lyle, a
slim man with crinkly hair, was training a replacement named Lance
Andreychuk, a man of medium height and trim figure, gold-rimmed
glasses, thinning blond hair, and a dark mustache.

I awaited my fate with trepidation, hoping that someone even more
junior than myself was wrestling with fiberglass, and was relieved when
Warner assigned Bonnie, a tall, thin young woman with flat cheekbones,
to train me on what I thought of as Doreeta's job, the next one down
from insulation. I was a bit less relieved when I saw how much stuff
there was on that job, which was called remotes. First I had to attach a
black box about the size of a paperback book—a controller for the
antilock-brake system—to a plug in the engine compartment. I had to
press hard to push the plug into the box, holding it in front of my chest,
and my pectoral muscles were sore by day's end. That was another

aspect of line work I hadn't anticipated—all the shoving, pulling, yanking, pushing. I had figured that things would fit together easily. No, everything went in hard, which, I suppose, it had to, so parts weren't rattling around all the time, but it was no wonder that these jobs produced sore backs, wrists, and shoulders.

Next part of the job was the long black fuzzy thing that went around the window frame, but I just had to insert the metal end of it into the door and leave the black part hanging out of the frame. Then I had to insert a rod into a hole in the inside of the door and attach a palm-size metal doohickey to it and secure it with three screws (little short screws, not the inchlong black ones that I shuddered to see at insulation). The doohickey was called a remote. At the next station, an X-shaped part called the regulator, which raised and lowered the window, would be attached to the remote. There was a tricky wiggle to inserting the rod into the hole, and that took a while to get down. It was quick work with two of us on the job, but new muscles, tendons, and ligaments hurt. I could see for the first time why people would want to stay on one job, although, to an outsider, that would look like a sentence of early death. When you got it down, it could be a breeze.

At lunch Bonnie invited me to sit with her and her husband, Nick, and a couple of friends down in Trim 1. B shift had constructed a table made from a large wooden spool set on end and had nailed several two-by-fours together to make benches. Sheets of pink plastic were nailed to the surfaces to make seats, and an umbrella was perched over the table, constructed of two-by-fours and cardboard. On the umbrella someone had hung a sign: CLUB GM. COULD YOU IMAGINE A LIFETIME, a play on a Club Med advertisement carrying the tagline "Could you imagine a week?" A very nice job by B shift. We were joined by Jan and Dina from Trim 1.

At breaks people did the same things all the time. You might have thought people would want to do something different every day. You might have thought that I, as a reporter, would use each day's half-hour meal break to go exploring a different corner of the plant. You would be wrong. First off, I was just too damn tired. Second, we had to cram any kind of personal business—resting, eating, making a phone call, talking to a friend, visiting the washroom, cleaning up—into one thirty-minute meal break and two twenty-three-minute breaks, stuff one might take a few minutes here or there to do in the normal course of an office work-day. Third, you just didn't go barging into another department and plop yourself down at a table with a cheery, "Hi, folks. I'm Sally from Trim Two. Mind if I eat lunch with you here today?"

I was not on remotes for long. The next day I was busted back down to fiberglass along with another Ste. Thérèse visitor, Christine. We had a bunch of extra people for some reason, so Warner had to double us up on some jobs. Lance took over from Warner and found something else for Christine, so I was back on insulation alone again. Damn, I hated that stuff. It occurred to me that it was a flat-out humiliating job, my ass in the air, bent over the front of the van, bent over the side. Couldn't even stand up like a person. I left a "hi" note for Lorne and the B-shift gang taped to the workbench, but I didn't find any reply the next day.

My one consolation was that at last I was getting so smooth at the job that I could work ahead. I carefully tucked insulation panels between other people's work areas and piled a few vents on the workbenches several stations up the line, after being sure that the inhabitants were working even further ahead. I was two trucks ahead, into Trim 1, when I looked up from the engine cavity to find Rolando, the Trim 1 supervisor, standing over me. "Nick has to inspect his trucks," Rolando said, adding that I wasn't supposed to work ahead. Bonnie's husband, Nick, was the repairman in Trim 1. Apparently he felt that I was getting in his way, although I couldn't imagine what he was inspecting in an empty engine compartment. I was outraged that he had called the dogs on me without talking to me first.

But I was also still on probation, so I had no choice but to slow down and stay out of Trim 1. Tired, hot, filthy, I stood there, finally able to work faster than the line, waiting for the vans to come to me while everyone else was busily whipping parts into the trucks and walking off the line, headed for home. Nick started to work ahead about fifteen minutes before the end of the shift, but I had no idea what was going on with him, so I stayed where I was, and at three twenty-eight, with two minutes officially left on the clock, I was the only one there.

I thought, I'll be damned if I'm not going to work ahead now that I've finally got this job down. How is it that everyone else can work ahead but me? This isn't fair. Warner and Lance were poking around in my area at the end of the shift, and I asked if there was one rule for everybody about working ahead.

"You are supposed to remain in your station," Warner said.

"Oh, really," I said. "Look around."

"Management has lost control of the situation," he admitted.

"Glad we got this settled, fellows," I concluded. They looked at me, I looked at them, and the three of us knew what the situation was. They couldn't help me out; they could only mouth the company rule while tacitly admitting that it was more honored in the breach than the observance. I was on my own. I resolved to have a chat with Nick the next day and straighten this out.

If I made sure Nick was working ahead, I wouldn't be in his way, so next day I asked Nick nicely if he would be working ahead. He blew up at me, something along the lines of "You just don't get it! I have to inspect my trucks! I don't want to hear about it anymore!" I remained mystified as to how exactly I was a big problem for him, but it didn't seem like a good time to inquire. I was in despair. Since I was on probation, could I get fired for working ahead if this guy persisted in his tantrums? Why had there been no problem with the Trim 1 repairman on B shift?

My B-shift buddies finally left me a note, duct-taped to my workbench: "To the Long Tall Sally. Sorry for the delay. We just found a pen. It only took 3 days." I missed them terribly and was beginning to wonder if I'd made a mistake by changing shifts. The B-shift crowd had told me, "You won't like those people on A shift, Sally," and I'd thought they were kidding.

I was also dismayed to discover that Billy, a major reason for my transfer, wouldn't be staying on A shift very long; in fact, he wasn't even staying in Scarborough. The union had negotiated a transfer arrangement for those in Scarborough who wanted to go to work at the Oshawa complex, and about 130 were taking them up on it, including Billy. Others, such as Caitlin on B shift, were agonizing over whether to go, since a rumor had the plant staying open until 1994 or '95. So, by my second week on A shift, Billy was gone and I was stuck.

I hadn't seen much of his friends/my acquaintances in the body shop either, and the people on this shift weren't nearly as sociable. It was very quiet in my section of Trim 2 at lunch—no raucous card games. Ruth, a British-born middle-aged woman who was part of the team on a wiring job, called the TR9 job, always read a book and didn't want to chat. Three guys played something like cribbage. Others disappeared, possibly to the parking lot or roof to drink or catch a puff of weed. I brought in the *New York Times* one day to read on break and nervously slipped it out of my bag, thinking someone might comment upon this unusual reading material. I needn't have worried. Nobody noticed. Nobody cared. Besides, it wasn't that unusual. While the newspaper of choice was most often the tabloid *Sun,* the more serious broadsheet papers, the *Star* and *The Globe and Mail,* made regular appearances, and I once heard two men discussing mutual funds while looking at the *Globe*'s Report on Business section.

They seemed to be a morose bunch on this shift. Well, if no one wanted to talk to me and I was having a tough time breaking into the cliques, I had more time to look around and observe. Next to me, on taillights, where Elsie would have been on B shift, a daily circus took place. Tracy, the young woman doing the job, was about five feet, ten inches tall, had a cascade of curly dark-brown hair, black-eyed Greek good looks, and a completely guileless manner. She had half a dozen daily visitors to her job station, a parade of guys I called the Tracy Admiration Society. One day one of the society members appeared to be our local fence, as I heard Tracy ask him about earrings.

I made note of graffiti in the plant, starting with the body-shop departments nearest me, known as the Jungle. Someone had written on a pillar DARCY MEADE IS NO F-----G GOOD. Who was Darcy Meade, and why was he no fucking good? And why did the author of that graffiti feel he had to spare the delicate sensibilities of his body shop companions, inserting dashes for letters? You know, there's just no substitute for good breeding. A Catholic-school survivor, no doubt, who, despite his rage at Darcy Meade, who had—what? welshed on a bet? screwed his wife? rammed his car? served red wine with fish?—retained a sense memory of being rapped on the knuckles by Sister Anna Patrick's ruler when he used a bad word. I asked a passing inmate about the mysterious Darcy Meade, and, of course, he just shrugged. It had all been lost in the welding fumes.

As the days dragged on, Marlon, from my WHMIS class, ambled by (he looked like a young rapper in loose coveralls) to say hello. They'd put him in the body shop. Yes, his hands hurt, but—he shrugged—it wasn't too bad. I didn't believe him. Sometimes it seemed that the only friendly faces were those from other departments. A short, pale, balding man with a black mustache and a ready smile stopped to chat occasionally, and I learned that his name was Ed Donohue and he was a trainer in the body shop. Although he wore the ubiquitous blue coveralls, he said he'd been a supervisor but quit to go back to the line as a trainer. "What happened?" I asked, a little tentatively, hoping that wasn't too personal a question.

"No consistency from upper management," he said, and I got the impression he'd made decisions based on what he thought was company policy, only to be overruled later. His temperament was precise, sometimes picky, and he had no patience for stupidity, but because of his obvious intelligence, I leaned toward thinking that Ed's move had been more GM's loss than his. He'd been to college, forestry school in Sault Ste. Marie, and had wanted to go to school in Butte, Montana, but feared being drafted for Vietnam, he said. Apparently Canadians could have been drafted if they resided in the United States. Ed and I hit it off immediately, and I pegged him as someone who had valuable perspective from the world of management as well as labor.

Tracy was quite friendly, but she was taken off to the window-securing job, and the Tracy Admiration Society moved down the line. Bonnie was teaching taillights to a hefty woman, who was slow. The six-day weeks were wearing me down, and stirring loneliness into the mix made the days very gray. I'd been spoiled by the B-shift crowd, but I was partly to blame, too. I tried to engage Ruth in conversation, but she kept looking at her book, and it was clear that she preferred to read on breaks. So I didn't try. I waited for people to ask me to join them, and as on any new job, that was slow to happen. I had also assumed, foolishly, that there automatically would be more camaraderie in an environment where people were sharing hard jobs than in the world of cubicles and carpet.

Gradually, however, I learned the names of this new cast of characters. The woman putting in taillights next to me was Laverne, and she seemed a lot more placid than Elsie from B shift. Across from her, where Chris would be on B shift, was Ivan, originally from Yugoslavia: dark-brown hair, big eyes, slightly goofy manner, addressed me as "Solly," reminded me a little of a Schmenge brother. There was a skinny young guy with flying hair named Bruce. Bruce the Rock Star, I dubbed him, since he hooked up a boom box every day and blasted Guns N' Roses and Nirvana through the plant. Ruth, who was a transplant from one of the Windsor plants, made it clear she despised being in Scarborough. One day she was bitching up and down the line about the noises emanating from Bruce's boom box and had to be persuaded that calling the union about such a matter would not be effective. God, what a contrast to the cheerful crowd on B shift.

Bruce often hung around with a large young man named Phil Bumstead, also known as Bummer. I've often found that the bigger the man, the more good-natured. Big men have nothing to prove, and this was certainly the case with Bummer. He was stocky, with sandy hair, and looked as if he could heft an entire van himself. Although I wouldn't wish this on anybody, you'd have thought such a strong guy would have been firing guns in the body shop, not installing remotes in Trim 2, which is what he was doing and had been doing for the past two years. Bummer's and Bruce's substances of choice were mostly weed and sometimes booze, and they generally disappeared to the roof or parking lot at lunch.

Another big young guy in our department was named Kieran, but universally known as Stretch. He was just too tall for some jobs, especially the climb-in-the-van ones such as dashboard wiring or dome lights. Like most big young men, Stretch could hold his liquor, or whatever else he might ingest, but he didn't seem as devoted to substance abuse as Bruce or Bummer. He was a sweet, bright guy, and I caught myself hoping, as I had with Bernie, that he would rise above the line to a career outside General Motors. I wasn't sure how easy it was to advance from the line, but three of the four supervisors I'd met so far hadn't worked on the line—Warner, Lorne, and Rolando. Only Lance had. Line workers in Scarborough had little chance to show initiative or leadership as part of their jobs. There was a program that paid bonuses for suggestions that saved the company money or led to greater efficiency, but that was about it. We looked as if we were part of a great team, but we weren't; each of us worked alone. Because it was an old plant using the drag-chain assembly-line system, the new team concept, in which workers supervised each other to some extent, was unknown. General Motors wasn't the right place for bright young guys like Bernie and Stretch, and I wondered whether that was one of the problems with GM.

Our trainer was named Rob McKenzie, a redhead with a crew cut from Newfoundland, about forty years old. While Tony, on B shift, wasn't exactly Mr. Happy, Rob definitely didn't seem interested in socializing. Once he made sure that every job was covered at the start of the shift, he did crossword puzzles at the table just off the line or joined a group of cronies in the cafeteria for cards. Lance didn't seem to care, or didn't want a confrontation with Rob. The trainer was also supposed to be available to give washroom breaks, fix something that broke—like a hose or gun—bring a new battery from the charger to a worker whose gun was running down, and generally keep things rolling. But sometimes we had AR, or absentee-relief, people hanging around who could do some of that stuff also, and Rob was well within hailing distance in the cafeteria next to Trim 2. The question for Lance and for plant management in general was, I suppose, How strict do you want to be in a plant that's going to close in eighteen months?

Rob often hung around with Travis Allman, a wiry man who worked near me. Another one of the Newfoundlanders, Travis would climb into the truck on the passenger side just as I was leaning in on the driver's side with my vent and trio of vicious screws. One Saturday night both Travis's and Rob's breath could've lit ovens. Rob didn't often show up loaded, but Travis pursued the love of the hop and the grape with dedicated intensity. I learned to hold *my* breath for a couple of seconds when he did his installation and his face was a few inches from mine. I never saw Travis eat much—maybe a candy bar or a danish—but he nearly always had a John Player Special cigarette going.

Our version of Balthasar was a short Italian guy named Paul, known universally as the Wop. When I first heard his nickname, I thought, Now, this is too much. I really cannot stoop to that kind of name-calling no matter how much I am trying to fit in here. Besides, being half Italian myself, that word really sticks in my throat. And that poor man, how awful it must be for him to be the object of an ethnic slur every day. He really should file a complaint. Paul, like Ivan, seemed to come from Ethnic Central Casting. A cross between Jerry Colonna and Chico Marx, he talk-a like-a dis. He waved his hands and even had a black mustache.

Besides Bonnie, our AR crew included Ken Sui. He was from Hong Kong and looked as if he weighed maybe 140 pounds, but I saw him do many jobs faster and more efficiently than many a bigger man. José Venancio, a swarthy guy in his thirties who always wore a smile, was

■

from the Philippines. Glen Jackman, from Jamaica, was a member of the TR9 crew. He ran a couple of side businesses, including a vending-machine operation, and wore a beeper, but he cultivated a no-worries manner.

What a United Nations of a department we were. Among fifty people, we were Serbian, Chinese, Filipino, Trinidadian, Jamaican, Italian, French-Canadian, English-Canadian, American, Greek, Irish, British, and Newfies, nominally a part of Canada, but really a nation unto themselves. I'd expected to meet more first-generation immigrants than at any other workplace I'd known, but I was surprised at the wide range of homelands represented in our department. At my former workplaces I'd shared cultural and social attitudes with people who'd grown up in America or Canada, but I was discovering that the recent arrivals I was meeting possessed fresh viewpoints.

So that was my world: Trim 2 and the body shop next door. The office staff at the front of the plant was another world, as were such important departments as skilled trades (electricians, carpenters, and the like) and maintenance. Skilled trades had their workshops at the front of the plant. I didn't see too many members of the maintenance department on a regular basis, since many worked the midnight maintenance shift. Women made up only about 15 percent of the workforce, but they had been there since the Frigidaire days. I heard that Canadian Auto Workers Local 303 pursued a militantly antimanagement stance, nurtured by the older men who were working-class veterans of the British Labour Party and younger, sixties-inspired radicals who had joined the van plant in the 1970s. The plant manager's name was Don Dornan. His signature appeared on notices, but I couldn't tell you what he looked like.

Five weeks after I started the job, I felt strong one night. I'd gotten a good night's sleep, and everything seemed to click into place. My legs were steel. I swung the heavy diesel fiberglass panels out of the big metal bin with one smooth motion. I changed the gun bit and fingered the screws like a gambler rolling dice. *Zip, zip, zip,* my biceps and triceps contracted to pop in the screws, and I just felt stronger, not sore. I didn't need the hockey elbow pad anymore.

I obtained a box-cutting knife and with quick, efficient sweeps of the blade sliced off the flaps of the large boxes that held the vents, the more easily to fish them out. I lined up the boxes of screws and washers neatly and formed an intimate bond with the black screws. When the job didn't hurt anymore, my mind subdivided into compartments. One box was doing the job: step, step, heave, swing, bend, push, clip, step, step, step, bend, shove, shove, shove. One box was off thinking about anything else: friends, what I had to do at home, my romantic life, my family. And one box grooved on the robotic beauty of a repetitive physical task. I was Chaplin, Buster Keaton, Marcel Marceau. Time turned elastic on the line once I could see the Zen of a taillight. I was so good and so fast that I became master of the line. I played it like a piano, working ahead two or three jobs, reading a newspaper or book between trucks.

The line went down for a few minutes, and even that didn't fill me with blessed relief. It was just down, big deal; more time to read. When the line started again, I didn't need to jump up immediately, because I'd worked a truck ahead, so I could nonchalantly look up, look back down at my book, and casually get up when I saw the next job approaching my station.

The drag chain no longer owned me. I had triumphed, won the battle. But who would win the war? Conquering this job brought me intense satisfaction, but that feeling had little to do with the specifics of this particular job. In the course of my working life I had taken great pride in acquiring the skills of my trade: how to write news for broadcast, how to write a newspaper feature, how to conduct an interview, how to condense a complicated topic. Mastering my current occupation required no new skill in handling fiberglass—it could have been any hazardous substance—nor did I learn anything about driving in screws

■

that I didn't know before. Meeting the physical, and therefore the mental, challenge, was what mattered to me, and that was a new sensation.

I rejected the use of the word "mindless" to describe the jobs, although that was exactly how many line workers referred to them. Something in the human soul needs to take pride in work, and that pride, despite relentless cheerleading by the company, was as often lacking as it was present, just because the jobs were so monotonous. But mindless? No, people did many things with their minds to survive the years on the assembly line.

My newfound strength deserted me a few nights after that. It went in waves. Some nights, or days, were better than others. Sometimes I just felt draggy, my feet a bit swollen. One night a muscle in my left foot became sore as the shift plodded on. Hadn't happened before, who knows why it happened then. You do one little thing a bit differently, unconsciously, and something new hurts.

I always glanced up at the latest from the Message Deity above the body shop, and he came up with a pithy aphorism that seemed appropriate for me: "God made our bodies so we can neither pat ourselves on the back nor kick ourselves too easily." I learned that another display box above the aisle, close to the message box, showed the number of trucks built the previous day and quality numbers that corresponded to the average number of defects per vehicle. Good numbers were considered to be four hundred or so vehicles per day and fewer than four or five defects per vehicle, Lance told me. He also said I had missed two trucks in the past couple of days. From the way he said it, it didn't seem to be that unusual, but he warned me to pay more attention. The Message God was right. I shouldn't have been patting myself on the back that easily. I'd probably worked ahead a little, gone back to my station to have a coffee or look at the paper, and hadn't noticed one go by undone. Now that I could do the job easily, I'd really been trying to achieve quality—making sure the insulation wasn't crooked, that I had installed the right kind of insulation for the diesels, that the three screws went all the way

into the metal. At the same time, since the job didn't demand all my
mental energy, I was spacing out occasionally and missing trucks, obviously.

I discovered, from somebody else, that Nick the repairman's problem was that he had to check whether a couple of screws had been
installed in the doghouse, and my working ahead put the fiberglass
panels over the screws before he could check them. Other repairmen
simply pulled back the panel a little to see if the screws were there, but
Nick didn't want to touch the fiberglass. When he wasn't there, it was
easy for me to work ahead, and I was regularly out the door fifteen
minutes before the end of the shift. One night I was in such high spirits
that I bounced along the still-moving line of vans, slapping each one,
yelling, "Yes. Out of here! Get the fuck out of here!" and a couple of
people even cheered.

In mid-December General Motors said it would have the details of a
major restructuring plan available within a week, and the lag time between the two announcements threw the rumor mill into overdrive. I
asked Dave, a guy with a Harley-Davidson tattoo, what he thought was
going to happen, and he replied, "You're an American, you tell us."

"Oh, sure," I said, "I'll just phone up [GM chairman] Bob Stempel.
'Hi, Bob. Sally here. Scarborough Van Plant. Say, Bob, what's the deal?' "
Harley Dave laughed.

Paul (the Wop) said he'd heard we'd be on short work week when we
got back from Christmas vacation and we'd get a pay cut of three dollars
per hour to keep the plant open. That pay cut sounded a little dicey to
me, since they'd have to reopen the contract to do it and I couldn't see
the CAW giving up that much in wages. Yet another rumor had the life
of the plant extended beyond 1993.

Seven days before Christmas, General Motors lowered the boom,
announcing the closing of twenty-one plants and the elimination of more
than seventy thousand jobs. I watched GM chairman Bob Stempel on
the news that night and mused on how I could well have been at such a
news conference, grabbing the news release, running for the phone to

call the Reuters newsroom, trying to beat Dow Jones (no cell phones for us in the late eighties), asking questions ("Mr. Stempel, when do you think you'll be able to announce the size of the charge to earnings?"). The big company seemed to have a remarkably nimble sense of timing. It had announced the closure of the Scarborough Van Plant just before people left on summer vacation, and this one came just in time for the festive season. In Scarborough, supervisors distributed the four-page press release, but reaction was muted and resigned, since our plant already had its head in the noose. Of far more concern was a GM Canada statement that the future of Oshawa car plant #2 was in jeopardy, since the company was phasing out production of the Buick Regal and Chevrolet Lumina at that facility after the 1994–95 production year. Many Scarborough people who weren't ready to take a transfer to Oshawa just then were pinning their hopes on going to work there after the van plant closed. It was only a thirty-minute drive away, compared to a two-hour drive to the St. Catharines engine plant and foundry, two and a half hours to the London locomotive and armored-vehicle plant, or five hours to the Ste. Thérèse car plant.

"All this company gives us is bad news," said Laverne.

"I think that's the only kind they have," I replied.

On the way in to work the day after the bad news, I remarked to a very nice material-control guy whose locker door, a couple down from mine, had been decorated with the simple word COCKHEAD, "Who would have thought we'd see a year with the breakup of the Soviet Union and General Motors?"

"Yeah, two ailing giants," he said.

I tried the same line on Monty Allen later, and he responded, "Yeah, both dictatorships."

At lunch I asked Ed Donohue what he thought about what was happening at GM.

"Is it the workers' fault or management's or both?"

He thought a second and said, "Both. In the seventies they were just pumping out these trucks and cars. Anything the union asked for, it got.

'Sure, here's five bucks an hour more, just keep turning 'em out. We don't really care how well they're made, just make 'em.' "

American hustle had built General Motors into the world's dominant car company after World War II as the factories of Japan and Germany lay in jagged ruins. Thirty years later, hustle had rotted into arrogance and GM was sick with the disease of bigness. It wasn't the only automaker that had failed to anticipate competition from abroad, but Ford and Chrysler had managed to turn themselves around, while GM seemed to lurch from crisis to crisis, losing market share, fighting pitched battles with the union, cutting staff and capacity to get its suddenly unwieldy costs in line. I'd read that GM's executive culture was mostly hostile to new ideas, in love with bureaucracy, heavy-handed in its labor relations. Ed's analysis confirmed something I'd sensed when reading, or hearing, that the poor quality of the workforce was running GM into the ground. You can go only so far in blaming the workers. In the end it was management that set the tone, and what I'd seen so far was clearly uninspiring.

Communications with the shop floor, from what I could see, were rather dismal. The mysterious "John Short, Personnel Director" signed all company bulletins. I imagined a fifty-five-year-old lifer, burly, balding, a smoker. We were not given any idea of the financial health of our plant, how it stacked up against other GM plants, whether we were meeting production targets. Maybe our supervisors were told all this, but it was never disseminated in any structured way down to the line. In the absence of facts, of course, rumor rushed in. In addition, management was constrained by the fact that in a unionized workplace certain communications (benefits, working conditions) had to go through the union. I got the impression that management had, figuratively, thrown up its hands and left much of the communicating to the union.

Several school tours wound through the plant that fall—high-school or college kids. One of the stops was right across from Fiberglass 'R' Us. As they were getting their lecture on the robots, I wondered if they also got a lecture on the people. Their attention wandering, some of the kids turned to stare at me and my insulation. I hated it when people watched me work. Go away! Stay in school! This job won't be here pretty soon. Do you really want to sling fiberglass every day?

Christmas arrived in the auto plant. I found a red envelope attached to my workbench with black tape and SALLY written on the front. Inside:

"Merry Christmas Sally Baby! from your admired. BALTHASAR." (I think he meant admirer.)

"Merry Christmas Sal from your Pals 'B' Shift."

"We miss you kid!"—Caitlin B.

"Merry Ho Ho Popeye! Your arms must be big enough by now"—Clyde Barrow

"Ho Ho Ho. Merry Christmas all the best"—Keenan

"Hope You Enjoy Your New Shift"—Marilyn

A sweeper—big, unshaven, rough—whom I'd seldom seen, went out of his way to shake my hand and wish me a merry Christmas. In Trim 2 we ordered a catered buffet, set up on a picnic table near the repair station. Very nice, too, for twenty dollars each: a turkey, cheeses, side dishes, juice and pop, a log cake. Supervisors didn't have a problem with Christmas lunches; in fact, Lance paid his twenty dollars and dug in. Our half-hour meal break acquired a pleasantly congenial feeling. Billy heard of the festivities in Trim and shook his head, saying that in the body shop they wouldn't be sitting around eating quiche. It would have been impossible to set up a lunch table over there, what with the sparks flying and hose tangles. I started to feel a little warmer toward my line-mates. Laverne said she didn't know what she'd do after Scarborough closed. Ivan said he didn't feel any Christmas spirit, because of the fighting in Yugoslavia and because he celebrated the Orthodox Christmas on January 6. He'd been on the taillight job thirteen years, he said, and liked working overtime, although there hadn't been much of that lately.

"Solly, I have bought a house. Even if we go into 1993 here, it won't give me enough money."

"Why don't you apply to go to Oshawa, Ivan?" I asked.

■

He shook his head. "I don't know. You don't know where you stand."

Toward the end of shift Lance told everyone not to work ahead out of the department. Everyone ignored him. Hey, it was one of the few joys we had around there. The next day Lance and Rolando made appearances on the line, Rolando at the end of Trim 1, Lance at the beginning of Trim 2, attempting to enforce the no-work-ahead order, but it was a losing cause. No one stopped. As I carried ten pieces of insulation, five clips, and five air vents past Lance, I tossed over my shoulder, "I'm certainly glad to see everyone's behaving themselves and not working ahead." It was unenforceable. There were fifty of us and two of them. As Sidemarker Scott said, "Oh, gee, if we work ahead, they might take our jobs. They might even close the plant. Maybe in 1993!"

Lance came down the line with our checks, just before we were due to leave for our twelve-day Christmas–New Year's break, and gave each of us a little present—a one-dollar lottery ticket. We chatted a bit. He had started out in Scarborough hanging mufflers on the chassis line—forty-five-pound parts, he said. "None of this sticking in wires," he said.

"Forty-five pounds—but you're not a big guy," I said.

"I'm a lean, mean pleasure machine," he smiled, and I rolled my eyes, tickled at his mild flirtation.

"What was it like for your first weeks?" I asked.

"Your hands," he simply said. "Sometimes I was numb, you know? Beyond pain. It's amazing what the body can do."

After last break a youngish man wearing glasses, slacks, and a green V-neck sweater slowly came down the line, pausing briefly to greet each worker. He looked vaguely familiar. As he approached me, I piped up, "Who are you?"

Then I spotted his name tag as he said, "Don Dornan, plant manager."

"Oh," said I, "good to meet you." Like members of the royal family, he had perfected the art of giving me a firm handshake while simultaneously looking me in the eye and looking past me. He wished me a merry Christmas and moved on.

■

# THE TRANSPLANTS

O rdinarily one would have thought a twelve-day vacation would have been welcome relief. It was, but I knew I wouldn't be able to keep up my strength and would pay for it on the other end. I went skating a few times and worked out at the health club, but nothing equaled a seven-hour shift on my feet. When we came back in the new year, they ached, as did my legs, as did my chest from banging into the front of the van. I was never unaware of how I felt physically—tired or fresh, dragged out or bouncy—and it was a running theme that underscored every day at work. Like nursing-home residents, we talked incessantly about our aches and pains ("Sally, I'm not feeling too good today." "What's the matter, Laverne?" "I think I have a pinched nerve in my back."). Leaving the cafeteria, I passed a young man in body-shop coveralls flexing and unflexing his hands, and my heart went out to him. When my legs ached, I complained to Ivan, but he would have none of it. "You are young, Solly. I have fifteen years on the line, and I am older than you." He was right, too. Once we were ribbing a TR9 worker about his easy wiring job, and he snapped, "I'm climbing in and out of these vans. I'm working on my knees!"

One cold, dark morning, as I lumbered from my car, clumsy in heavy parka and work shoes and laden with lunch bag, I quit. I had had enough. About two months into this gig, I decided I simply could not do this anymore. Oh, what relief. I reasoned it out. It made perfect sense. I had done it enough to know what it was like. I really did not need to

■

know any more. I convinced myself I would not be wimping out. Two months was plenty. When the place shut down, maybe I'd go and talk to some people about it. Jesus, who cared, anyway, about this dopey, dilapidated corner of GM's attic? Then I went and did it for eight more hours. And eight more ... When it came down to marching into the supervisor's office and saying, "I'm gone," I just couldn't do it. This story isn't about leaving, it's about persevering, I told myself, and what has gone before will be for naught if you give up now.

I started talking to some of the women who used the same washroom and made the acquaintance of Kathryn, a cheerful person with curly blond hair who was a bright spot in the body shop two columns down from my station. A few women worked in the body shop, and they had my undying admiration. On break she took me down to show me her job. The "ladders"—that is, the floor frame that resembled a ladder—emerged from the orange plastic shroud of the robot station, and Kathryn and her partner put spring hangers on them. "A fellow was once caught by one of the ladders and dragged," she said.

"God. What happened?" I asked.

"He had a broken leg. They called an ambulance," she said in a matter-of-fact tone.

Several weeks later I saw a job almost kill a man. An inspector named Brad squatted, checking something, in front of a truck that was moving slowly along on the line. His dark-blue lab coat must have caught on something, or he lost his balance, because he fell and screamed as the van continued to move over him. Travis, of all people, realized what had happened in a second, dashed over, and pulled him out from under the van. I was right behind Travis, but he had Brad out as I asked him where it hurt. "My knee," he said, grimacing and rocking in pain. He was driven to the medical office and several days later returned to thank me for helping him. But it was really Travis the lush whose quick action saved his leg.

Workplace safety seemed to be an on-again, off-again thing at this point in the plant's life. I'd heard that years before, wearing safety glasses had been mandatory on all jobs, but nobody enforced such a rule now. We were called individually to the supervisor's office on occasion to read safety pamphlets on, for instance, preventing back injuries. Under law we had the power to refuse unsafe work, and the line stopped several times during my tenure when workers cited unsafe conditions. Still, there were dangers built into the workplace, and things happened. The body shop was the most dangerous place to work, and I knew personally of two men who had sustained deep cuts resulting from accidents.

The no-working-ahead foolishness continued after Christmas. Lance bent my ear at the end of one shift, asking me where I'd gone on vacation, telling me that he and his wife had visited Boston. It was a pleasant conversation, but I wondered if he wasn't deliberately slowing me down. Another night Rolando and Lance again stood at the respective end and beginning of their departments, observing all the activity, but they did not actually prevent anyone from working ahead. Everyone ignored them again. I pictured a couple of old sheriffs out West, maybe Andy Devine and Gabby Hayes, rocking on their heels, watching a vicious gang rob the town bank. "Yep, jes' standin' here, enforcin' the law. Sure enough." Since it was hard for me to carry insulation panels past them, I was forced to go around on the other side of the line. This is stupid, I thought, hustling my parts, both physical and industrial, down the line. "It's 1:15 on a Saturday morning. Guys, give us a break. If I were a supervisor, I wouldn't enforce this stupid rule." Then I realized that was, perhaps, exactly what they were doing.

The line went down for a full hour one night. A flashing yellow light, high above the aisle, was the signal that something in the paint shop had messed up, I was told. Bummer, intent upon extending the season of good cheer, was working Travis's job across from me and mixing whiskey and Cokes, hiding the bottle in among the parts boxes. The soul of courtesy, he asked, "Sally, do you want one?"

My tolerance for drink had declined with the years, but that night I was feeling frisky and knew that the good dinner I'd had would cushion the alcohol. "Okay, but don't make it as strong as you like it," I said.

The spiked can of Coke was pretty heady anyway, and I sipped it over the two hours post-dinner. For the first time I did my job mildly swockered. Time did pass more quickly. This tastes all right! A person could get used to this, I thought. I guess I have arrived. Three months into this and I'm drinking on the line.

In that respect I was fitting right in. Billy Davis was right. Drinking ranged from a lunchtime beer or two in the parking lot to pints of Scotch drained over the course of a shift. I learned that when a guy moaned he'd had a "hard night," he didn't mean a bout of insomnia or walking the floor with the baby; it meant a night of drinking and a wicked hangover. I estimated that at least one third of our fifty-person department drank on the job, which was, of course, one of the couple dozen things strictly prohibited in the wallet-size pamphlet of rules we were given on our first day.

Alcohol made my face flush and my feet swell, so I wasn't prone to excess, but I couldn't deny that drinking made the parts prettier, the night shorter, the thoughts mellower. I sometimes tucked a beer into a nest of ice in a cooler and stashed it in my car's trunk, where it awaited me at the meal break. I and more than a few of my co-workers would head out to the parking lot for a quiet half-hour liquid break in our cars or vans, some alone, some with a friend or two. You kept the bottle down on the floor, just in case a GM guard was wandering around, but nobody poked flashlights into cars. I couldn't see that it was much different from having a glass of wine at lunch when I wore a suit, except that then I could take an hour or two.

Alcohol and drug consumption affected the quality of the product we were producing, of course, from the Iron Water Balloon that dented a truck to Bruce's occasionally sloppy wiring jobs. Truth to tell, though, anyone could do most of those repetitive jobs half bagged, and a large man on a strenuous job could certainly knock back two or three at break without being drunk. Most of the workers who drank weren't dumb enough to mess up their jobs completely. Besides, the attitude went, the repairman would catch the occasional loose wire or missing screw (as-

suming the repairman was sober), and management didn't seem to care
that deeply, as long as the trucks got built and the average of defects per
vehicle was held down to four or five. No one searched bags on the way
in or out, unless you were leaving early. The parking lot was only fitfully
patrolled. Lance confirmed it for me when he told me that the attitude
among supervisors, and even among their managers, was "These are hard
jobs. Let the guys have a break." Scarborough had an employee-
assistance plan for those with serious substance-abuse problems, and
people did find their way to the counselor's office, but they couldn't be
forced to go.

One member of our department, Tyrone, really needed detoxing. A
thirtyish man with handsome blue eyes and a solid gut, Tyrone lived in a
small town that was an hour's drive into the country from Scarborough.
He made a unique first impression upon me when he arrived to do my
job so I could go to "the store" for another couple pairs of coveralls. "Slip
one of the winter vests under the coveralls," he said, referring to the
quilted, insulated vests often worn by guys who were in and out of
the plant all day—those who drove the vans out of final repair into the
parking lot, for instance. Barry Harvey, another trainer, was nearby and
urged, "Yes, Sally, get us a vest." I was a little scared of guys who would
make such a suggestion to a newcomer. Would they pull some nasty
prank—glue my locker shut? run a key down the side of my car?—if I
refused to steal from the company store? "I don't think so, guys," I
replied, giving them a look that said I was too smart for this sort of thing.

On several shifts, even in the mornings after that long commute,
Tyrone could have fueled up a couple of vans by breathing into the gas
tanks. Apparently he also liked to mix his substances. Tyrone called in
late again one day, and another worker remarked, "Ah. Snowstorm in
Tremont." He showed up for work two days in one two-week period, and
I wondered how this man kept his job. Then he went on some sort of
extended leave, and I didn't see him anymore.

One night, sitting in my car with a cold one on a break, I mused on
how I would cut down on the substance abuse if I were Don Dornan.

■

First, send a notice around saying that management would not tolerate any drinking or drug-taking on the job and security was going to be tightened immediately, including bag searches at the gates and regular patrols of the parking lot and the roof. Admit this may seem heavy-handed, but that the problem was serious and must be stopped. Looking through everyone's bags would, of course, create a huge pileup at shift changes, so instead do random searches of, say, every tenth person, and keep doing it so all got the idea. Have the guards do random bag inspections within the plant, too. Patrol the parking lot on meal breaks every day and evening. Patrol the roof. Confiscate booze, pot, etc., and suspend people. Then I, switching back to my line-worker persona, laid out why these measures might not work. They wouldn't prevent anyone from going off site in order to consume. They wouldn't stop anyone from getting tanked before work, unless supervisors were to administer Breathalyzers, hardly a practical notion. It would add to the oppressiveness of the atmosphere, giving management a factory full of hostile workers. Besides, the place was closing in a year or so, the vans were rolling off the line, so let it be. I finished my beer with a satisfied swig, slammed the car door, and strolled back in to smack fiberglass around for another four hours.

It was beginning to seem as if I'd be on insulation for the duration. Sometimes, when I'd enter the plant, hear the familiar *squeak, squeak,* put my coat in my locker, and pull on my safety shoes, it seemed like home. Other times the place still scared me. But if I was destined to wander in forests of fiberglass forever, at least the Line God smiled upon me. Lance arrived with extremely welcome news. An engineer named Ercole had redesigned the air vent I installed, so that it fastened with a plastic push screw. I wouldn't have to change bits, even use the gun at all for the vent, just push it in. Ercole the Engineer, a short dark type wearing a polyester shirt, came by to check out the new arrangement. I was wearing a white mask, and Rob McKenzie said, "Dr. Kildare loves it."

Lance also came along. "How's the new push screw?"

"Much easier," I said.

"Our only goal is to make you happy," he replied brightly, which made me lean against a van, weak with laughter. He also said I'd done a good job the day before—"A hundred percent defect-free." I hadn't been missing any more trucks. Lance's comment made me feel great for hours, out of all proportion to the minute he'd spent telling me. It was one sentence, but that "attaboy" made all the difference for a while. No matter how simple the job, I was doing it well, and someone had noticed. I recalled that when I was a reporter in Florida and we'd had a busy day, my editor made it a point to say, as I was getting ready to go, "Good job today," and I left eager to come back and conquer the world next morning. His praise meant so much to me that when I became a manager, I always tried to motivate through encouragement. Lance's words made me feel for the first time that I wanted to do a good job for General Motors, that I mattered, that someone cared.

Apparently a lot of workers felt that no one cared, because a few days before my three-month anniversary, the big day that would mean I had passed probation, Bummer asked, "Gonna take your ninety-first day off?" I said I wasn't planning to. "They don't like that, but some people do it, kind of a 'fuck you,'" he said.


I began to have a regular lunch table and regular lunch buddies. Location: a table inside a bank of lockers across from Trim 2. Characters: Ed, Tracy, and Murray, a trainer in Trim 1 often known as Spaz. Murray had bright brown eyes and a bristly mustache and favored jeans, country music, and Desert Storm caps. I once saw him putting in some false teeth, and he explained that he'd lost three in a "misunderstanding on Yonge Street." Murray, like Ed, really knew where the bodies were buried, and imparted the delicious information that Rolando used to be a baker. I pictured Rolando in a white toque and apron, at the beck and call of every housewife who needed a birthday cake. ("I said *yellow* icing.") He had had a couple of businesses, and that one went belly up.

■

Apparently he also had a brother who was a GM exec and a brother-in-law who was management in Scarborough. "Don Dornan's right-hand man," Murray said. While I could imagine Ed wearing a suit to work, that image didn't fit Murray at all, and he once characterized meetings and paperwork as "that stupid faggy shit."

Murray also warned me about working ahead through Fred Melvin's station. He pointed down the Trim 1 line to a small, thin man who was leaning against his workbench, staring straight ahead and mumbling to himself. "He's off his noodle," Murray said. "You've got to go around him. He doesn't work ahead and he goes ballistic if anyone works through his area."

Assorted characters made guest appearances at our lunch table on an irregular basis. One day a huge man, mostly beefy, not fat, in light-blue coveralls open nearly to the waist joined us and launched into a tale of how he'd gone to a strip joint the night before and seen "Chesty Morgan" or some such hugely endowed woman and how her massive breasts reminded him of boxers' punching bags. He didn't say it in a cruel or violent way (actually, his tone was more of awe); that was just the image that came to mind. I tried not to show that I was both shocked and embarrassed at this talk. I couldn't fathom what kind of reaction was expected from me, so I just kept my mouth shut and listened with what I hoped was a knowing half smile.

My tolerance for regular, garden-variety vulgarity, especially if it was genuinely funny, could be quite high. I didn't particularly care for it, however, if it was really stupid, insulting, or directly aimed at me, such as the time Barry Harvey said, "Sally. Fold your arms" (in other words, make cleavage). I ignored him. I also ignored Bruce the Rock Star when he asked, "What's the front of your T-shirt say?" on a day when the T-shirt I was wearing had some slogan or brand name written directly across the chest. There was a guy named Jack Morgan who painted black primer around the windshield opening, a job that was right next to my locker. He gave me a little wooden frog that jerked off when you pulled a string. I pretended it was mildly amusing and eventually gave it back to him in a week that had also seen the previous two incidents.

At the end of one particularly tiring week I lost my patience. I had cut the sleeves off my coveralls, as many did, because after you washed them, they shrank a little and got tight across the upper back. So, to protect my arms somewhat from the fibers, I'd cut a pair of stretchy cotton sleeves off a big roll in the supply closet and taped the top ends to the shoulders of the coveralls. Toward the close of one Friday day shift I was hot, tired, itchy, and diligently working ahead past Rob and Barry Harvey, who'd been communing with Mr. Coors during the shift. They'd hidden the beer cans in a box of foam blocks on Travis's workbench. Barry decided it would be cute to rip off the piece of tape on my right shoulder.

I yanked off my glove in order to replace the tape and spat at him, "If you *ever* do that again, it will be the last thing you do!" Ruth and Bruce heard the commotion and wanted to know what had happened. "I don't care if they want to get loaded. But I'm sick of strong men standing around and watching me work. And do not fuck with me!" I couldn't believe Lance didn't see this stuff. Of course he did. Everybody knew, and nobody did anything about it.

Then a new problem developed that made the tape-ripping incident seem ridiculously trivial. One evening, when a vicious winter storm hit Toronto, I discovered that my gas pedal was frozen to the floor. I took a cab home. Next day a plump man named Lloyd, who sported a goatee and worked in another department, offered to help me get my car running again. Out we went to the parking lot; he helped get the car going, and I thanked him. Couple of days later I was sitting on my workbench, and Lloyd sneaked up behind me and pulled the strings of my apron, undoing the knot.

"Cut it out! I am not in the goddamn mood," I told him. Since the car incident he'd been getting a little too friendly. Nevertheless, I soon felt a little bad for snapping at him. So when I saw Lloyd next, I resolved to be pleasant. He didn't give me a chance, because as I was working at the front of the truck, he grabbed my rear end.

"Damn it, Lloyd! Don't you ever do that again!" I yelled at him.

"Gee, okay, okay," he replied and quickly walked away.

Upset and confused, I kept working, thinking, That's a sexual-harassment charge right there, but should I make a big fuss about it? Obviously Lloyd was a jerk, and if he refused to stay away from me, I would have to take formal action against him. Should I do so for one boorish encounter? That wasn't what I was there for, to discover the ins and outs of the harassment procedure. However, I went ahead and asked Ed what the procedure was, knowing he could keep knowledge of the incident to himself.

"Tell Lance," he said, "and Lance will speak to Lloyd's supervisor."

"I think I'll let it go this once," I replied, "but if it happens again, that's it."

"Up to you." Ed shrugged.

Lloyd didn't join our lunch table in the next few weeks, and the occasional sight of him made me sick. But he must have realized he'd behaved like an idiot, because he didn't come near me and I didn't have to apply for official wrath to rain down on him. I searched my behavior to see whether I'd given him any kind of encouragement, but of course I hadn't.

Although I had good reason to keep quiet, I felt bad that the incident would go unreported. In essence, I'd let Lloyd get away with it and possibly feel free to try the same stunt with another woman. Sexual harassment, while still alive, was less common than it had been years ago. The company was trying to change the atmosphere, and harassment rules made a big difference, to the extent that some guys now complained, "You can't say anything to a woman." Pinups were mostly banished to the insides of locker doors, although a few survived out in the open. We were given a couple of hours off the line to attend a human-rights talk in the plant that defined sexual and racial harassment and how it wouldn't be tolerated. Times and attitudes change slowly, however. I heard one ominous story, but was never able to check it out: A young woman in another department had filed a sexual-harassment case but it had been dismissed, and later she'd found her car heavily scratched.

I wasn't surprised that a tough, mostly male working environment bred rough behavior, and I didn't rate dirty jokes as high on the scale of offensive behavior as a physical assault. It wasn't as if I'd never been the target of a risqué remark in the white-collar world, because I had. Besides, I wanted to experience a more earthy working environment, and there it was. The difference was in sharing an off-color joke and being the butt of one, and I was getting tired of the latter. I asked Tracy if this stuff bothered her.

"No," she said. "All the guys I grew up with were pigs. When I first got here, they tried to shock me. They'd show me all kinds of things, and I'd just laugh," she said, tossing her hair, which had just been permed and made her look like the eighties version of Cher.

Of course, as soon as I decided that every male in the plant walked on his knuckles, Valentine's Day arrived. Travis, loaded by 2 P.M., stepped into the truck and slurred at me, "Sally, I didn't gesha a Valentine's Day card, but here's a heart," and he made a little heart with his thumbs and forefingers.

Big Dave, the Chesty Morgan fan whose antiperspirant never seemed quite strong enough, stopped by, saying, "Sally, I want to show you something," as he pulled a little black box out of a plastic bag. I was wary of Big Dave since that conversation about the strip joint, but I saw that the black box contained a delicate glass heart pendant with two tiny cloth roses in the center. "I'm going to give this to my wife after work today," he said as I admired the jewelry. He then pulled a Valentine's Day card out of the bag. It wasn't one of those tasteless nudge-nudge, wink-wink cards that are supposed to be funny; it had a sweetly affectionate message. He said they were going out to dinner that night.

I smiled. "Guess you'll celebrate pretty hard."

"No, I don't drink much anymore," he answered, and my stone image of him as Factory Gorilla suddenly cracked.

I was still having problems with Nick the repairman. I looked to be sure those two screws were in that he was supposed to check and I tried not to get in front of him at working-ahead time, but one day I mistakenly put in a couple of panels before he was done with the van, and he had to do a repair under the insulation. Sure enough, I found Rolando standing there, but he was pretty cool about it, merely asking, "Did Nick explain to you about working ahead?"

"Yes. It was an accident, Rolando."

I reckoned that Nick had cost me hours in the plant, and the Message God seemed to be obliquely commenting on the situation with "Experience is something you get just after you need it."

The winter was marked by paint-shop problems. On one particularly arctic day, the line was down for two hours. Ed Donohue said they had trouble getting the ovens going if it was too cold overnight. He took me, Tracy, and Ruth on a tour of the paint shop. It was amazing up there. The line wound around and around, up and down, like some mad carnival roller coaster. There was a little cafeteria off the paint shop and, near the windows, a profusion of plants—potted palms, ferns—a greenhouse in the unlikeliest place. "There's a guy up here who does all this—this is his baby," Ed said. He pointed out the window to a wooden deck, complete with trellis, that lay under a dusting of snow. "You should see that deck in the summer," Ed said. "He's got sunflowers, cherry-tomato plants, all kinds of flowers."

When we returned to Trim 2, we found that someone had stolen the battery charger from our supply closet. Theft was a recurring problem. Not only did batteries walk away, but whole Makita guns disappeared. The plant was full of tools that were very tempting targets—a Makita gun and batteries retailed for around $150. Auto parts walked out the door all the time. One of the stacker drivers told me about the infamous Timmy Flack. They got onto him eventually, and called the police, who found about $100,000 worth of parts, tools, and other equipment in his garage. Management seemed to take theft more seriously than drinking, but again, security could have been tighter. One incident astonished me. A sweeper in our area was fired for theft. A couple of months later I saw him back at work and asked Murray what happened. "The union went to bat for him, but he's on restriction. He can't go into certain areas of the plant."

If all kinds of stuff went out of the plant, a similar wide variety also came in. Some of it was purchased wholesale legitimately; some fell off a truck. One guy came around regularly, while we were working, with a duct-tape-secured box full of homemade peanut brittle, of all things, which he would sell by the piece. He also sold industrial-size boxes of plastic wrap. Where did this stuff come from? If he was able to sell these things to us while the line was running, what was his real job at GM? There were guys with leather jackets, perfume, sweatpants and T-shirts, comforters, food such as meat or fish—selling in the plant or out of vans and station wagons in the parking lot. Hot cigarettes and liquor, smuggled in from the United States, were regularly offered. One night I bought a carton of half-price cigarettes. Several months before the plant closed, the Mounties arrested a guy who had been selling cigarettes and liquor out of a red station wagon.

One effort to combat stealing and booze-stashing drove Ivan, and lots of other people, around the bend for a while. Someone decided to rearrange our work stations, starting with Ivan's. They put in new workbenches, removed the metal racks that had held taillights stacked about eight feet high, and installed new, lower ones. The idea was to increase visibility. Ivan was livid that he hadn't been consulted about the new setup. Over the past nine years he had carefully nurtured his work area. He'd brought in bits of carpet to put on the workbench so the taillight lenses wouldn't scratch when they were laid on the bench just before he needed them, and so he could sit comfortably, his back against the metal racks, and eat his lunch and read the paper on breaks. Now everything was out of whack and more difficult for him to reach. He called the

■

union committeeman, poor guy, and jawboned to him about the work-station changes.

Several weeks later, when I was on right-side remotes, I arrived to find my work area rearranged in such a way that my job was harder. "Lance," I said, "if I could get this big table moved about ten feet that way, then I'll be able to pick up the parts more smoothly and the job will go easier." He said he'd see what he could do, but days passed and the table failed to move. Finally I spotted the general foreman, Lance's boss, and asked him if I could get the table moved. It was much too heavy for me to do alone. All right, he said, and a couple of guys came along shortly and helped me shift it. Lance was not pleased.

"You went over my head on this," he said.

"Lance, nothing was happening, and I had to get this done. Where's all this worker-empowerment bullshit?"

I got the impression that Lance didn't want to make waves with his supervisors. It seemed like such a small thing, but when you worked on the line, your world was small. Anything that rattled the little cage you had meticulously decorated was infuriating. Why not at least ask the workers who live there for seven hours a day whether they have any suggestions for rejigging the area? I'd read a great deal of blather about how companies had finally figured out that the worker knew the most about the job, and workers were involved in quality circles, decision-making, even budget-setting, but these Macho Management incidents made that seem like so much consultant hogwash.

A new addition to our lunch quartet was Neal Callahan, a short fellow from Belfast with a snort of a laugh, an awesomely profane vocabulary, and a profound lack of respect for any human. He was taking math courses in order to earn a high-school diploma and had four credits to go. I noticed that he had a scar across his throat running from ear to ear. A car accident? I wondered, or a major fight, or worse, a horrible assault? After I got to know him, I worked up the courage to ask him about it.

"It's a long story," he answered.

"Looks like you were lucky to survive," I said.

"Yeah, I would have missed all this."

Just before one break, Don Dornan led a tour of white shirts and name tags past our section. I told Laverne I'd blow a little fiberglass on them. As she looked on, delighted, I held up some panels in front of the fan as the group listened to Dornan talk about—what else?—the robots. Dornan's face also appeared on the bulletin boards, courtesy of a Van Express plant memo that announced we had achieved a COVE average of 4.9 in the previous week, the best since that audit system was put in place in the mid nineties.

"Although we are in times of significant financial restraint, I want to give recognition to our achievement by providing coffee or tea to all of our Scarborough Van Plant people throughout the day in our cafeterias."

I headed to the cafeteria for my free coffee and discovered that the large-size cups had been removed. Then again, people were carting away two and three cups of coffee at a time for themselves and others, far more than could practicably be consumed. It would not be the last time that the workers twisted a management gesture that was meant to be generous.

One night, having worked ahead, I was leaving about ten minutes early and I bopped over to my locker, as per usual, which was next to Jack Morgan's windshield-primer job. This wasn't the greatest job in the world. You had to grab a gun, which was attached to a hose, which snaked into a drum of acrid black goo. You hopped up onto the tongue of the carrier in front of the truck, leaned over, squeezed the trigger, and painted the goo around the windshield opening. Too little pressure on the trigger and you didn't get enough out and had to go over it. Too much pressure and it dripped into the truck and, more important, on you. The fumes from the primer were wicked, although the job area had its own ventilation hood. Some people liked it because once you got it down, the job took way less than two minutes and it was the only task on that job. The fumes didn't bother Jack or the woman I'd seen doing it on B shift. Maybe their tissues were saturated. Jack used his spare minute and a half per job to sit at the picnic table in the small locker area and create wild abstract drawings with ink and Magic Markers. But one major drawback to the job was that you were pretty much tied to the work area, although I did once see someone working ahead—he'd managed to get some of the primer into a little can and was using a brush. Tricky, that: You had to be delicately sure you didn't drip any on your co-workers who might be doing a job in the truck at the same time.

On that particular night Morgan was out and one of the Windsor transplants, Lee Argus, was doing the job. Usually Lee, who had a generally pleasant personality, was a free-and-easy AR, wearing civilian clothes, giving people breaks, kidding around. That night I nearly didn't recognize him. He'd gotten a haircut, so his hair was standing up short and spiky. He was suited up in dark-blue coveralls, work boots, mask, and safety glasses. Still, the fumes and the constant stepping up and bending over had wiped him out. All his usual vitality was gone. I waved as I went past, but his look was death. I have seen a job kill the light in a man's eyes, I thought.

In the months following GM's restructuring announcement, the Canadian Auto Workers union battled the company and its own membership as it tried to secure an agreement covering mandatory overtime that might keep Oshawa Plant 2 open. The sour whiff of panic arose from news articles and dispatches as local politicians and union reps faced the possibility of a layoff of thirty-eight hundred people. In the midst of all this, Oshawa Local 222, which included Plant 2, held a tainted election for local chairperson, in which 160 ballots literally fell out of one of the election-committee members' socks. The moderate candidate, who was willing to entertain the idea of concessions to save jobs, squeaked in over the hard-liner (whose name was on those fragrant ballots) opposed to concessions.

We were discussing the Oshawa controversy at lunch one day and the talk turned to our own workplace family, CAW Local 303. "This local is a joke," spat Murray as he and Neal talked of cliques, power grabs, and yes, ballot-box stuffing. "Last election here, a guy had the ballot box in his house overnight," Murray said. Great atmosphere, I thought; they're cynical about the company *and* the union.

GM announced it would be laying off 750 people at its four plants in St. Catharines, near Niagara Falls, due to slow sales. We in Scarborough, however, had all the work we could handle. We were still working Saturdays due to the weather-related problems we'd had and because of a shutdown in Lordstown, Ohio, which was the only other plant making the full-size vans.

We received a notice that the SUB (Supplemental Unemployment Benefits) fund was depleted and benefits for those laid off would be cut 20 percent for those with less than twenty years' seniority. Layoffs in Ste. Thérèse, Oshawa, St. Catharines, and Windsor had taken their toll. The SUB fund tops up unemployment benefits (usually) to something like 90 percent of take-home pay (which sounds like a lot, but tax is taken out of that and there's no overtime), but it looked as if that was being whittled down. Not comforting news for those looking at a job-free future.

The adjustment committee gave us the results of the YMCA survey. About twenty-three hundred out of a workforce of twenty-seven hundred had participated, testament to the good sense of giving people time off the line for the interviews. Overwhelmingly, people wanted information on how and where to look for jobs, how to write a résumé, on financial planning, interview techniques, and vocational guidance. As for retraining, various trades were cited by many, also computer skills, and perhaps surprisingly, management training. The committee said it was looking at ways of meeting the need for retraining and information.

The plant's top union official, Red Rolland, posted a two-page letter with disheartening news: The 140 Scarborough workers who thought they were transferring to Oshawa last fall with a good shot at permanent jobs were about to have the rug pulled out from under them.

■

"It appears that Oshawa management is attempting to convince their Detroit bosses that the Oshawa complex can be run more efficiently in the hope that Detroit will put another product in the car plant," Rolland wrote. The 140 were to be laid off indefinitely, but the letter informed us that the union and the company had agreed to give them the option of returning to the Scarborough plant, although at entry-level jobs in production departments only. This last bit was highly significant. It meant that people with high seniority who had worked their way to a job off the line—say, stacker driver (material-control department)—would be coming back and crunching welds in the body shop or hanging mufflers in chassis (production departments). Rolland's letter said the group of 73 workers, which included Billy Davis, who had taken the option of returning to the van plant (the rest were indefinitely laid off, but hoping for a return to Oshawa) contained people with as much seniority as seventeen years.

But what about the workers from the other plants who had come to Scarborough to fill the vacancies left by the seventy-three? Well, they would be offered voluntary layoff, which wasn't as crazy as it sounded. Someone paying rent in two locations might be glad to go home and survive on unemployment insurance and SUB for a while. If GM didn't get rid of enough workers by that method, the company would go to the top of the seniority list and offer early retirement. After that, top-seniority people would be offered a buyout.

Rolland's letter ended with a timely warning: "If this local union is not prepared to look after people who worked here for as long as 17 years, how can we expect other local unions to look after our interests during the course of 1993 negotiations when all the items in the master agreement relating to our rights need to be renegotiated?"

Despite his call for support, the return of the magnificent seventy-three still exploded into a huge controversy. A fractious meeting at Local 303's hall degenerated into chaos. Members of the plant council were pointing fingers, calling each other "liar," accusing some folks of voting against the returnees. Much to my surprise, many were not particularly glad to see their union brothers again. "They left," Ruth said succinctly, adding that she was not interested in taking a voluntary layoff because of the uncertain hiring situation in Windsor. No one's job felt secure.

The seventy-three were caught in a very nasty vise. They'd gone to Oshawa in good faith, hoping to get a jump on the van plant's closing. But they had the least plant seniority, so when an indefinite layoff came up, their heads were on the block. Red Rolland had gone to bat for them and, it was said, overruled his own plant committee to return them to jobs in Scarborough. But when they came back, they were treated like India's untouchables. I ran into a guy in Trim 1 who came back from Oshawa. He had ten years' seniority and said, "I'm on the lousiest job on the line. I feel like I'm getting punished, and I didn't even do anything."

In the midst of all this gloom, I was glad to see that Billy Davis was back, although we were no longer involved. He went straight back to bopping out welds in his old department. Since I was making friends in my own department, his return didn't mean quite as much as it would have when I was so lonely. Billy, who didn't care for confrontations in the first place, hated the whole Oshawa situation. He said his union rep wouldn't even talk to him. "My own shop committee voted against us," he said, shaking his head.

GM actually came up with some good news, saying it planned to call back twenty-seven hundred workers to Ste. Thérèse to build a new generation of Pontiac Firebirds and Chevrolet Camaros. In fact, GM was closing the factory in Van Nuys, California, that made those cars and moving production to Quebec, which indicated to me that free trade was not necessarily to blame for the closing of the van plant, as the union liked to maintain. Like many U.S. and Canadian unions, the CAW opposed the North American Free Trade Agreement (NAFTA) even before it was put into effect on January 1, 1989. While American unions feared the loss of jobs to low-wage Mexico, the Canadians historically feared the loss of tariff barriers and other measures designed to keep jobs from going south to the United States. Example: the 1965 Auto Pact, in which the Big Three automakers agreed to produce a certain proportion of vehicles in Canada in return for duty-free access.

Canada, with a population about one tenth that of the United States, has always feared becoming merely a distribution site for major U.S. companies. Domestic beer brewers, for instance (basically Labatt and Molson), were a powerful political lobby and always enjoyed protectionist measures. The thinking I heard many times went, "Budweiser could service all of Canada from one distribution center in Chicago." In other words, we have to make it hard for them (beer companies, car companies, whatever) to do that and easier for them to set up production centers in Canada—or require them to license a Canadian beer company to make their brand, as is the case in that business. Blaming free trade for the van plant's demise was convenient and neatly avoided a more complex analysis of the situation. The leadership of the CAW sincerely believed that there was nothing in free trade for their membership, but using free trade (and CAW President Bob White's favorite phrase, "the corporate agenda") as the catchall bogeyman for the factory's closing also suited the union's purposes. A membership angry at the forces of management is a militant membership and one more likely to view the union as its champion and less likely, perhaps, to reflect upon the fact that the union cannot, in the end, prevent a plant from closing. Other explanations—that the plant was old, small, couldn't be expanded and might just have come to the end of its useful life—were too easy and devoid of the proper emotion. The union also continually hammered the point that the van plant was profitable and, having paid off its mortgage years ago, it surely was. Rolland kept referring to it as a "gold mine," which begged the question of whether it was profitable enough, compared with modern plant capacity.

I believed that some politics entered the decision: GM had taken a lot of flak as it closed plants and threw thousands of people out of work in its home state of Michigan. More than once Scarborough people mentioned Michael Moore's deliciously audacious film *Roger and Me,* in which he tried to confront then–GM chairman Roger Smith in order to ask him to go bowling and explain why GM had devastated Moore's hometown of Flint. It wasn't a total coincidence that Scarborough's twenty-seven hundred jobs were headed for Flint. After all, GM had to work with the political and labor establishment in Michigan, and moving twenty-seven hundred jobs, even if it was nowhere near the number lost, could probably be held up as a good-faith gesture.

The Ste. Thérèse announcement cheered the Quebecers up, although it would be months before the factory was ready for their recall. I wondered how long such a product would last. Who was going to buy those souped-up sports cars in the early 1990s recession? The eighteen-to thirty-year-old men with no jobs? Infuriatingly, a newspaper article quoted a GM suit as saying that the life of the plant would depend upon a quality product, making the point that those workers had better not mess up, or else. I saw it as blame-the-worker time again, totally ignoring the roles of design, management, and marketing.

Eric Weil, a hawk-nosed, eighteen-year GM veteran, said he couldn't wait to go back. He was sharing an apartment with John Mullins, a sour-faced man on window install. John possessed an Anglo bias against French-Canadians, but had some pretty cultivated taste in reading. (Once, I noticed he was reading *Dear Theo,* Van Gogh's letters to his brother, and we discussed art for a few minutes. Another time he had Kingsley Amis's novel *The Old Devils.* "It's very well written," he intoned.) Many of the Ste. Thérèse people were doubling and tripling up in apartments near the plant and faced a five-hour drive back to Montreal to see their families on weekends, then the same routine in the other direction less than forty-eight hours later. People on layoff from Windsor, a four-hour drive away, also shared sparsely furnished rentals. St. Catharines workers who were called to Scarborough were looking at a ninety-minute commute, which meant leaving the house at about 4:30 A.M. for the day shift. "GM gypsies" were all over the United States, too. Workers at a Tarrytown, New York, van plant that shut down were offered jobs in another GM facility sixty miles away, forcing many onto a numbing treadmill just to keep a good-paying job.

We acquired a kind-faced lady from Quebec, named Bernice, with reddish hair and glasses. She was on left-side remotes. Her English was only fair, but I was able to find out that she was a passionate fan of hockey star Mario Lemieux. She was the salt of the earth, from small-town Quebec. If Bernice's voice were a vegetable, it would have been cabbage. She looked to be about fifty years old, with the flat-footed tread of those who have worked at manual labor all their lives. She found it hard to get up to speed, though, especially pushing the brake-control module into the plug.

Bonnie was helping her and was fairly annoyed about it.

"Well, she's old, Bonnie," I said, hoping to arouse some sympathy for Bernice.

"If she can't handle it, she should leave," snapped our young AR.

Another Quebecer, named Léo, was put on right-side regulators across from Carolyn, a placid lady who'd been on left-side regulators for several years. Léo and Carolyn looked to be in their late fifties or early sixties, and I couldn't help but feel sympathy for those nearing retirement who were doing this work. One time, during the working-ahead hour, a short, wiry, older, Italian-looking lady came down the line, doing a job I wasn't familiar with, and the first thought that popped into my head when I saw her was, She should be home playing with the grandchildren, not slogging the day away here on the line. I caught myself wondering if I wasn't being condescending, whether some of these older folks weren't tougher than I was, and wasn't "playing with the grandchildren" perilously close to "go home where you belong, little woman"? I concluded that I wouldn't want to be patronized and shouldn't make quick judgments.

A plantwide survey made the rounds, asking us if we wanted to start the day shift at six-thirty instead of seven. A week later the reported results were that 68 percent of the plant voted to start at six-thirty. I was raging. As it was, I was getting up at five forty-five to get in before seven. Now I'd have to roll out at five-fifteen, sheer agony for a night person. "I don't care what they say, I am not getting up one minute earlier!" I vowed to the lunch-table crew. The survey was fixed, some said, a sham meant to disguise the fact that the company wanted everyone to leave at the same time so it wouldn't have to open the gates half an hour earlier for the body shop. The body shop used to start half an hour before the other departments in order to build stock, so if there was a problem during the shift, the rest of the line could keep running. The company decided that it preferred a coordinated start-and-finish time. I saw the malevolent anti-working-ahead forces gathering. With the gates locked until shift end, where was the incentive to work ahead?

As the Oshawa prodigals returned, there were new (to me) faces all over. I saw Travis and Ivan, who apparently didn't mind their return, greet three acquaintances with smiles and handshakes. Off they went to the office, and not too long thereafter Lance came down the line with a pale, small man in tow.

"Sally, this is Kurt. He'll be learning your job." I looked to the ceiling and mouthed "Thank you." Kurt was about my height, but I weighed more than he did, or at least as much. I reflected that there seemed to be so many amazingly thin men working here, not nearly the proportion of hulking brutes I'd imagined. Kurt had short, almost crew-cut hair, a spotty complexion, and gentle eyes. But he also came equipped with one of the most acute cases of autoworker attitude I'd seen so far.

He thought that Lance was an asshole and wasn't crazy about being back in Scarborough. "It's a pigsty," he said, adding that the Oshawa plants were cleaner and the hoses retracted, so people weren't tripping on them all the time. When I suggested dividing the job, he instantly took the vent-and-screws part of it, natch, not the fiberglass. Kurt came in every day with a plastic lunchbox and ate like a starving Ethiopian— couple of sandwiches, fruit, juice, cookies. I could have killed him. Where did he put it? He didn't read on the job, though he carried a model-airplane magazine in his lunchbox. When I saw a notice about an information session on skills upgrading, I asked Kurt if he would be going. "No," he said shortly. He finally took a turn on fiberglass and put diesel insulation in a truck that was supposed to get the regular kind. He shrugged when he realized his mistake. "Oh, well, that owner will get a little extra." Not wishing to seem like a company toady, I let it go. Nothing happened. It wasn't easy to make conversation with the taciturn Kurt, who often just stood looking down at the workbench between jobs, but he told me that his dad, Gerhard, also worked here as an inspector in the paint shop and his mom was Chris on B shift. I asked him to give her my regards.

My own parents continued to be interested in and amused by (that was Mom) and interested in and disapproving of (that would be Dad) my work, but an unexpected boost came from Dad. I was talking about how many hours we were on our feet, and he said, "You should get some of the support socks I wear for fencing."

"What are they like, Dad?"

"They are knee-length, and your legs feel great."

A week or so later I opened a package with two pairs of dark-blue and one pair of brown support socks. I wore a pair the next day and felt as if I were walking on cotton candy.

# E I G H T

■

# L A N C E

Kurt was my salvation. It looked as if I was getting off insulation for good, but my joy was tempered by apprehension. Spaz and Ed advised me to be cautious and find out what my new job would be before giving up the old one. What classic mixed emotions. I was eager to ditch fiberglass, but I dreaded the inevitably awkward and painful process of getting up to speed on a new job. Would it involve even nastier material? Could I work ahead, or would I be tied to the workstation? (Although the starting-time change meant that the gate nearest the parking lot didn't open until the end of the shift, the guard station at the front of the plant was still open, and nobody bothered you even if you were walking out half an hour before end of shift. It just meant you had to walk a little farther back to the parking lot. So everybody still worked ahead.) Which muscles would be sore this time?

Everytime I saw Lance, I asked, "Where am I going?" The second time he pointed down the aisle and said, "We've got a place for you over there. It's called the Pit."

"No, Lance, not the Pit!"

"The body shop for you, so stop asking! Remember, me and the gateline foreman are like this," and he crossed his fingers. The gate line was an area of the body shop where the sides of the van came together and were welded to the floor. The roof frame was built there, too. As for the Pit, there were actually a number of troughs cut in the floor throughout the plant, in order to get at the undersides of the vans, and none of them were particularly pleasant places to work. In the body-shop pits, you had to mig weld over your head, which meant that sparks fell on your head and you had to wear a cap with a leather neck flap and a leather jacket buttoned up to the neck. If another welding job was located over your head, you worked in showers of tiny points of fire. I had looked into some of the pits in Respot on my way to the main cafeteria and thought they were the most desolate work areas in the entire plant. Usually there was only a hard plastic chair down there—no posters or pinups—as if the inmates realized it just wasn't possible to brighten up the Pit.

I laid off Lance for a while—he really didn't know where I was going—but I guess he was tired of seeing me sit and read the paper (Kurt and I were doing half hour on, half hour off), because he had me join the dome-lights team for half a shift. The only thing bad about that job was that you had to climb into the vans and twist your neck around to install the little ceiling light. Ed brought the chilling news that the body shop needed eight people. There were dust balls in the plant that had more seniority than I did, so I couldn't imagine what might keep me from HELL: MAIN OFFICE. I had to bug Lance again.

"Lance, where am I going?"

"Okay, that's it. Roof rails. You'll never hold a pencil again in your life." I instantly caught an acute case of sorry-I-asked. He didn't know I was a writer, yet he had managed to describe the worst fate possible for me. I felt as if my days were numbered in Trim 2, which made every day seem more like Malibu Beach compared to the gulag across the aisle.

Then the news came that Bernice was to be transferred to the body shop, along with two or three other people from Trim 1—all from Ste. Thérèse. Although these people had far more seniority at GM than I did, they had arrived at this plant after I did. However, the Quebecers felt that it was very unfair that the Oshawa returnees, who supposedly didn't have seniority for thirty days, as part of their returning deal, were not the ones to go. I thought they were right. Despite the controversy their return caused, the ex-Scarborough people clearly had more buddies in the right place—i.e., the union—than the Ste. Thérèse people, who were far from their friends and advocates and would be going back home and out of Local 303's hair anyway.

"I hate to see her go," said Rob. "She's not gonna last over there." Our trainer's sympathy surprised me, but I was beginning to sense that his tough, "quit complainin' " attitude hid a heart that could warm up to a fellow human in trouble. I couldn't believe how dumb this move was. Bernice found remotes a tough job. Did GM really believe this fifty-something woman would be able to tackle a two-hundred-pound welding gun, or was there such a thing as a light-duty job in the body shop? Bernice was petrified at the thought of HELL: MAIN OFFICE, and I could see her getting badly injured over there. It wasn't right. I was younger and stronger. Something had to be done about this situation. An effort had to be made.

I agonized for a day, then made my move. Before work I went in to see Lance and offered to transfer to the body shop in place of Bernice. I knew this would be seen as unfathomably dumb, and I was afraid it was. I still wasn't the world's most graceful autoworker, and recalling stories of broken legs and other injuries caused the bottom to drop out of my stomach. All the jobs looked terrible over there; what was the entry-level job?

Lance had spent some time in the body shop and advised me to stay away if at all possible. "There was an even worse job than hanging mufflers. You had to weld part of the roof, clamp down a part, and climb in and out of the truck. I did that for one day as an AR, and I was ready to hang myself. Twenty bucks an hour or not, that was slave labor. Nobody should have to work that hard."

He was right, I thought, but when I described that job to Billy Davis, he brushed me off with "Lance used to complain a lot." The macho creed cropped up often, among men and women: No matter what the pain, shut up and bear it.

Once I told Travis, as we were doing our jobs, that I felt tired, and he snapped, "All you're ever doing is complainin' how long the day is!"

Quickly trying to lighten the mood, I said, "Okay, it isn't long, it's short."

He was sorry for having yelled at me, because he softened immediately and made a joke. The attitude seemed to be "Look, everybody knows these jobs hurt. Talking about it makes it worse." Funny, though, that the same person who spouted the macho creed would the next day reminisce about how awful some job or other was. Depended upon a person's mood.

"Lance, I know the body shop is rough, but it sort of fascinates me. I would be okay."

"Are you crazy?"

"No. It would be a challenge."

"Forget it. How would you like to clamp your hand? How would you like to get flashed—get a faceful of sparks? Or how about tattooed?"

"What's tattooed?"

"Bits of hot metal in your skin. Or how about mig-welding so much that your eyes are bloodshot? You think you hurt now. Over there you're always like this . . ." He grabbed a phantom gun, braced himself, and mimed pulling the trigger, over and over. *"Ka-chunk, ka-chunk, ka-chunk* . . . all day."

"Day in and day out."

"That's right. Your hands always hurt. I got away with five stitches."

"Where?"

"In my hand. Or how about the tip of your gun flies off and you're covered in water?"

"Water?"

"Yes. It cools the gun. You think the line stops? You go over there, you think you're going to get some good job? There are some horrible jobs there. How about a job where you have to put in sixty welds? Sixty. How about knife-edge? The workers named it. You have five guns on that job. You never get ahead. And the worst part is when you're working away and you look up. And everyone else is gone."

Lance turned my offer down flat, commenting, "Well, you've got character, Sal." He said it wasn't his decision, that rigid seniority rules applied. He didn't think sending Bernice there was terribly smart, but there wasn't anything he could do.

So I got Bernice's job—left-side remotes—and I became a slave of the line once again. There's too much stuff on this job! was my first thought. The second was that my pectoral muscles were starting to ache like crazy from pushing the antilock-brake module into the plug. I had three days' training on the job, but my first day alone recalled my initiation into The World of Fiberglass: a meat grinder of unrelenting, unceasing labor. No sooner did I finish one truck than I had to start on the second. Didn't bring the newspaper in because I knew I'd have no time to read it, although maybe it was also because someone finally did notice which newspaper I read. Eric Weil kidded me that "the *Globe* isn't a paper to bring into a factory."

My second day alone on left-side remotes wasn't much better. My shoulders and arms hurt with every job, and I fought stark, staring exhaustion. The feelings of pain and panic . . . Hello, old friends. You're always waiting, aren't you, just around the nearest pillar on the line, ready to pop out, bloody jaws grinning?

Ed bopped past and said, "Smile!"

"I am sick of assholes coming by and telling me to smile, because I don't fuckin' want to smile, because I'm too fuckin' sore. I want to be in a bad mood!"

Ed quickened his step, and who could blame him?

I let some jobs go for the repairman, and I hadn't done that in ages. I was too sore to pull the brake module out of the clip if it didn't go in right the first time. I was so wiped that I dropped screws in the door and forgot to put a little colored sticker on to signify that there was a screw rattling around in there. Was it caught later on? God, I don't know. Is it possible someone bought a GM van with a screw loose (the van, not the customer)? It's possible. Sorry about that, GM customer. That was my best on that day.

It was days before I could work ahead even five minutes. There were no forays to the parking lot with Ed, Tracy, and Spaz. I was so shackled to the line that I would hardly have had time to get out there before I would have had to get back. A sweet-faced young woman named Charlene from St. Catharines was on my old insulation job, which now looked like a dish of double-chocolate ice cream with whipped cream and chopped nuts compared to left-side remotes. Apart from missing one vent, Charlene handled insulation with aplomb, and I was awed. It had taken me two months to get really smooth at it.

Lance was doing more job-juggling, and he offered Ivan a new position repairing and testing the TR9 wiring. Lance told him, "I need someone reliable. Please don't tell me no." Lance could be pretty persuasive, and he played a valuable card with Ivan, telling him there would be lots of overtime.

"He knows how to push my buttons, Solly," Ivan said, agonizing—as only Ivan could—over whether the new job would be more or less hassle. He sat down at our lunch table one day, and Neal and Murray groaned slightly. They regarded him as an old-country hick. I told him to take the job and get off taillights after thirteen years.

"I have turned down every job—chassis, UR [utility relief]." Ivan was reluctant to leave his comfortable post and wasn't sure enough of his English to take anything with more responsibility. After Ivan left the lunch table, Neal snorted, "He's tighter than a whore's pocketbook," and it was true. For instance, Ivan never bought a newspaper; he'd always ask to borrow a section or two of someone else's or pick one up that'd been left on a table. In the end Lance couldn't push quite enough buttons. Ivan's fear of the unknown was stronger than the tantalizing—but vague—possibility of a bigger paycheck.

About ten days after she was shanghaied, Bernice returned to Trim 2, along with John Mullins. A bunch of people laid off from the St. Catharines plants had arrived in Scarborough with the least seniority of all, thereby supplanting the Ste. Thérèse people in the body shop, and once again we were overstaffed.

"Too many is almost as bad as not enough," said a harried Lance.

"But doesn't someone have a master plan?" I inquired, half jokingly.

"Nope. Personnel just says, 'Go back to your area.'"

John Mullins was told to sweep up, but no one could find any brooms. Bernice relaxed at the lunch table, and I asked her in French how her job was in the body shop. Unfortunately, I could not understand a word she said in return, but she waved her hand and curled her lip, so I figured that was description enough.

After I'd been on left-side remotes awhile, Rob took over one day, saying that Lance wanted to see me in the office. "You're in trouble," he said. That's it; I'm being fired, I thought. I went to the office, and Lance said, "You're in shit. Have a seat." He left me to stew for a few minutes, but I saw one of the trainers, pumped him for info, and discovered I was to be offered right-side sidemarkers.

Lance returned, threw himself into his desk chair, and tapped the desk for a few seconds, thinking. "I'm putting Bernice back on her old job and Paul [the Wop] is going to the TR9 repair job. I don't have to go through the seniority list. It's a choice job, and I don't think you want dome lights," he said. I didn't realize it at the time, but dome lights was actually a pretty good job. Sidemarkers, however, was way better than remotes.

"Sure, Lance. I'll take sidemarkers," I responded, trying not to jinx it by showing how eager I was. "I've done it before," I said, to indicate that yes, this was a completely rational decision on his part.

However, when I returned to the line and relayed this news to my colleagues, it was not met with unfettered joy. John Mullins, now training on c.v. secure with Eric, was annoyed that he wasn't offered Bernice's job. And the prevalent view was that I had way too little seniority to get sidemarkers right off the bat. Tracy, of all people, called the committeeman to complain.

"Nothing against you, Sally. I just don't think it's fair," she said.

Things happened pretty quickly after that. Murray said at lunch that Lance "was getting his ass reamed by a committeeman." Supposedly sidemarkers was classified as a "secondary" job, which meant that Lance didn't have to go through the list. But Spaz said that the departments agreed all job openings would be "primary," to cut down on the beefs.

"So I shouldn't get too comfortable on sidemarkers," I said at lunch, sighing. Paul the Wop trained me on right sidemarkers. It had one more task than left sidemarkers (which was a really prime job and which I'd done on the other shift)—a wire at the back that I had to curl up and shove through a hole in the floor. He was incredibly fast at the job and had a massive callus on his left forefinger from putting in the clips. I was slow, of course, but recalled the days when I did the other side and was able to get twenty minutes ahead.

I still flinched every time someone passed by and called him the Wop, and finally I asked him, "Paul, doesn't that bother you?"

"No, because you know what a wop means?"

I knew, but answered, "Okay, what?"

"It means a *man,*" he said, giving the last word such proud emphasis that "wop" seemed to be a title of highest honor. He was pretty much right, too, since the word came from the Neapolitan dialect word *guappo,* which meant a rascally fellow.

I liked his take on it, the way he'd made an insult his own and turned it on its head. From that day on, since even he called himself the Wop and nobody knew who you were referring to when you said "Paul," I fell right in, and he became the Wop to me, too. Nobody from the outside would have understood it, but it just became a nickname, like Spaz or Stretch, or the Trim-1 trainer from Newfoundland who was called the Codfather.

I wasn't with the Wop long on sidemarkers. Early the next day Lance arrived to inform me that he had to open the job and a guy named Jerry, with six years seniority, wanted it. No way, said I.

"I'm getting flak, and I want to keep the peace since the group is working so well together," he said, essentially appealing to me to be nice and not make a fuss. No way, I decided. This was the Little Big Horn. I was offered this job, and I was going to fight to retain it. I had passed probation and was tired of feeling pushed around. Even if I was doomed to defeat, I wanted to start getting some respect as a Person to Be Reckoned With.

"I want to see my committeeman."

"Well, why don't you switch with Jerry and we'll call the committee-man?"

"Why don't I stay right here and you call the committeeman?" I replied, reasoning that possession was nine tenths of the law. Dave Whipper, a slim fellow with prematurely gray hair (and no wonder), showed up. He said that secondary openings were to go by seniority, according to a plantwide agreement. Lance apparently didn't realize this.

"I've been doing this job, and I want to file a grievance," I told him.

"I'll get writer's cramp, and it'll be torn up anyway," Whipper said.

"Too bad," said I.

Off he went to consult a higher authority, and I worked away. Lance passed. I did not look at him. Whipper returned and said there was no grievance. We argued back and forth a little, but I realized I would be going down in flames.

After lunch Ed passed by and said, "If Lance tells you to move, the one thing you don't say is no."

"Oh, I know, I've just made my point."

Shortly thereafter Lance appeared with Jerry, and I went quietly.

"Nothing personal," Lance said.

"Nothing personal," I replied. I had provoked a confrontation that I figured I would lose but that wouldn't backfire on me, because it had started with Lance's mistake. Working on the line, feeling like a beast of burden, had made me angry with a kind of free-floating, powerless re-sentment that was ready to fight should a convenient battlefield appear.

I got Jerry's job on right-side remotes, which was harder than sidemarkers because it had bigger parts, but better than the left side because it had no brake module. Nevertheless, it was like a completely new job, because everything was backward for me, and I was slow and

■

awkward again. The Beauville models, which came along about one in ten, had an extra bit: a chrome strip that went on the inside of the door and was secured by four really small screws. I had to put a tiny screw on the magnetic tip of the gun, hold in place the chrome strip, which was only an inch or so wide and a couple of feet long, and aim the screw at one of the holes, while, of course, the whole bloody thing was moving. José Venancio, the AR, had some time free and did some chrome strips for me, which qualified him for sainthood, if the Vatican wanted to ask me.

Things got better, and one Friday night the musketeers ordered Chinese food to be delivered on break and went to the parking lot for beer at lunch. It was truly an exercise in time management that we could get so much done on a twenty-three-minute break and thirty-minute lunch. But if the Chinese food order was there already, and you worked ahead three trucks, that gave you a twenty-nine-minute break. Similarly, at lunch, if you worked ahead four trucks (which took some doing), you had thirty-eight minutes to rumble out to the parking lot and back.

It was quite the jolly Friday night. By last break Rob, Bummer, and Eric had entered a state of happy liquidity. Bummer playfully put a little sticker on my back that read HOT, which was usually stuck on a parts box that had to get to the line quickly. It was done with good humor. I thought it was funny, and I left it on all night, causing much amusement. Bummer, who was training as a UR and had time off the line, mixed whiskey and Cokes as usual, and shared the remote job.

Everyone seemed to be in a mellow, lubricated mood. As I took a break by the workbench, I watched Bummer's broad back working up the line a little and slid into a sentimental, alcohol-induced reverie. I held my can of spiked Coke. "This is for all the men and women who put their bodies on the line to make a living. This is for those who work in pain and just do it, over and over, to get through the night."

Not long after, Lance stopped by my remote station to ask how the job was going, and I told him truthfully that it was going well. Neither of us mentioned the Sidemarker Affair again, and neither of us held a grudge about the other's actions.

Lance lingered for a few minutes, and we fell to talking about the topic that was more and more on people's minds: what to do after the plant closed. Lance's promotion to supervisor wasn't permanent; it was just for the duration of the van plant's life. His future after the closing was a big question mark. He could well find himself back on the line in the Oshawa truck plant, if he decided to stay with GM. His father had worked "joe jobs," he said and he was tired of joe jobs, but he was married and a baby was on the way.

He said he would be attending career-counseling sessions, offered by GM, and dreamed aloud while I worked and listened.

"I want to get out of the auto industry; I've been in it too long. I wouldn't mind working in an office, wearing a twelve-hundred-dollar suit to work. It's time for a clean job."

"It's a different world, Lance."

"I know. I was there. I was a company rep for a telephone company, but the company was absorbed."

"Was your job a casualty?"

He nodded. "I wish I had the education."

"Why did you leave school?"

"I was stupid. If I knew then what I know now, I'd have taken business courses. I'd like to be a company rep or a PR rep."

PR. Now he was talking my field. When all this was over, maybe I could do something for him. For now I smiled.

"With your luck, you'll be hanging mufflers in Oshawa," I kidded him.

"Bite your tongue."

I was beginning to be intrigued by Lance, so I asked him if he had time for a coffee one afternoon after the day shift. Besides Lorne O'Halloran, he was the most engaging supervisor I'd seen so far, and he possessed experience that Lorne (and Warner and Rolando) didn't: He'd moved up from the line. He seemed bright, restless, outgoing, possessed

■

of a quick sense of humor. Not a yessir-GM plodder like Rolando and, to some extent, Warner. So what was his story? Why was he walking that path, and where did he hope to go?

We settled in at a coffee shop in the Eglinton Mall. It was two blocks west of the plant and one of the two places where you'd always run into someone from work, the other being Gene's bar and hamburger grill, located two blocks east of the plant.

"Let me ask you something, Lance."

"Anything."

"How did you come to be a supervisor?"

"Well, I was over in chassis, slugging mufflers, and they came around with applications," he said, lighting a cigarette. "From the first day I started with this company, I said, 'Someday I'm going to wear a white shirt.' So I sent it in, and one day my boss came to me and said, 'You have an interview at ten o'clock.' Well, I was wearing coveralls, I had ripped off the sleeves, and I said, 'An interview? Looking like this?' He said, 'Don't worry, they know you work on the line.' So I cleaned up the best I could, and I went in. There were three generals and Warner Lyle, and they just fired questions at me. 'What would your priorities be as a supervisor?' 'Quality, safety, production.' 'How important is safety to you?' 'Extremely important.' 'Why do you want to be a supervisor?' 'I think I know what it takes. I've seen the good ones and the mediocre ones.'"

It was hard for me to picture him in blue coveralls, dirty, shoving a muffler into the underside of a van every two minutes—this man sitting before me in his tan slacks, black short-sleeved cotton shirt, suede lace-up shoes, gold-rimmed glasses. The only remnants of life on the line were the hard-muscled arms.

We talked about extracurricular activities, and I found I was more of a typical blue-collar sports fan than he was. My favorite spectator sport was baseball, then hockey, both of which Lance could take or leave alone. I played softball and hockey, skied a little, and hated golf. Lance was the classic golf obsessor—the latest equipment, articles, videos—

and a skillful skier. He'd known Billy Davis from the body-shop days, but the only activity they really had in common was golf, since Billy's softball, hockey, and bowling activities didn't interest Lance at all.

I didn't envy the line supervisor's job. The first step on the management ladder is often the toughest. You're the filling in a corporate sandwich: closer to the people you're supervising than you are to top management, yet subject to pressures from both. In Lance's case, he oversaw fifty people, which meant that on any one day maybe up to half of them represented problems or tasks he had to manage. Quality screwups brought his bosses down on his head. Disciplinary action meant acres of time and yards of paperwork, so you let some things go . . . as long as the jobs got done. What kind of image will work best, day in and day out, with your workers? Should you be a good guy and take the chance that some of your people will try to walk all over you? Should you be a real hard-ass and have fifty people hate you? Some of them will hate you anyway, the minute GM gives you that white shirt with the van-plant logo on the breast pocket.

Lance and I had struck up a rapport, but to his credit he didn't allow his natural friendliness to override his duties as supervisor. In fact, I received my first reprimand around that time. On the remote job the small rods had a couple of clips on them that were put on in a subassembly job farther off the line near Lance's office. The operator would attach the clips, then bring a box of assembled rods to the remote station. One day I watched with glee as my pile of rods dwindled and no new ones appeared. I'd once seen Laverne run out of taillights and saunter with a smile on her face down to the phone at the tool locker to call Lance's office. That was good for four or five trucks before Claude, one of our area's stacker drivers, hustled along with more taillights. So I let the rods run out. If we were missing a part and couldn't finish a job, we were supposed to put the rest of the parts in the truck, so the repairman or trainer could do the job once the part was found. But if I couldn't put in the remote, then the next person couldn't put in the regulator and the next one couldn't put in the window and the next one couldn't secure that window, so the parts piled up merrily in the trucks. It was a joy to see Léo Arsenault's eyes light up as he approached the first truck with his regulator, only to find the remote parts lying on the floor. I thought it would be clever not to tell anyone (hey, the repairman will pick it up shortly) and was happily placing channels and remotes on the floor in the passenger side of the van when Barry Harvey came bustling down the aisle with a box of rods and Lance right behind him.

"Hey, it's not my fault the rods ran out," I said as Barry started up the line to do the half dozen jobs that had gone by.

"Come on, Sal, you know you're supposed to notify me or the trainer if you're getting low on parts. That's part of your responsibility, not someone else's. Consider this a reprimand."

"Yeah, okay, Lance."

The future weighed heavily on Lance, as it did on many people in our doomed workplace. Over another coffee Lance said that in a way he was not that sad the plant was closing, because he felt his options were limited at GM.

"I just have a high-school diploma, and the highest I can go is a level seven [a general foreman]. At GM they want that university degree. But I know people with university degrees who don't know anything, and I have tons of practical experience," he said, smoking a cigarette as usual.

"I agree, Lance. You could sell, make commissions, and earn far more than you're getting at GM." It was easy to picture him as a salesman. He had style. He liked his toys. He drove a black four-wheel-drive sport-utility vehicle.

Lance allowed as how he didn't necessarily think much of degrees from some of the universities around Toronto, "but if you go to a school in the Ivy League, they have the best information, the best seminars. A degree from Harvard—that means something."

He looked at me for confirmation, though God knew why, since all he really knew about me at that point was that I was American. This man is amazingly sharp, I thought.

"Yes, an Ivy League degree does open doors," I agreed, thinking that mine were in an envelope somewhere in one of my file cabinets. I was tempted to tell him, but I couldn't. I didn't want him to know just yet. The plant had another year or so to go. It was too early.

"It's never too late, Lance. I know a man who had a successful career as a lawyer, then around age forty became a priest. I know an engineer who's contemplating going to medical school."

Even as I said this, I earnestly believed it, but I also knew that Lance would likely never acquire the education he missed so keenly. Married, soon to be a father—the man needed to earn a living more urgently than a degree. He spoke of education as something he'd thrown away, only to realize its value too late. I hoped that Lance could channel that burning desire to improve himself into a better job, a better life. He was standing at a crossroads, but vandals had run off with the street signs.

After we talked, I bought a couple of frames, dug my diplomas out of the drawer, and hung them on the wall of my home office. I had taken them for granted. Mother had always made such a big deal about her degrees, and I thought I'd be more modest, more egalitarian than that. Meeting Lance showed me how foolish I'd been. Now I saw those pieces of paper as symbols of a dream and an accomplishment that should rightly be a source of pride.

# M A R I A

I'd been working in Scarborough less than a year, and winter was fading when Lance informed me I was to be trained as a "floater," that is, someone who could fill in on more than one job. I wasn't quite up to the status of an AR, but to paraphrase Neil Armstrong, it was one giant leap for mankind from the line. When you trained on each job, there was an inevitable break-in period when you were sore and slow, but I was getting much stronger and felt sure I could get through the awkward stage more quickly. Besides, there were two great advantages: You weren't tied to one job, and there was often lots of idle time if no one was on vacation or out sick. In a plant with a more stable workforce I would have been surfing insulation for years before moving to a more desirable line job, never mind a floater job.

Around this time Warner Lyle, Lance's predecessor, left for Oshawa, and we were invited at meal break to a small going-away party in one of the meeting rooms on the office level. There was pizza and cake with GOOD LUCK WARNER written on top in colored icing. The white shirts stood in a clump and talked mostly with each other; we production operators did the same. We gave him a gift certificate to Collegiate Sports, a sporting-goods store. The irrepressible Ivan kissed him on both cheeks, exclaiming, "This is how we do in Europe!" The other supes presented him with a plaque commemorating eighteen years of service at the Scarborough Van Plant. After the presentations, the good soldier Warner stepped forward to say a few words. Since he never said more than a few words at any time, I figured this would be brief. He said he was sorry to leave Scarborough because "without all of you, there would be no Warner." I assumed this meant he was thanking us, although he appeared to be saying he would literally disappear without us.

My life as a floater began when Lance brought a fifty-something woman, dressed in jeans and a T-shirt, to my right-side-remote job and asked me to train her on it. He introduced her as Maria Carlisle, and she said she was from the Windsor trim plant. I set to work teaching her remotes, and she was slow at first, but as the day wore on, I found myself enjoying showing her the job. She laughed at her clumsiness and praised my skill in such a natural way that I didn't feel she was being insincere or trying to flatter me into doing more work. Unlike Kurt, she had no chip on her shoulder whatsoever; in fact, she tried so hard to do a good job that you wanted to help her.

Her smile crinkled up the corners of her black eyes, which were deep-set and had dark circles underneath. She wore her black hair short in a side-swept style, was about my height (five-feet-four), and had a shapely, womanly figure. She smoked like a building torched for the insurance money and drank her coffee black, but that seemed to be about it for any abused substances. Her voice—pitched a little high and a little sharp, with a faint echo of the flat tone typical of Windsor and nearby Michigan—usually had a laugh buried in it. Her worst curse was, "Oh, frig," which harkened back to my Catholic-high-school days and the girls who would say, "Oh, sugar," instead of "Oh, shit."

I asked if she'd like to have lunch together. Somehow she didn't seem to be the type to go drink in the parking lot or blow weed on the roof. Maria had been working at Windsor trim for a few years, but the van plant was as alien an environment to her as to me. "At the trim plant we sat down at sewing machines. We wore dresses to work!" There was a greater proportion of women at that plant, and the place could be a bit cliquey and gossipy, she said. Her reaction upon first seeing the van plant's huge, filthy, noisy assembly line was similar to mine upon seeing the body shop for the first time—sheer terror. She and her friend

Marnie, who'd also come up from Windsor, were sharing a sparsely furnished apartment in Scarborough. Like the Ste. Thérèse transplants, they headed for Highway 401 on the weekends, driving four hours west as the Quebecers motored five hours east.

She was picking up right-side remotes fairly well, but Lance said I couldn't have the next day—Saturday—off as he'd promised me unless Maria was up to speed, because he didn't have a lot of extra bodies on the weekend. I had been invited by a friend to see *Love's Labour's Lost* at the Stratford Festival (which I didn't tell Lance) and desperately wanted the day off. By the end of the shift Maria was fairly wrung out, but she graciously said she could handle remotes alone so I could have my day off. I made a mental note: I owe her. I knew she wouldn't be okay, but I selfishly wanted my time off and figured an AR would be around to pick up the pieces.

Come Monday my suspicions were confirmed, but I had other fish to fry, since I was now learning a new job, one that used to be performed by a shy woman named Carolyn: left-side window regulators, the X-shaped part that raised and lowered the window. Until now my jobs had involved rather light parts, with the possible exception of the diesel insulation panels, and they didn't go in every truck. Regulators, on the other hand, weighed a good five or so pounds each, and installing them wasn't all I had to accomplish in two minutes. It also included installing two switches in the power trucks and climbing up on the back of the truck to tuck a wire in behind a clip. I had to tape my fingers to install the switches, since it took some force to bend their stiff little clips. You had to build your own stock: putting together the switches with their little frames. You also had to dip the end of the regulator in a bit of white grease that, of course, found its way onto your clothing by the end of the shift. How did Carolyn keep up with this job? I wondered, but I was also wise enough now to know that if you did anything long enough, you got it down.

No sooner had I been on Carolyn's job for a couple of days than I learned the other side, where Léo Arsenault presided. It was the next workstation down the line from Maria. José Venancio was doing Ber-

■

nice's job, and I caught the tail end of a conversation he and Maria were having—something about Mexico. I listened harder, between the screams of the guns and the blams of the body shop, and heard José say, "The sun's getting hot. I better put on some more tan lotion. Hey, our drinks are empty. Where's the waiter?"

"Maria, what's going on?" I asked.

"Oh, José and I often 'go away,'" she replied, looking a little embarrassed. If they were working near each other, Maria explained, she would ask, shortly after the line rolled, "Where are we going tonight, José?"

"Okay, we're at a luau in Honolulu, drinking rum punch, and everybody's dancing," José might reply.

Or, "We're on a cruise ship, relaxing by the pool, and the buffet just opened." They would take it from there, exploring the various facets of a resort stay.

That night, as I interrupted their idyll, they were lying on a beach in Mexico, ordering another round of margaritas. "Hey, José, isn't your wife jealous that you go on all these trips with Maria?" I yelled across the line.

He grinned. "That's all right. She knows."

"It's so much fun. Makes the time go faster, too." Maria smiled.

Well, I wanted to get in on this, so I asked if we could make it a threesome, and José, delighted at the prospect of "going away" with two women, readily agreed, as did Maria. We toured most of the Caribbean in the ensuing months, and Maria was right. It was hard to think about how your shoulders were aching or how break was two hours away when you were filling in the details of an imaginary vacation in the sun.

A couple of days later I trained on TR9s with Eric and discovered what a choice job that was. A team of five or six people was on TR9s. We each took a number between one and five or six and read the production schedule to see which wires we had to install in which truck, each truck having a number. Each of us started several trucks up the line, since it took more than two minutes to do a TR9 job. But there were no guns involved; you worked completely in the truck inserting and installing wiring, and the shorter you were, the better. Stretch, Bonnie, and Bruce the Rock Star were TR9 regulars, and Stretch had a devil of a time with the job. We carried homemade stools, cushioned with scrap foam and well wrapped with duct tape, and sat on them in the truck to pull the wires with a homemade hook. If you were too tall, your head was bent over like a crane with a broken neck. The alternative was to scare up a pair of knee pads and kneel on the truck's grooved metal floor, not an attractive alternative. You had to feel around in the channel where the roof met the side of the van, while looking down, so you didn't slip and smack yourself in the eye with the hook. It was hard at first, like any new job, but once you got the hang of it, it was easier to work ahead on than most jobs, and you could carve out an hour mealtime.

If I had a free half hour or so (still astonished every time at this small miracle), I'd drift down to Maria's job station, sit on the workbench or on the stool that swung out from the workbench, and chat. She and her husband, Tom, who worked in a warehouse and shipping facility in Windsor, lived in a semirural community near there. She dropped out of high school to marry Tom Carlisle and get out of the house. Maria and Tom were hot. She showed me an early 1960s picture of them, barely out of their teens—Tom, lanky in blue jeans next to a motorcycle, and Maria, jaunty in capri pants. When they were a young couple, she said, they always had friends dropping around on weekends for beer and a party.

"We had such good times, Sally, and Tom and I still have fun. We're always hugging and snuggling with each other. The other night my son said, 'Will you two knock it off,' and Tom said, 'Hey, I miss her.'" She had an innocence about her, a playfulness and sense of fun that didn't seem to have dimmed at all over the years.

Maria and Tom had four sons: Ronald, Ted, Donny, and Keith, now all adults or nearly so. She sounded like a bright and imaginative mom. When the boys were young, Maria would do such things as have a rainy-day picnic on the living-room floor. She expressed an old-fashioned sense of sacrifice for her family. She would often say that something had been her "duty" as a wife and mother; I hadn't heard anyone speak like that since my father. I couldn't quite relate to that point of view, but I respected it.

She had good reason to marry young and get out of her parents' house. When she was growing up, she endured some vicious physical punishment from her father, a man whose vocal commitment to Jesus Christ and to his church did not preclude beating his daughter. She told me once that she tried to make the hitting less painful by telling him, "It's okay, Daddy, it doesn't hurt." I flushed with impotent anger when she told me this, but she had put the past behind her and often saw both her mother and father. Her father had changed as he'd aged, she said, becoming kinder and less rigid.

"Really, he's a different person," she said, with a little wonder.

The warmth and cheerfulness of her personality was such that, even if you didn't know she had four sons, you'd have described her as a mom. She was so easy to talk to, she became the mom confessor of our department. People I had pegged as absolute clams would talk to Maria. She liked that; it made her feel needed. She easily wore the mantle of the advice-giver, the knower of secrets. As a professional interviewer, I could only envy her.

As far as I could see, Maria only had one real vice. Bingo. The more she told me about her bingo habit, the more I saw that when it came to gambling, the men played cards, went to the track, or bet on football pools and the women went to bingo.

Not that Maria described it as a problem, just as fun. But I was startled when she said, "The money doesn't matter. When I win, I give it away."

"How can you do that? I'm so tight with a buck that I hate to gamble in the first place, but if I win, you can bet I keep the proceeds," I declared.

"I just like to play. Last week, I won a hundred dollars, and I gave it to Ronald," she said as I shook my head. She added that one reason she liked working, besides the money, was that she ended up going to bingo too much during layoffs.

I found myself gravitating to Maria quite a bit. We always found something to talk about. She was funny and lively, and she laughed at my jokes. Back then, when I was childless, I got bored listening to people, especially women, who talked about their kids a lot, but Maria loved her boys so much and discussed them with such enthusiasm that I was eager to meet them. One was a college student who had married a deaf woman and become fluent in sign language. Another was going for a career in health care. The third had been laid off from a warehouse job and was looking for work. The youngest still lived at home and was going through the late-teenage I-hate-my-parents phase. They had lost a fifth child to cancer at the age of six. I started to tell her a bit about myself, but I wasn't ready to doff the Iron Mask yet. I could discuss my family and the guys I was dating, and the fact that I was looking for The Real Thing.

Once I told her I was using a phone dating service called Telepersonals and I'd met a couple of nice guys that way, along with a couple of oddballs.

"Sally, that's too dangerous. I hate to think of you doing that."

Annoyed at her cluck-clucking, I snapped, "That's easy for you to say. I would give my right leg to have the family you have. What am I supposed to do, Maria? Sit around and look at the wall? Date somebody from in here? From what I've seen so far, if they're not married, they're losers."

Later that day I emerged from my grouchy mood and apologized for being so crabby. As I said I was sorry, Maria had tears in her eyes.

"Sally, I'm sorry, too; I just wasn't thinking. I feel closer to you than anyone else here," she said, which surprised and pleased me. Everyone seemed to be Maria's friend, and I actually found myself jealous, like the schoolgirl who wants the popular teacher all to herself.

One day she looked tired, the circles under her eyes more pronounced, and I asked if she'd gotten enough sleep, which, considering all the coffee she drank, was a legitimate question.

"Sometimes I'm in a lot of pain. I'm being treated for breast cancer, and when it gets close to the treatments, sometimes the medication doesn't work," she said.

She went on to tell me that she was allergic to chrome and rubber. Part of her job on right-side remotes was, of course, installing a chrome strip, but she was able to handle it if she wore gloves.

"Maybe you should have stayed home in Windsor," I tentatively suggested.

"But I like being here," she answered, much to my surprise. What was to like? A long commute? Bunking with a roommate? Working on the line?

"I've never been on my own in my entire life," she continued, "and now I'm living away from Tom and the boys and I can take a break from being Supermom. You know? Sometimes I got tired of being Supermom."

I was amazed. I had had no inkling that there was another side of Maria besides a totally committed wife and mother. One night I learned that Maria's desire to work away from home was even more powerful than I thought. At about 11:30 P.M. I noticed her leaning on the big box of remotes and went over to her.

"Oh, I just feel so dizzy," she said.

"Do you want a break? Do you want to go up to the ladies' room and lie down?" I asked, quickly concerned.

"Yes, I think so."

"Rob!" I yelled down the line. He was at the TR9 station. "Maria doesn't feel well. She needs a relief!"

Rob came running down, I hurried back to finish a job, and José, who wasn't on a job, helped Maria across the line and sat with her at the picnic bench.

"Oh, I feel so silly," she moaned, but her eyes were wet and she just didn't look well.

"Maria, I have some fruit juice and an apple in my bag. Do you want some?" I asked as I worked away (channel, rod, remote, screw-screw-screw). She shook her head.

"I'm calling security," said Rob. He got on the phone, and Lance came down in a couple of minutes. Maria was holding her head in her hands and wiping away tears.

"Call an ambulance!" Lance ordered.

She sagged against Lance, who sat with his arm around her, talking quietly to her. She looked barely conscious. A security guard came, along with a union safety officer. The medical team arrived shortly thereafter with a gurney. They lifted Maria onto the gurney, and two nurses opened a large medical kit and started giving her oxygen. I finished a job and went over.

"She is being treated for breast cancer. She also has a Medic Alert bracelet. It must be in her purse, since she's not wearing it."

Lance looked at me, stunned. I crossed the line, got her purse, and handed it to one of the nurses, then had to dash to do the next job. "Let's get her out of here," said the older nurse. The line hadn't stopped, and the open van doors were brushing past the medical team. They wheeled the gurney into the aisle, loaded it on a cart, and took off.

Later I asked one of the plant's ambulance attendants, who happened to pass by, where she was taken. Scarborough General, he said. The Wop said she had had a heart attack.

"Paul!" I said sharply. "Don't you dare tell anyone Maria had a heart attack. You are not a doctor, and you don't know."

"I'm-a not a doctor, but I have-a esperience," he replied. I could imagine the rumor mill springing into action.

I urged Lance and Rob not to blab about Maria's condition. "She told me this in confidence, and she's entitled to privacy." They promised.

My emotions ranged far from work that night. Go home, Maria, I thought, please get out of here and take care of yourself. For the remainder of the shift, the usual dramas seemed petty next to Maria's crisis—a rumor that Saturday's overtime had been canceled, denied by Lance;

■

news that the guards had actually caught somebody drinking—Bummer and a guy from Trim 5—and they'd been suspended for three days, according to one account, and for a week, according to another. I might have gotten a chuckle out of their adventures, but next to Maria and her courage, they just seemed like brainless screwups.

I thought we might have seen the last of Maria in Scarborough, but she was back a couple of weeks later. The doctors thought she'd had a minor stroke. Astoundingly, she wasn't on any restrictions and went back to right-side remotes, puffing cigarettes and drinking black coffee.

"Maria, are you sure you're going to be okay?" I asked her.

"Sally, I feel so embarrassed about getting sick. Really, I'm much better," she said.

Maybe it was an attempt to get Maria to drink better coffee, but we decided to get in on the illicit-food-sales trade in the plant by running a coffeepot. GM's contract with TRS gave the food concessionnaire exclusivity, of course, but surreptitious food and drink stands flourished, with nary a squawk from management. Across in Trim 5 a guy dragged in a couple of cases of soft drinks and a cooler full of ice and sold pop at a nice profit. His retail price was the same as the cafeteria's, and he was closer to a lot of workstations. It was more convenient during a long, hot shift to step over to Joe's cooler and hand him a buck than to wait for break and go to the lunchroom.

Coffeepots blossomed everywhere. TRS coffee was the typical barely palatable brew produced by a cheap grind, hardly cleaned pots, and overenthusiastic warmers, which was why I tried to mute the acidity with plenty of cream. The coffeemakers and electric kettles were plugged in to the GM power supply—which was supposedly verboten, but obviously tolerated.

Maria and I bought an average little Mr. Coffee, foam cups, filters, some good-quality coffee, sugar, and milk, and set it up on the right-side-remotes workbench. It was instantly popular; the coffee didn't rot your gut as badly as TRS's swill, and we charged only twenty-five cents per cup. We got an immediate lesson in the economics of coffee-by-the-cup sales: Even charging our tiny price, we made money. Of course, our only overhead was the cost of supplies; the workbench wasn't charging us rent, and we weren't paying ourselves a salary. Still, I thought, if coffee shops charge more than a dollar per cup, the profit margin must be pretty healthy.

Our coffee station got to be so well known, especially at the beginning of the day shift, that we had to keep an eye on the machine while a pot was brewing, lest our customers raid it in the middle of the brew, thereby weakening the entire pot. They were pretty honest, too. At twenty-five cents, nobody stiffed us, as far as we knew, and the plastic container with the change in it was never stolen. We stashed the supplies in Maria's locker and the milk in a nearby fridge.

After about a month we had an amazing surplus of more than twenty dollars, enough to get a couple of pizzas for the department. We also had a worn-out Mr. Coffee, a modest household appliance being whipped into making four and five pots a day. So we bought a catering-strength coffeemaker with a spigot, which was a bit more of a production to lug back and forth to Maria's locker, but could stand up to the daily strain. The capital expenditure of about forty dollars ate into profits for a while, but we were soon back in the black.

A few weeks later Maria got sick again. At last break I was sitting with her at the picnic table as she said, "Oh, I feel so tired." When we started up again at 11:53 P.M., I decided that someone else could do her job for the last hour. So I called Ken Sui over and told him that Maria was feeling very tired. He willingly took over the job, and she sat at the table, her head in one hand. I wanted to call someone, but she wouldn't let me, so I suggested she go upstairs to the women's washroom to lie down on the bench there.

A few minutes later I looked up, and Maria wasn't there. Rob came along and took over my job, asking me to check on her. Lance, standing nearby, said, "Oh, no, not again."

I dashed up to the washroom, and she was lying on the bench, but she didn't look as pale as she had the last time.

■

"Don't worry about it. It's just the last hour; someone else can do your job," I assured her.

Later I saw her sitting at the picnic table near the office.

"Maria, really, how are you feeling?"

"Oh, much better now."

Her doctor told her to reduce stress, so I suggested wearing earplugs to cut down on the pounding from the robots across the aisle in the body shop. I wished she would stop smoking and eat a healthier diet.

I was overjoyed to discover that Maria and I were both Scrabble fans, so when I was on Bernice's job for a couple of days, I brought in a Scrabble game and we set it up on the picnic table. We started the game at first break and played until lunch. We'd work a truck or two ahead, then take a turn. She was very good, and our scores were usually very close.

A few days later we didn't get to finish our second Scrabble game. Maria had a fit of the shakes and felt ill after lunch, and Rob took over for her. Ivan, Leo Arsenault, and the Wop came over to ask if she was okay, and the Wop got her a coffee. She had neglected to take her medication.

"It's because I'm in pain a lot, and if I don't take the medication, I get the shakes." On break she confided that she couldn't stand the thought of possibly having to have an "operation"—i.e., a mastectomy.

"I won't do it, Sally. I couldn't go through that."

I didn't know which words to choose. "It's an awful thought, Maria, I know . . . but when it comes to your life, it's a decision you might have to make. But I hope not." I almost felt a little angry at her, scared at the idea of losing her and thinking, Maria, come on, a mastectomy is better than death! All the same, I knew that if it were me, I'd try anything first rather than lose a breast to surgery.

I got to meet Tom and two of their sons, Donny and Keith, one day when they came by for a tour of the plant before the afternoon shift. I liked Tom right away—a combination of a nice Al Bundy and a better-looking Homer Simpson. The day shift was in full swing as we started the tour at the body shop. When we got to Trim 2, I heard a scream of joy—Keenan, Caitlin, and Marilyn had spotted me. I ran over and we gabbed through ten minutes of who-was-where. The big news was that George, who had helped me with the three screws so long ago, had gotten fired for decking a supervisor with the c.v.-install power box.

As our group was meandering along next to chassis, Tom asked, "Are those the only robots?" meaning the ones in the body shop.

"Yeah, that's it," I answered.

"This place is pretty labor-intensive," he observed, quickly identifying one of the prime reasons the plant was closing. As we walked through the plant, pointing out various jobs to Tom, Donny and Keith, I felt detached and sad. So many of these people were strangers. I work here? I look like these people when I work? People do these jobs? How can they? Later that night, as I ruled the narrow kingdom of left-side remotes, back in my apron and coveralls, opposite Maria, she said, "It looked different when we went around today."

"Yeah," I replied. "Worse."

She nodded.

Watching our colleagues work on the line, we felt ashamed of being dirty laborers, little cogs in a big machine. Once we were actually doing the job, immersed in detail, performing mental gymnastics to make the time pass, we didn't think of ourselves that way.

I hadn't mentioned that I was a writer, but Maria told me one day that she'd written some children's stories. We had something in common! I was falling deep in friendship-love with Maria. What talents and resources this woman had. We were such different people, yet we were forming a most unlikely friendship: the highly educated professional from New York City and the high-school dropout from Windsor; the single woman yearning to find a long, solid relationship again and finally ready for babies and the long-married woman with four sons.

She didn't know it when she came to Scarborough, but Maria was searching for herself and finding it in a strange place, the decrepit old GM van plant. Funny where voyages of self-discovery take us. She didn't do anything wild. She didn't have an affair. She roomed with a gal from back home and wondered at being a woman on her own, responsible only for herself for a time, away from her five-guy family, much as she loved them with all the strength of her heart. She was reflecting upon her life, performing that essential exercise called taking stock, looking at where she was and where she'd be going and just thinking about it, weighing it, stretching the canvas of her own image.

I saw parallels between Maria's state of mind and my own at the time. Working at the van plant allowed us to explore hidden parts of ourselves. Feeling independent was so important to her that she was willing to brave a serious health crisis. For my part, I stayed in this grungy workplace in order to discover whether I could meet the challenges of a world totally unlike one I'd ever known.

I followed many stories in the last year and a half of the Scarborough Van Plant. A man from Windsor, tired of lonely weeknights, had an affair, driving his marriage perilously close to the rocks. Another man tried to give me an engagement ring he'd intended for his girlfriend. They'd broken up and he said he had no use for it anymore; I handed it back and told him that I hoped they could work things out.

When I thought of all the van plant stories I knew—there were many more, of course, outside my ken—and braided them into one tale with many threads, Maria and Lance emerged as my main characters. They were the two people I knew for whom the van plant's closing meant the most. The plant's imminent demise threw their lives into sharp relief. They were chasing their hearts' desire—the one, to know herself; the other, to better himself. I admired their quests and was silently cheering them on.

# D O W N T I M E

At 2:30 A.M., after about three beers and a couple of shooters, Stretch wasn't too steady. He was trying to stand anyway, egged on by a jeering crowd of Trim 2 citizens celebrating Eric's recall to the Ste. Thérèse plant. We were wedged into the "lounge area" of Gene's bar near the plant, where the large-screen TV and a bit of carpet provided that touch of the Ritz so lacking in the orange Early Formica decor of the rest of the place.

Gene had locked the front door from the inside and closed the blinds on the front windows at 1 A.M., as usual. Legally, no alcohol could be served after one. However, GM workers came off the night shift at that time: yet another tough-luck aspect of working factory shifts. At these times—feeling sweaty on a summer night that's still warm at one, but with enough residual energy to want a cool, golden beer and some conversation—I again recalled my old white-collar life and remembered how easy it was to get a drink after work when work ended at 5 P.M.

Factory work and the law made criminals of us. After the evening shift, GM workers who wanted a cold one had several choices: You went to your home, someone else's home, or a vehicle in the parking lot with a cooler thoughtfully stashed in the trunk. If you wanted to buy a brew and socialize close to work, you went to Gene's.

I always assumed that Gene was paying somebody off, since the restaurant sat right down the block from a courthouse and a police station, but I never heard with any certainty that this was the case. I did hear that Gene would throw everybody out and close up instantly if a fight broke out, so maybe he relied on the discretion of his patrons to keep him out of trouble.

I'd heard about "the legendary Gene's" before I set foot in the place, mostly thirdhand tales of arguments, who-was-seen-with-whom, who got really tanked, who lost a bet on the World Series, who went there at lunch and didn't come back. This must be the real thing, I thought, a low-down, grease-and-grit, body-parts-flying, shot-glass-crunching, blue-collar bar.

I wanted to go, but felt as chicken as I did when I went to England at the age of eighteen and wouldn't go into a single one of those comfy pubs alone because I thought they were rough, like American bars. If I entered Gene's by myself, I feared, everyone would turn around, glare, and start throwing bottles, yelling, "Phony! Get out!"

The first time I walked into Gene's, I was with Maria, and we were going for a drink in the broad afternoon light after the day shift. A few heads turned, as is normal in a place where there's a good chance you'll know somebody coming in the door, then turned away. Intensely self-conscious, I tried to look around to see if I knew anyone without making it obvious I was looking around. Among the first people I spotted were Dave and Chuck, Billy Davis's friends from the body shop, who looked at me as if I were invading holy workingman's space. I quickly looked away to talk to Maria.

Our lunch passed quietly. Someone we knew stopped by our table, a couple of unshaven guys sat at the bar with beers, a sullen young wait-ress with a tight black top and a short black skirt took orders, the corner television soundlessly broadcast a Blue Jays game. As I chatted with Maria, I continued to glance around furtively to see if anything colorful was happening—knife fights, punches flying, a woman throwing a drink in a man's face.

I was disappointed. Drinking at Gene's, I discovered eventually, was nearly an extension of working in the van plant. Half the clientele was in grimy coveralls. I saw the same people there as at work. They talked about the same things they discussed at work. It was the cafeteria with a liquor license and slightly better food.

After my initial foray with Maria, I began to feel quite comfortable hopping over to Gene's to kick-start the socializing engine. I went to Gene's once for a real meal in the middle of the night shift. I was working an overtime shift on a quality-checking assignment off the line and was able to slip away for a full hour of dinner. I remember feeling so deliciously human, so at peace with the world after the luxury of that long sixty minutes.

Even those tied to the line would sometimes dash over to Gene's for a lunchtime beer. Most went back to work. Some didn't and caught hell for it the next day. I couldn't quite understand the point of using that precious half hour to run outside, jump in the car, drive two blocks, park the car, quick-step into Gene's, down a couple of beers, and rush back, not until I sweated up a whole desert of thirst doing a tough job one hot night. Then I performed the whole hurry-hurry routine around the corner, and that cold Labatt went down like water. That one beer was enough to take the edge off the second half of the shift and made it just a teensy bit more bearable.

By the time I found myself there at 2 A.M. watching Stretch attempt to stand on a chair, I'd completely lost my self-consciousness. "I'd like to propose a toast to Eric Weil," Stretch began. Echoing the movie *Wayne's World,* shouts of "Hurl! Hurl!" greeted him. I yelled, "He needs a c.v.!" a reference, immediately understood by all, to the time a supremely hungover Stretch relieved himself of breakfast in a bin of c.v.'s, or side windows.

At the instant shout of laughter and delighted glances in my direction that followed my remark, something clicked. Sitting between Maria and Barry Harvey, a beer in my hand, I felt I belonged. Who doesn't love making a well-timed funny remark? But more than that, I'd struggled for so long to fit in, groping for the right thing to say in so many situations, never really knowing whether I'd hit the target. That night an absolute bull's-eye.

■

My social life wasn't always this lively. There were times, at the beginning, when I despaired of ever socializing with anyone outside work—or inside work, for that matter. Transferring to A shift specifically to see Billy, Chuck, Dave, and Sharon had proved to be misguided.

Although the body shop was across the aisle from Trim 2, Billy was buried deep in its entrails at the opposite end of the plant. I saw him sometimes going to or from a cafeteria, and occasionally he stopped by my workstation, but he clearly did not want to hang out with me. He much preferred being with his guy friends at work. I hadn't asked him to keep my background a secret, but he respected my privacy and didn't feel the need to blab about it.

I sighed. All right, if Billy and I shared a little too much personal history, then perhaps it'd go easier with Dave, Chuck, and Sharon. Shortly after I started at the van plant, remembering the lively New Year's Eve Billy and I had spent at Dave's place, I went to visit Dave at break time, threading my way through the welding guns and hoses of the body shop. He was sitting in the supervisor's office with the lights off. The supervisor had gone for a coffee, and the light from the plant threw the little office into a dusky gloom.

Dave was leaning his head back against the wall. It was 9 A.M., two and a half hours into the morning shift, and his eyes were hollow from fatigue. I think I asked how his day was going. "Christ, twelve years in this place. I could have had a decent job," he said, referring in an oblique way to the inertia that had kept him pounding out welds instead of applying for forklift driver or even supervisor. "Why don't you apply for supervisor?" he asked, looking at me with a black expression. "With your education, you'd be a cinch."

I pretended he was kidding, replying, "I don't know about that, Dave. I just got here," then left quickly. The fantasies of rejection that my fervid imagination had conjured up when I first walked into the plant as a worker had just come true—quietly and with a sting. This was a totally different Dave from the guy I'd met socially. New Year's Eve Dave liked me; Van Plant Dave hated me. But he was the same Dave, and I was the same me. Maybe I'd caught him on a bad day, I thought, refusing to acknowledge what was going on, and I tried to be friendly a couple more times. One Christmas at the plant I searched him out just to say "Merry Christmas," but he replied, "Oh. Yeah," and turned away.

I had to speculate about what was going on in his head, since he wouldn't talk to me, but it was obvious that he couldn't understand why someone like me—an educated woman with a career—would show up on the line one day. I guess it would be like suddenly seeing your bank-branch manager or high-school principal wearing dirty coveralls, shoving in transmissions on the chassis line. It was my worst fear come true, that I would be pegged as a dilettante, an impostor, or worse, a spy, and rejected. This isn't fair, I thought; he's refusing to get to know the real me. He's rejecting a symbol, an image. Besides, I have nothing but the best intentions.

I recalled Billy's remark that people who go to work in Gucci loafers "look down on us as factory trash" and thought there might be some kind of justice in the way I was being treated by Dave, that people in shirt-sleeves routinely rejected people in coveralls. I didn't think that crossing the line would be without problems, but I had thought that the problems would be ones I could solve: enduring the physical challenge, trying to stay friendly and open-minded, reporting and writing as best I could. Since I believed that people were people, despite class differences, I didn't realize how lonely it would be.

Sharon was different, but she didn't have time for me. Whenever she saw me, she smiled and had a friendly word or a wave. Treading water in a sea of loneliness, I felt that she threw me life preservers of kindness. But she worked a second job as a waitress to support herself and her son, so she was always on the run. In whatever time off she had, Sharon played fast-pitch softball with the men. I admired Sharon without reserve.

So it was six months or more before I dug into the social life inside and outside the plant. One of my first social events was with a group of people who were as much outsiders as I was, the French-speaking workers from Ste. Thérèse. In my immediate area the loudest person around from Ste. Thérèse had to be Maurice, a large man with an impressive black mustache. He worked across the aisle from Trim 2 in Trim 5, installing seats. On his way to the cafeteria he often walked up the line bellowing, *"On s'en va!"* ("We're going home!") He was most definitely not shy about speaking a great deal of French and very little English.

The factory supported some fairly skilled softball teams that were beyond my level, but Maurice decided to organize a game of fun softball. Several days before the weekend he was signing people up for his team, which he called The Turkeys, in English. I gladly signed up, and on a sunny Saturday afternoon I met a group of the Quebecers in the plant parking lot, preparing to go to the softball field.

It was about midday, and they were pulling on cans of Labatt '50' beer from coolers in the car. It was Mardi Gras, a picnic, and the Marx Brothers, all in one. Much laughter, loud talk (of which I understood a tenth), jokes, exclamations, even a burst of song. I chatted with a couple of people I recognized who spoke English, and eventually we all headed for the field.

Maurice, captain of The Turkeys (or *Les Dindes,* I suppose), had me in stitches. He was like a host on one of those crazy TV variety shows so popular in Quebec. He put on an umpire's chest protector and a baseball cap, both backward, a pair of glasses with no lenses, and marched up and down the sidelines, making emphatic pronouncements in French. God knew what he was saying, but the effect was hilarious. The Labatt '50,' chips, sandwiches, fruit—all came out of coolers in a steady stream.

Very few of these folks could play ball, even a little, but they gave it a wonderful try. I was stationed at third. As luck would have it, an early batter hit a good, hard smack my way—right into my glove. This play can be fairly easy if you're in position, but it makes you look like God. A great shout arose from my teammates and Maurice, who was now behind the plate, umpiring after a fashion. I bowed.

Ironically, because we couldn't communicate that well and they didn't know much about me, they accepted me. I tried to stop caring so much about making contact with the people I'd known before and turn my attention to people I was meeting for the first time.

One early social outing came as a result of Bruce the Rock Star passing out fliers advertising a gig by his group, Burnt Offerings. I'm a rock-and-roll fan, so I went to see whether Bruce had any talent. The band was appearing in a basement club not far from the plant. The ceiling was low and the opening group played at ear-shattering volume, so I retreated to the pool tables at the back of the club, where I ran into Bummer. After a break Burnt Offerings came on and immediately swung into Jimi Hendrix's "Purple Haze," setting a high standard of guitar skill right off the bat. I wondered at the wisdom of that, but Bruce was brilliant. He had lightning hands and played with a minimum of stage attitude, just rapt attention to the music. The band played a couple of original songs that Bruce had written, and they were pretty good, too. I remembered I once saw him reading Kafka on the line, and he had laughed when I asked if that wasn't redundant.

Maria, Bonnie, and I decided to organize a Trim 2 bowling night. None of us had been bowling in years, we thought it would be fun, and since it was the great blue-collar sport, I saw it as a perfect fit with my working life. A week or so later our group included Bonnie; her husband, Nick; Maria; me; Jan from Trim 1 and her husband; and Frank, Maria's Windsor friend, currently residing in the chassis department. We chose tenpin bowling mainly because I'd never seen, much less played, the fivepin version.

Jan's husband was better than most of us, but Nick did all right. Nick and I got along fine now that I was off insulation and no longer getting in his way. The rest of us were bowlers in the 100- to 150-point range, complete with gutter balls and body English urging stray pins to go down. Frank committed the crowning gaffe of the evening when he released the ball on his backswing. We nearly fell off our chairs with laughter; we couldn't help it. "Stupid fuckin' game," he muttered sheepishly.

Our group got together for a few more bowling nights and a couple of Chinese buffet dinners. Generally a good time was had by all, although I felt a bit edgy in the early going; it's not easy to talk to someone when you're the Woman Without a Past. Many people didn't talk about their work history much because they didn't consider it that interesting. If I answered a question with a smile and, "Oh, it's a long story," people took the cue and accepted the fact that I didn't want to answer. Being closemouthed, in fact, was a pretty good way to get along and a prevalent attitude.

If I was the Woman Without a Past among my blue-collar friends, then I became the Woman Without a Present in the white-collar crowd.

I really had to bite my tongue one evening at a gathering at the home of Mike Malloy, then Canada editor of *The Wall Street Journal*. A friend of ours, a former Associated Press reporter, had married a woman I'll call Wanda who then was in the public-relations office of the autoworkers' union. I'd had one or two brief contacts with her in my Reuters days, but as far as she knew, I was freelancing now.

We were relaxing in Mike and Ruth Malloy's living room after dinner when the talk turned to the autoworkers' union, always a high-profile entity given the economic importance of auto manufacturing and the dynamic profile of its president, Bob White.

Wanda was talking about sexual harassment in the workplace and said one of her predecessors in the public-relations office several years ago had gone into one of the GM plants on business. "When they saw her on the floor, the men all began banging tools on the workbenches and on the equipment, because they saw a woman in the plant. It must have been awful," Wanda said, shaking her head.

Wanda's audience, a group of educated, middle-class professionals sitting in the warm glow of the Malloys' book-lined living room, made sympathetic noises. She continued, "I just can't imagine what it's like, to do those jobs. Bob White says the worst part is what it does to your mind."

Although he'd performed manual labor early in his working life, the president of the autoworkers' union had never actually held an assembly-line job. I resented, just a little bit, the idea that he knew how it was.

I'd lived this scene so many times—a social gathering of educated, middle-class folks—but never with this perspective. They looked so comfortable, so nice in their liberal-politics reasonableness. I was to all outward appearances one of them, but I felt as if a huge gulf yawned between us. They thought I was still in their world, but my double life split my emotions. I had more in common with the people in that living room than I did with Dave or Billy, but I also felt I'd purchased the right to see myself as an autoworker with pain and perseverance. As they talked about my work, they had the best intentions, but they had no real idea what they were talking about. I was doing it every day, and I couldn't say a word. As I listened to them clucking about the poor autoworkers, my thoughts turned completely unreasonable. (Don't even wonder one word out loud about how bad you think my job is. Until you've done it, and done it again and again, you are an effete bunch of wets who don't even realize how lucky you are in life. And don't you dare extend your moist sympathy to that dirty man or woman in coveralls, because there, but for the grace of a God who is having his little joke, go you.)

These were my friends—hell, this was my tribe—and in my self-righteous fury I wanted to smash them.

# ELEVEN

# THE
# DOG DAYS BARK

Rob came down the line as I was picking my next set of wire harnesses at the TR9 station. I was there because Bruce the Rock Star had a gig that night.

"Check pool! Who wants to get in on the check pool?"

"Every week I swear I'm not going to do this and every week—"

"Come on, Sally, quit jawing. Are you in or out?"

"All right, all right, I'm in. Here."

I handed a dollar to Rob, which he put into an envelope. Each week he chose a number from one through nine. When Lance gave out the checks at midday, we'd look at the last three digits of the serial number and the cents part of the dollar amount. Whoever had the most twos or threes, or whatever that week's number was, won the pool.

I think the last time I'd won anything was in the late seventies—a Christmas turkey at the Associated Press in New York. I didn't participate in the check pool every week, but I wanted to fit in and it was only a buck, so I lost money for several weeks. This particular week the number was five. After lunch Lance came along with those precious slips of paper. The Wop ripped his open. Two fives. "Ha!" he shouted. No fives for Rob. One each for Bruce the Rock Star and Travis Allman. None for Maria. Two for Stretch. I tore mine open and searched for the number. "Whoa! Three fives, Rob. Beat that!" Rob disappeared to canvass the other check-pool participants. No one had three or more, and I incredulously collected twenty-eight dollars.

People would bet anything on anything. During football season Lee Argus circulated the weekly NFL pool. For a couple of giddy weeks bingo cards were sold throughout the plant for the United Way: a dollar apiece, and each day a new bingo number would go up on the message display, between pithy sayings from the Message God. The prize was a hundred dollars. People were mad for the cards and bought four or five each, and I was no exception. Didn't win, though. Stretch did, and he treated us to beers in the parking lot. Betting appetites certainly weren't confined to the factory. At my various journalism jobs I bet on the date of the NHL playoffs, the first big snowfall, the Oscars, the Olympics, and a "ghoul pool" on which elderly public figure would die first (Jimmy Stewart beat Boris Yeltsin, Mother Teresa, and the Queen Mother).

As I climbed into the trucks to hook up my wires, I pulled a bandanna out of my pocket to wipe my face. After eight months in the plant I was experiencing my first hot weather. Summer turned up the burner under the auto plant, until the whole building cooked and simmered and even the machinery radiated heat. Winter was definitely the better season, once you endured that brain-numbing, I'm-a-human-icicle walk across the parking lot. If it got cold enough, there was the chance the paint shop couldn't handle it, and a really vicious snowstorm held the promise of parts running out or not enough people getting to work to run the line. In summer about all you had to hope for was a strike at one of the GM plants that supplied ours.

Summer in the van plant was added to the short list of times in my life when I truly appreciated the invention of air-conditioning, the others being when I lived in Florida and New Orleans, the wettest sweatboxes of the South. The supervisors' offices were air-conditioned, as were the offices on the upper story and at the front of the building. Perhaps it would have been impossible to air-condition a facility like the van plant, although I have heard of air-conditioned factories. Entire office buildings are air-conditioned, for heaven's sake, but they are more self-contained than factories, with their various large and small openings. It must have come down to cost, of course, and no one in 1952, when the plant was built, or 1974, when it was converted to vans, thought it was worthwhile. Maybe in those days it really wasn't possible, and retrofitting in later years would have cost way too much, but the end result was yet another sign that we were considered less than human, certainly less human than the white shirts and the office staff, though our labor was the rock theirs rested upon.

The sunny season also brought a new (to me) concept called "tag relief," a procedure that boosted output but from my perspective seemed like another effort to make my working life as miserable as possible. Although it sounded like a game children should be playing on the street, in reality we were all "it." No longer would we all take breaks at the same time, except for the main meal break. Each of us would now take the early break and late break at a different time while our job was performed by a Utility Relief person (UR). URs were Absentee Relief people or people taken off the line and trained on several jobs (Bummer and a couple of others). In this way the line squeezed out a bit more production, since it was scheduled to go down only one half hour per shift.

It wasn't hugely popular. For one thing, it was lonely. For another, in order to get all the breaks in, the UR folks started giving breaks half an hour into the shift, then starting half an hour after lunch, leading to some fairly weird schedules. On day shift, for example, when we started at six-thirty, you could find yourself taking the first break from 7 A.M. to 7:23 A.M., then nothing until lunch at eleven-thirty (four solid hours of labor), then the second break at twelve-thirty and nothing until quitting time at 3 P.M. The good part was that a UR usually wasn't as inflexible as the line would have been, and you could sometimes stretch a break by a minute or two.

Our first day of tag relief was a Saturday, and when we came in on Monday, the build number for Saturday was, sure enough, higher than usual, at 431, but the COVE number was 5.8, or an average of 5.8 defects per vehicle—also higher than usual. I pointed this out to Murray, and he replied matter-of-factly, "The quality numbers are always down when we start tag relief," mainly because a whole lot of people were getting up to speed on jobs they'd learned in two or three days, and they weren't yet as good at them as the regular operator.

Summer also brought the students. Although we all took the same two weeks of vacation in August when the plant shut down between model years for retooling, workers with higher seniority got more weeks off, so students on summer vacation were hired to fill in. Trim 2 acquired a cheerful young man named Marc Patrick who was studying industrial design.

The warm weather gradually intensified until we got hit with the inevitable: July and August. Clothing came off all over the plant as guys who used to wear coveralls now showed up in shorts and T-shirts or no shirts at all. At least they wore shorts. A lot of guys stuck with coveralls, and for those with dirty and/or dangerous jobs there was no choice.

One week the temperature relentlessly boiled up to a hundred degrees in the plant. I was unlucky enough to get Carolyn's job, left-side regulators, and I tied a bandanna around my forehead to soak up the sweat. About halfway through the shift Lance came down the line, handing something out from a small cardboard box. He got to me, and I saw he had a box of frozen Popsicles.

"Lime or orange?"

"What's this?"

"We get to hand these out when the heat gets too brutal."

"Oh. Lime."

It wasn't easy to try to eat a Popsicle when you had to do a job every two minutes. I bit off a good chunk, then had to put it down on the workbench, where, of course, it began to melt. And I had to handle it gingerly with my gloved hands, lest some white grease or black dirt get on it. It almost wasn't worth it—thanks anyway, GM.

Later that day, as we rounded the corner of the last hour at two o'clock, Lance appeared to see how people were holding up. By that time I was wrung out like a washcloth and wondering in a slow, spacey way how I was going to get through the last hour. I was also trying to keep an eye on a new person named Lauren, who was on windows and whose arms were killing her by this time.

I turned my head as Lance came by. "How much longer, Lance?"

No one there ever looked at me with greater understanding as he answered, "Only about an hour."

Léo Arsenault was out for a couple of weeks, so right-side regulators was open. It was the heaviest job that needed to be filled, and Rob was very fair about it, even noting on a pad who did it each day and rotating the job among the ARs and floater (me). He didn't have to do that; he could have just stuck me with it. Indeed, an AR named Jake, who'd been transferred from the other end of Trim 2, complained that I should be getting the job every day. I was beginning to like Rob. He really knew his job, card-playing in the cafeteria or not. He was easier to talk to once you'd known him for a while. People from the East Coast were like that; they didn't warm up to you right away. I thought he still looked at me a bit suspiciously and tended to dismiss any complaint, genuine or not, as whining. But he possessed a sly Newfoundland wit, as I discovered one day when I came in from root-canal work with the left side of my face swollen and numb.

"Rob, they froze half my mouth," I said thickly.

"Ah, Sally, why didn't they finish the job?" he replied.

We lost Charlene to a short-staffed Trim 2 on the B shift and gained a bouncy young blonde named Jody who went to stock car races with her boyfriend on weekends. She, too, picked up insulation quickly, to my dismay. A handsome man from the axle line who reminded me a little of Billy Dee Williams was transferred into our department and got a new job that nobody else wanted: climbing into each truck and sticking fuzzy strips on the dash that were designed to cut down on rattling inside the dashboard. His name was Rafe. He said he liked the axle line better, because he was used to it, although he'd had to soak his arms and hands the first few days.

When I was on right-side regulators one day, I noticed Maria feeling the heat. She got a little dizzy on second break, and I tried to keep her going when we were back on the line for the last hour.

"Gimme an M! Gimme an A! Gimme an R! Maria! Maria! Rah, Maria!"

She smiled tiredly.

"What did the Little Engine That Could say? That's right, Maria! I think I can; I think I can!"

I had to take my own advice shortly thereafter on a moderately warm July day. I started the regular shift at 6:30 A.M. on left-side regulators. Toward the end of the shift Lance asked if I wanted to work a double, since B shift was short-staffed, and I agreed. I was feeling pretty strong that day, and I wanted the money. The next day was Saturday, and we weren't working six-day weeks anymore, so I figured I could collapse and sleep in if necessary. During the ninety-minute break between shifts from three to four-thirty I went up to the roof garden, found a large, relatively clean piece of cardboard, and arranged it against an air shaft so I could sit on it with my feet up and read. I didn't dare nap for fear I wouldn't wake up in time.

When I went back down to the Trim 2 office at about ten minutes after four, I discovered that Lorne had taken the week off. Some substitute supervisor was there whom I didn't know. As bad luck would have it, I drew left-side regulators again, but the supe, noting I was pulling a double, said, "We'll try to get someone to give you a couple of breaks."

As I ambled down the line, I waved at Bernie at the sidemarker job and Balthasar at the repair station.

"Sal, ol' gal!"

"Bernie, how's it going?"

It was Old Home Week around the picnic table. Lively Caitlin was doing remotes on the right side. Marilyn was shoving in dashboard wiring. Keenan hurried over to gossip. Caitlin's brother, Clyde Barrow, had a pinched nerve in his neck and was out on Workers' Comp.

The line started to roll, and I swung into the familiar motions. It was one of those quiet nights. I saw Chas the musician heading into the cafeteria, but he didn't see me, so we didn't talk. I could hear Caitlin and Marilyn chattering, but from one workstation down I couldn't quite make out the conversation. However, I agreed to meet them for lunch at Embers, a bar/restaurant in the same block as Gene's, but a little nicer. There was carpet on the floor and the tables were wooden, not Formica.

Although it hadn't been unbearably hot that day, I was sweating and thirsty by lunch, bearing out Ed's observation that on the afternoon shift the plant held in the day's heat. At lunch I got into my car, drove like blazes around the corner, and knocked back an exquisitely chilled lager in ten minutes. We did some gossiping and catching up, then scattered for our cars to head back to the plant.

When I got there, I found that not all of us had headed back to the plant. Caitlin didn't return from lunch. I guess she decided that a cold beer and a cool restaurant beat manual labor and a hot factory. We were already shorthanded, and her disappearance didn't help matters much. I didn't get any extra breaks. I believed that people should have been fired on the spot for such behavior, instead of reprimanded or suspended a day or two. In this respect, union power was too strong.

The night ended as quietly as it began. I worked ahead a few trucks, then gathered with Marilyn, Balthasar, Bernie, and the others at the tool locker to put our guns away. No chance I'd be joining anyone at Gene's for a quick one. Except for the break between shifts, I had worked from 6:30 A.M. until 1 A.M., on my feet for 90 percent of that time. As I negotiated the fifteen-minute drive home, I felt a self-satisfied glow of triumph. I'd really done it—fourteen or so hours of physical labor, and I didn't feel anywhere near as wrung out as I did that first day I was on the job by myself.

I arrived home, the street dark and asleep, as it had been when I'd left at 5:45 A.M. I climbed the stairs to my walk-up apartment and went into the bathroom to wash up a little before going to bed. I looked in the

■

mirror. I was wearing shorts, and my legs were filthy where the hose had brushed up against me. My white Chicago White Sox T-shirt wasn't white anymore.

Although it was nearly one-thirty, I had to sit down at the table on the back porch, which served as a small dining room and had a view of the Toronto skyline about five miles away. I recorded the moment in my computer journal as the point at which I knew that not only could I cope with one job, I could handle it doubled.

Carolyn continued to be out, and I continued to get left-side regulators. My, but I was good, twirling the regulators like a Marine drill rifle. Carolyn's shoulder must have been bothering her again. Maria said she'd urged her to go to the nurse and get it checked out, but she wouldn't.

"I think she's scared," Maria said, and she was right. Carolyn didn't want to admit that the job was hurting her because she was afraid she'd be taken off it, contradictory as that sounds. She knew how to install two hundred left-side regulators per day, crimp the wire at the back, and put window switches in the power vans, and she wanted to stick with what she knew.

With the closing less than a year away, Lance was participating in a career-counseling course that the plant was sponsoring for its temporary supervisors. I was honored when he asked me to fill out a questionnaire that was designed to give him feedback on his management style.

He had about five others to give out. The folks running the career counseling were to put the anonymous replies together in a report for the counselee. I think I was honest and fair in my assessment—he was generally a good boss, but he sometimes had a my-way-or-the-highway approach. But I also made a point of noting that he was compassionate on "days when the air hangs thick and the parts grow heavy."

Toward midsummer we began the last of the 1992 model year. I learned another job: Travis's specialty, dome lights. Funny how we associated a particular job with the regular person who did it. Ivan Taillight.

Travis Dome Light. Scott Sidemarker. The last few days before the two-week plant shutdown, we counted down the numbers. One night the remote station ended at about number 25. When we came in the next day, number 240 was sitting there and we ended at about 480 that night. Barring total breakdown, we figured that B-shift Trim 2 would finish the next day at about midshift.

I had some easy nights before we left on vacation. With the students there, sometimes we were overstaffed. One night I built some stock for Leo and Carolyn on regulators, who were overjoyed, since Phil Bumstead, amusing guy though he was, never lifted a finger for anyone else. I continued to clean up the repair station, then sat with Lance and Rob in the office for about an hour, just shooting the bull. Everyone was asking everyone else about vacation plans. I heard that Stretch was going to Europe. Some planned to get away "up north," as they always said, meaning the lakes and summer cottages north of Toronto. One of the most charming things about the Toronto lifestyle was that even working-class people could afford a summer place: Canada's a big place with a small population, and there's still a lot of land, even within a couple hours' drive of a city of three million.

We were all looking forward to the next day, when we expected to do little but clean up. Since I had less than one year's seniority, I didn't get paid for a "short work week." The others got paid straight time through Friday. However, I had the option of volunteering to stick around and sweep, clean up, whatever, just to put in some hours. Lance wanted to know the day before whether I'd stay, but I told him I couldn't let him know until tomorrow. I'd like the money . . . but I could be playing a softball game tomorrow at 6:15 P.M., if we got out that early, and the thought of staying around in a factory when it was a beautiful sunny day out (assuming it was) and everybody else was walking out the door . . .

It was bad enough the night before when the body shop finished the build-out and left at about ten-thirty. Dina, installing door handles in Trim 1, looked as if she were about to cry, and I went over.

"Dina, what's the matter?"

"They're all leaving! It's the one time in my life I'm sorry I don't work in the body shop!"

A few minutes later I was down at the regulator station, and Léo was wearing the same face.

"Look! They're all going!" It was agony, it really was.

How strange to have the body shop silent for the last two and a half hours, the inmates freed and milling about the aisles before heading toward the door. The huge gate line moved on its track as usual, but the dozens of clamps held no giant metal pieces. Is this how it would be when the final shutdown came? One department after another . . . sayonara . . . nothing more to weld, to bang, to send down to the robots? Hands suddenly empty, bodies bereft of motion. The odd silence that isn't really silence, just the absence of crashing noise, replaced by the arrthymic squeal and squeak of something, somewhere rubbing against something else.

Next day, as I walked through the door, I saw a naked assembly line. No vans, just the carriages. The motor line was vacant—nothing on the hooks. But there were vans on the chassis line. As I passed the motor line, heading toward our department, I saw the end of the line, the last van, in Trim 5. Trim 2 was empty. We gathered around the office, waiting for Lance to distribute the checks. Everyone was in civilian clothes. I don't think I'd ever seen Rob out of his green coveralls, but there he was, in slacks and a shirt.

Maria had a medical appointment toward the end of vacation. The doctors were to assess whether the cancer had spread. I told her I hoped she would get the best news of her life.

Four-thirty came, the line started, the empty carriages moved, but no checks.

"Where the fuck is Lance?" asked more than one person. Lance appeared.

"I can't release the checks until I get the word."

He disappeared again, presumably to inspect the department and make sure all was cleaned up. B shift had left the place spotless—well, as spotless as a van factory could be. Anyway, the floor was swept and there were no parts lying about outside their boxes and bins.

Lance reappeared—by now it was five—and Maria piped up, "I've got the tar, and Sally's here with the feathers." There were mutters about a lynch party. He opened the office door and went to his desk, and the multitudes shouted with impatience.

"Come on, Lance."

"What's going on?"

"Fuckin' idiot."

The checks came out of his drawer, and he stood at his office door, calling names. You never saw autoworkers move so fast. As people got their checks, they asked, "Can we go? Can we go now?" Yup. And they scattered.

Maria and Marnie were heading straight for the highway and Windsor, as were Lee and Laurie. Leo and the other Quebecers were bound east for Montreal. Rob waved his blue piece of paper and shouted, "To the beer store!" He would be going home to a little seaport in Newfoundland called Bishop's Point. My check was healthy—more than six hundred dollars gross—due to nine and a half hours overtime the previous week. It was a warm, sunny day; I had a softball game to play at six-fifteen, and there was no way I was staying there.

"So long, Lance."

I walked out with Maria and Marnie. It was so eerie, seeing the empty line, a foreshadowing of what was to come next year. When the whole place was up and humming, the vans moving in their stately procession, you could be lulled into thinking it would go on forever in just this way. But on this day I realized that as a cyclone sweeps a house clear of its foundations, a great, nameless force could simply drain all the machines out of there, leaving a huge, whispering hulk.

■

# B E G I N N I N G
# O F   T H E   E N D

I didn't fear the two weeks off, in contrast to the Christmas vacation. Confident in my strength, I went hiking a couple of times, but didn't do anything special to keep in shape. I knew I'd be able to handle the work when we went back. I also visited Mom and Dad in New York, and we did the usual things: went to a concert, had dinner at our favorite seafood restaurant on Long Island Sound. Dad said he thought I looked tired, but later he was impressed when I helped him change a headlight on his car and I was able to tighten down a part without using a tool.

We went back on a quiet August Monday that was a holiday for everyone else in Ontario but that we'd given up for a four-day weekend at Labor Day. So it was up at 5 A.M., make the thermos of coffee with half-closed eyes, pack the lunch, decide not to take coveralls since it would be an easy day (Ed had told me that start-ups always went slowly), and head out the door. My newspaper had not yet arrived when I left at five to six, and there were no newspapers in the boxes by the plant gate, knocking my morning routine off-kilter and putting me a bit out of sorts.

Seeing Maria in the parking lot cheered me up, and I walked in with her and Marnie. Maria had spent time at the family cottage. She looked okay—gained a couple of pounds, which she blamed on daily banana splits. "Never have a cottage near a dairy," she laughed. As we walked through the doors, we noticed immediately how quiet the place was: the empty line, no early clanging and buzzing from the body shop, a lot of gaps among the boxes and bins along the line, waiting for new stock. Even the little creaky bird of greeting was silent. Absolutely nothing moved. It seemed like an arthritic old patient, bedridden for a couple of weeks and trying to get up again, testing stiff joints.

Maria, Marnie, and I sat at the picnic table. Lee and Glen sat down for a while, and Jody joined us every so often. Stretch showed us his snapshots from Tivoli Gardens. He came back from Europe with sixteen rolls of pictures. At six-thirty the line slept and the body shop was silent. Ed came by and said a welding gun was malfunctioning on the first job on the line. We sat, read newspapers, drank coffee and caught up on gossip. At about eight-twenty the robots swung into action, and the unholy racket from across the aisle forced us to chat in somewhat louder tones.

Nothing was happening in our department, save Lance coming by and informing us there was to be a group picture at nine forty-five. I wandered out by the front gate and headed over to the mall to pay my Visa bill and get a newspaper. Come to think of it, I could have driven home, gotten my paper off the front porch, and come back. The morning was turning humid. With tired eyes I squinted up at a weak sun peeking out from some clouds.

As I walked back to our department with my paper, I saw that Job One had been loaded on the line at the beginning of Trim 1, right at the foot of the ramp from the paint shop. It was dark red, and it had descended from the paint shop on its dolly by elevator. It was rolled along the aisle to the ramp and pushed sideways until the carriage hooked onto the line. And there it sat, the object of intense attention from half a dozen shirts, including Karen Stinson, the only female general foreman.

At nine forty-five we headed over to column J11, at the west side of the plant, where two benches were set up for what felt like a high-school yearbook photo. It was for the commemorative book that the company was producing on the van plant. As we got into position, looking at the camera, someone said, "Say 'layoff' now." Another voice said, "This is stupid. I'm not going to smile for this." Mug shots of the last culprits.

After we drifted back to our department, I was chatting with Lance, who had driven through New England for his vacation, when Karen came up and said the line would be starting at ten-forty, which it did. However, it also stopped shortly thereafter, and the Lone Truck still wasn't up to our stations by lunch, so I headed up to the paint shop and spent half an hour in the comparatively fresh air. I was doing Bernice's job that week, the *quatrième semaine* (fourth week) of her *cinq semaines de vacances* (five-week vacation). But the cursed module had been taken away, since the antilock-brake systems that year didn't need it. The left-side remote was now easier than the right side and life was beautiful.

Job One reached us at about noon, and Maria and I joked about calling for a break, falling behind, and working ahead. "Now, let's see, how does this go again?" I asked her as we installed the parts. Some people didn't know what to do with themselves if the line wasn't running. Ivan had his guns all hooked up, parts neatly arranged and ready to go a full half hour before the first truck got to him. "Relax, Ivan!" I yelled down the line.

The next job, a dark-blue number, didn't get to us for another half hour. I wish they could have done it all at once and let us out early. Still, it was an easy day, and we were done by two-thirty. Lance told me, Jody, and the Wop that "they" were really going to be cracking down on working ahead. After Lance left, we kicked that idea around. "I'll believe that when I see it," I commented. Maybe they finally would chain us to our workstations. Solve the problem right there.

Next morning I saw the chassis line empty and Trim 5 empty, but our department full. What a letdown. The new schedule had begun, and the Trim 2 line—as well as Trim 1 and Trim 3—was full. The line went down at least half a dozen times after lunch, but I still felt supremely cheated at getting only one really easy day. Late in the shift a van came down the line with RAT JOE spelled out in gray foam bits. A couple of schedule pages were taped on the van, one reading RAT WILL HANG, with a primitive drawing of a hanged man. It seemed to be addressed to Trim 3.

Maria seemed to be in good spirits after the vacation, but it was a façade. She'd had a cancer treatment and was facing the thing she feared the most. "Sally, it looks like I'm going to have to have the operation. The doctors think the cancer has spread."

"You know I'm pulling for you, Maria." I hoped she was wrong or the doctors were wrong. For all her courage, there was something fragile about Maria's spirit, something that made you want to protect her, and I feared the effect a mastectomy would have on her psyche. I didn't want to have to visit Maria in the hospital. I wanted to will her into health.

Our return from vacation and the cool, energizing breezes of autumn woke us up to the inescapable fact that the closing was just nine months away. If some weren't aware of it, the Message God obliquely reminded us: "Value time over money. It cannot be replenished."

People began discussing their options. Red Rolland and the CAW team had negotiated a generous plant-closing agreement that gave Scarborough people preferential hire rights at other GM plants and covered a variety of buyout, early-retirement, and retirement choices. The choices improved with greater seniority, of course, but even newcomers like myself could count on a year's unemployment insurance, plus a top-up for a few weeks. With twelve years at GM, the Wop figured he could get about thirty-nine thousand dollars if he chose a buyout and left the company, but he said he wanted to work so he could retire at age fifty-five. Ivan said he wanted to get work at another GM plant. I asked him why. "Do you know how much is funniss?" he responded. I was momentarily nonplussed, until I realized he was saying a furnace costs two thousand dollars.

Ed Donohue began a computer course. Murray seemed lost, one day joking that he wanted to take a buyout, buy a Harley, and go to Texas with me, the next day admitting he wasn't making any plans because he didn't know what kind of plans to make. I noticed Jan Lennon in Trim 1 reading a textbook on one break and asked her what she was studying.

"Locksmithing," she replied. "Might be something steadier than this," she said with a resigned smile.

I asked Rob if he had any plans.

"Don't know, Sally. Oshawa, I guess," he said.

Léo and Bernice would be heading back to Ste. Thérèse, as soon as it was up and running.

No amount of course offerings would help Claude, the stacker driver. He had nineteen years in Scarborough and said he didn't want to apply to Oshawa because he didn't want to commute.

"What do you want to do?" I asked him.

"I don't know. I never wanted to 'do' anything," he said.

Though I came from the world of hustlers and bustlers, I had a sneaking regard for Claude's attitude, slack though it seemed, and I sympathized with him. He just wanted a job to go to every day, and he'd had one. Now he was supposed to have a résumé? Take career counseling? Learn interview techniques?

Billy Davis was thoroughly soured on the idea of Oshawa and said he planned to "take the summer off" and enjoy collecting unemployment and SUB. He was single, with a fairly inexpensive apartment, and he feigned unconcern about imminent joblessness. Brad, the man who was pulled out from under a truck by Travis, said he might have a chance to work for a relative in Alberta, caretaking some buildings. "I don't want to work in a factory again," he said.

Pierre, a Ste. Thérèse person from the body shop, said people from his plant were going on a two-week training course to learn new production methods to be used when the plant reopened to make all those hot Camaros and Firebirds. "Brainwashing," he called it. "They say they are going to show us films of how Japanese work. And they are going to give us lunch." Pause. "A bowl of rice."

I was a little annoyed that Pierre seemed to be dead set against the new training before he'd even seen it. Then I thought, Well, how would I feel if I'd been going along, doing my job for years, no complaints, then suddenly I'm told it's been all wrong and Japanese people half a world away have been doing it better and I should sit down and learn from them? I guess I might be a little resentful. Normally, though, the Japanese didn't loom large as villains in our working lives, since Toyota, Honda, et al., hadn't entered the cargo-van market in any significant way. Also, castigating Japan was a relic of the 1970s and 1980s. With the advent of NAFTA, Mexico and the United States were seen as bigger threats from abroad.

When I was doing right-side remotes, I used to keep my legs limber by constant stretching. If I had a spare moment, I'd do ballet stretches, extending one leg, propping a heel on the workbench, and bending down to my knee. This was remarked upon and laughed at by José and Rob, then taken in stride as one more departmental eccentricity. One day when I was on left-side regulators, I glanced over at the body-shop station where three men in ghostly dark-blue coveralls swung up half the floor and slammed it down on the jig. There was a break in the action, and one of the men was doing a stretch, propping up a foot shod in a heavy, clunky body-shop work boot that had a steel flap over the tongue as well as a steel toe, onto a waist-high barrier that stood between the job station and the aisle. I tucked this away in the back of my head and took a good look at him the next time he headed for the cafeteria and passed near my job station. Tall, sandy hair and beard, long hands, nice hazel eyes.

We were both in line in the cafeteria when I mustered up the courage to speak to him (you must remember, these blue-coveralled, dark-shades-wearing, welding-gun-wielding body-shop guys looked intimidating). "I've seen you stretching from across the aisle. I've only seen dancers do that."

He seemed slightly surprised that a woman he didn't know was addressing him and momentarily unsure of what to say. "I take karate," he replied with the beginnings of a smile, "and we do a lot of stretching for martial arts."

That was fairly interesting, so we sat down to chat. His name was
Cam Peters, and unlike nearly every other Cam in Ontario, it wasn't
short for Cameron, but Camille. My interest was piqued further, and he
explained that he was from the province of Prince Edward Island, a little
place off the New Brunswick coast on the Gulf of St. Lawrence side,
and that his family originally was French and their name was Pitre,
anglicized to Peters when the British took over in the eighteenth century. Easier to blend in when French families right and left all over the
Maritimes were being shipped out in the Great Expulsion, or *Le Grand
Dérangement,* of the 1750s.

He was somewhat shy, but possibly worth getting to know better, so
I decided to step up to the plate and take the first swing.

"Would you like to go out for a beer sometime after work?"

"Oh, I don't drink, but sure, I'll go out."

Several night shifts later, when we were still getting out at twelve-
thirty, we drove in two vehicles over to—not Gene's, on the theory that
there would be a ton of people from work there—but a place named
McGinty's a little farther west on Eglinton Avenue. There was time only
to order one before last call at 1 A.M., but the place stayed open past that
time, so Cam ordered a ginger ale and I had a beer. It was a weekday
night and not much was happening—a dart game winding up, some
television-watching over by the bar—so we were able to find a table and
a couple of chairs and some quiet space.

I wasn't interested in revealing everything about myself, so I didn't
ask Cam Peters a lot of personal questions, but I did discover that he'd
worked at Scarborough for about eleven years. Mostly we discussed the
local and national politics of the day: a vaguely socialist party had formed
the provincial government, while the middle-of-the-road Liberals held
sway nationally. His politics were right of center, he was an intelligent
observer, and while I might not have agreed with him on all counts, we
had a spirited discussion. At the end of the evening I used my usual exit
line: "That was fun. Maybe we could do it again sometime."

But in the ensuing week or so no invitation was forthcoming. He patronized our coffee stand, I made friendly chitchat, but no invite. Generally, I believe, there's no sense in taking things personally when you barely know someone. So I asked Cam out a second time—again for a casual encounter. Cam agreed to meet me at a pub after work. Again a pleasant time. I learned he had an eight-year-old daughter, Melody, and had grown up in a family of eleven kids on a farm.

I used my standard exit-line-when-I'm-interested, and Cam smiled. Now, the next part of my procedure was this: If the guy doesn't call after you ask him out twice, give up. He's not interested, and you don't need someone to hit you over the head with a baseball bat. After the second time Cam Peters disappeared. I did not see him for five days. This was noticeable because he'd been passing by our area three and four times a day.

"Oh, well," I said to Maria, sighing. "I can take a hint. *C'est la vie.*"

I sought advice from another member of the male gender: Spaz. "Murray, what do you think is the deal here? I thought we were having a good time. How come he's not asking me out?"

"Cam Peters, you say? Oh, yes, I know his cousin, Burleigh Myers. Well, Sally, they're from PEI."

"And so . . . that would mean what?"

"People from PEI, they're . . . different. You'll see."

I had to be content with that, since Murray refused to be any more forthcoming.

After five days Cam sailed into view once more and began filling up at our coffeepot again. I did not bring up the subject of going out, and neither did he.

Bernice returned after a few days in Atlantic City. I'd missed her. Her English was improving greatly, so in a slow moment I taught her the phrase "I am bored to death," only it came out "I yam bore to debt." I repeated it, then she did, several times, till it sounded like gibberish and we were both giggling. I was back to floating. Before the line started, I walked up to Léo, who was chatting with Carolyn.

"It looks like we gonna go home early today. B shift only made forty trucks. They have a lotta repairs to do—the lot is full," said Léo.

Carolyn added, "They pulled six trucks off the line to inspect them, then they chose six more and they were no good."

At this moment Lance passed by, and I yelled, "Lance! What's up?" He motioned me over.

"Is it problems with the brake system?" I asked.

"It's a lot of problems. I was here all weekend."

"The weekend! Jeez, what for?"

"We were inspecting and repairing trucks. We have been running shit. Paint problems, trim problems, everything. They had people down from Detroit."

"But why now, Lance? What are we doing that's so different from what we did before vacation?"

"They're cracking down harder."

He left, and I headed to where Rob and Bonnie were sitting at the picnic table. I was reeling.

"Did you hear about this mess?"

"I hear Detroit is so fed up with this place, they're ready to close it down right now," Bonnie said, pulling on a cigarette. "You know, everybody has an I-don't-care attitude, but I'd rather have another six months than have it shut down now," she added, and Rob and I agreed.

For the first couple of hours I trained on the channel and window-subassembly jobs—pretty easy jobs and, as Jake the AR said, "takes five hours a night." Three hours into the shift Jake said Lance had told him we'd be done for the day shortly. Apparently a lot of problems were stemming from the creaky paint shop.

Since the shift was due to end early, I asked Lance out for a beer. I told him there was talk Detroit might shut us down immediately, and to my surprise he didn't scoff at it.

"That could well happen."

"What do you mean? Flint isn't up to speed yet."

"They will be by October, and those people have been out of work for a long time. They'll work seven days a week."

"But why now, Lance?"

"Look, we've consistently missed our quality targets, management has been very lax, and it's catching up with them." He paused, then added, "We lost a big order."

"How big?"

"Four thousand trucks."

"Whew. Who's the customer?"

"Ryder."

"Wow. We've built tons of trucks for Ryder. Did they go to Ford?"

"Yup."

"The Econoline van."

"Yup, better quality." So that's why people from GM Detroit had been crawling all over the plant.

Thursday's results were 354 built, COVE 5.9—there was a nasty quality number right there. Lance said only ten trucks per day were inspected for the COVE number. Our department, he said, was showing up pretty well. We were meeting our targets.

The next day we were told we would work only three hours, but Lance asked for volunteers to stay for a quality-checking assignment. After nearly everyone had gone, those staying—me, Marc, Patrick, and Jake the AR—assembled by Lance's office. We headed over to the axle line, where there was a large open space and a ramp to the outside. Several vans were driven in; we were given checkoff sheets and a clipboard. I worked with Steve, a heavyset, amusing guy from chassis who knew Lance when he used to work on the chassis line and still played golf with him.

We started checking vans, and it quickly became apparent what the problem was—bad paint jobs. The electricals were okay on all of them—headlights, taillights, etc.—and the occasional body problem—a bump in weather stripping, say—could be easily corrected. But the paint! If you walked around the van and just gave it a glance, it looked fine. But get up close and you started to see drips and sags, tiny bubble clusters, bits of dirt in the paint. "What the hell. Did these guys forget how to paint over the vacation?" Steve snorted.

The next day the build numbers told the sad story: seventy-seven completed, 5.3 average defects per vehicle.

As the summer wound to a close, the students went back to school and tag relief ended. The URs had no assignments for a while. Bummer spent his time on the roof drinking and smoking, sometimes with Bruce the Rock Star. Jake said he'd heard that Lance didn't want floaters and wanted only two ARs for the north end and two for the south end. It looked as if it would be back to the line for me.

In the midst of all this quality madness Maria had some news that was truly of high quality: Her cancer had not spread, and she would not have to have surgery. We celebrated with lunch on the rooftop-garden patio, which was in full incredible bloom—cascading ivy, giant sunflowers in pots, blooms covering the wooden archway over the steps leading from the patio to the roof. Maria lit up a cigarette, and I told her I would throttle her if she didn't quit smoking.

"Sally, I would just be a nervous wreck without my cigarettes. I wouldn't know what to do with myself. But I'm trying to cut down on smoking," she promised.

One night I helped Ken Sui with window subassembly and channel subassembly and unwittingly also speared that day's quality rating. When Jake had trained me on the job, he told me he never used a metal flap on the machine that pushed the window and sash together. Only later did I realize that the flap held a bracket in place and a few windows I'd done had shifted slightly. Once installed, the sash had cut the channel—the black stuff lining the window opening. One of the guys on the window-install job told me. Nobody else seemed to notice, so I could only assume that final repair would find the ones that had been cut. I felt genuinely disappointed. I'd been trying to achieve quality, and I'd been thwarted by lousy training. Or was I passing the buck? I wondered. How could this have been avoided? I should have realized that Jake was just being lazy and used the metal flap, even though he'd said I didn't need to. I wondered if anyone had studied whether training would be best handled by special training officers or by the workers who know the job best.

The line went down yet again when I was helping Ken, so that our subassemblies were done by second break. Ken said he would cover for me if Lance came looking for me in the last hour. So at the start of second break I strolled toward the main cafeteria (I felt like putting my hands in my pockets and whistling) and just kept going out the main security gate. I walked down to the hourly parking lot and was on Comstock Avenue one and one quarter hour before the end of the shift. I can't say I felt particularly guilty about it. "Take it while you can," said Maria.

Next day I was on window subassemblies again, and Ken said I could leave at lunch if I wanted to, and he'd cover for me. I couldn't quite bring myself to do that. Walking out after half a day seemed too outrageous; I felt I owed my employer more than that. I was going to sneak out at second break again, but Jake the AR terrified me with stories of people fired for doing just that.

I headed over to the axle line. I maintained a home vegetable garden, and I'd been told that the best place in the plant to find scrap lumber that could be used for tomato-plant stakes was at the axle line. Wooden sticks about three feet long were used as part of the packing, to keep some of the parts on the axles from shifting. The axle operation was literally a sideline where a number of parts were put on the axles, which then merged with the main line. When I got there, I saw Bob Murphy, a guy who often used to join our Five Musketeers group. I had known he worked on the axle line, but never knew quite what he did. Jesus, it looked like a brutal job. The axles moved along on large hooks, and Bob's job was to heave the leaf springs on the axle. Leaf springs are long and thin and made up of layers (leaves), not coils. They run lengthwise down the vehicle and act to absorb road shocks. They are one of the few parts that have survived, nearly without change, from the horse-drawn-carriage days, the others being, mainly, wheels and seats. It seemed to be an all-male crew over there, and they looked rough. Bob, who was tall and slim, with thinning red hair and pale freckled skin, looked like the token human.

Bob's job was considered too arduous for one man to do for eight hours, so he and another man spelled each other. Which wasn't too bad a life, once you were strong enough that the job wasn't a strain. They had quite a little lounge back there on axle line—microwave, TV, a couch that was made almost completely of duct tape.

However, as I was chatting with Bob, a hulking fellow suddenly loomed before me, holding four stakes. "The hardwood is better for the garden. Won't rot as easily."

I ventured a look up—way up—at him. "Oh. Thank you."

Another guy came over. "Is this tape okay?"

He held out a roll, I nodded, and he bound the stakes for me, wrapping the tape at the ends and in the middle, so I could carry the wood without fear of splinters.


A tiny three-paragraph story caught my eye in the paper: GM CLOSES VAN NUYS PLANT. The story said that the last Chevrolet Camaro rolled off the production line in Van Nuys, California, ending forty-five years of production. "Camaros and Pontiac Firebirds that once rolled out in huge numbers—257,000 were built in 1978 by 5,100 workers—will now be assembled in Ste. Thérèse, Que." The Van Nuys plant was down to twenty-six hundred workers by 1992, and the story said the closing was "another blow to manufacturing employment in Southern California." A union official said that Canada's national health-care system cut the price per car by six hundred to eight hundred dollars through lower

■

benefit costs. After that, when I spoke with someone who wanted to blame only free trade for Scarborough's demise, I would point out that the trade pendulum sometimes swings both ways.

Good news for the people in Oshawa came at roughly the same time. GM said that it would retain production of the Buick Regal and Chevrolet Lumina at Oshawa for at least two more years, partly due to the overtime agreement reached with the union earlier in the year. This caused some relief among the Scarborough denizens, but GM Canada president George Peapples was quoted as saying, ominously, "By the time we reach the mid-1990s, we're going to be building more cars with less people."

GM also confirmed, in a terse announcement, that the Scarborough Van Plant was definitely scheduled to close in 1993, and they gave the month: May. If the closing took place on May 8, I realized, I could celebrate a birthday and lots of job losses all at once.

The adjustment committee announced that an adjustment center had been opened in the plant, essentially an office with space for the committee members and lots of brochures. The committee said in its announcement that it had tried to respond to the results of the needs-assessment survey done by the YMCA. It also said that eight hundred sixty workers so far had taken one or more of four courses: English as a second language, English and math upgrading, blueprint-reading, and basic computer awareness.

One day at lunch Ivan announced, "I am taking forklift-driving course."

"That's good, Ivan," I responded. "Is that what you want to do?"

"I don't know, Solly. I just want to keep job at GM. Maybe it will help."

I turned to Cam, who had joined us. "What about you, Cam? Are you taking a course?"

"I don't need a welding course. I need a welding job," he said.

I decided to try one of the courses to see if they were effective. Out of all the possibilities being offered—such as air-conditioning repair, forklift-driving, blueprint-reading, computers—I decided to take a forty-five-hour carpentry course. I knew darn well that some of the really technical stuff, such as air-conditioning repair, I'd never use, nor would I enjoy banging my brains against something for which I really had no aptitude. Carpentry was practical; I could use its skills in real life, and I toyed with the idea of entering a "nontraditional" career for women. I liked physical work; maybe there was something I could do in the construction field while developing different areas of writing—magazine articles, perhaps even fiction—anything to get out of the nine-to-five office routine.

Our first introduction to carpentry knocked the last idea right out of my head. Those of us interested in the course were invited to a preliminary information session held in a meeting room on the office floor at the front of the plant. About twenty-five attended. Union rep Doreen Cooper was among the union group leading the meeting, and of course I was the only woman in the audience. The director of apprenticeship of the carpenters union, a tough, smart guy who courteously addressed us as "fellas and lady," told us bluntly that 40 percent of his membership was still unemployed due to the recession, and an apprentice had to put in seventy-two hundred hours before becoming a licensed carpenter. Guys on layoff got called first, of course. It would take two to three and a half years for me to become a carpenter, and I knew that even if I might have been cut out to work on a construction site, I didn't have the time it would take to get there.

A fellow with a Quebec accent who said his name was Armand spoke up, saying that he thought it would be a nine-hundred-hour course, but a union rep replied that "we don't have the money." The forty-five-hour cost to the union for our group was about $13,000.

Armand was not appeased. "We need retraining, and a forty-five-hour course will not get a hell of a lot between my ears. There's not enough bloody money there." The union rep explained that the union had a total of $500,000 from the government and GM for retraining for the Scarborough people. As the meeting broke up, I heard Armand tell

■

the guy next to him, "I can already build a shithouse—that's what this [course] will tell me."

Our classes were held at the carpenters'-union training center, north of the city and a forty-minute drive from the plant. It was pretty well equipped: a large, warehouse-type space sectioned off into work areas— here a half-built staircase, there a doorframe. Our group of fifteen men and one woman (here we go again) met in an area that combined school-room desk/chairs with sawhorses and worktables.

Our instructor, Norm Wesley, was a solidly built man in his fifties who dressed in gray coveralls. I was to discover he did not wear anything different to class. Within minutes I realized that anything this man didn't know about carpentry could be put in a pillbox and rattled. He was telling us what to expect in class and describing some simple proce-dures. I was fascinated and completely lost. He was clearly speaking a foreign language. I attempted to hang on as he sped along, rattling off something that sounded like "You'll ratchet your dadoes and hitch a rabbet edge there where the molding meets the miter box."

Most of the guys seemed to be getting this stuff, and I realized from how far back I was starting. If they hadn't worked as carpenters, most of them had had some sort of woodshop experience, even if it was only high school or working on a house renovation with fathers or brothers. Why hadn't I spent more time in Dad's basement workshop? When I brought Papa something to fix, I really wasn't that interested in how it got fixed, just that it did, and I had absolute faith that Papa would find an ingenious way to fix it.

Our first carpentry lesson was a throwback to the Stone Age—liter-ally. We sharpened tools. Maybe it was the Bronze Age.

"We're not going to be using power tools in this course," Norm told us, because proficiency with hand tools was essential as a base skill for good carpentering. Sounded logical to me. The first tool we were handed was a simple chisel, whose ancestors were probably used to invent the wheel.

Norm took us over to a bench holding several grinders, we donned our safety glasses, and he showed us how to sharpen a chisel. The grinder went round and round, the chisel got nice and sharp, no problem.

Off we went to try it ourselves. I put the safety shield down on the grinder, started it up, and held my chisel against the rough, spinning surface. I was to discover that Norm could make a lot of things look easy. I had to move the blade of the chisel over the grinder with a steady touch or it came out unevenly sharpened. If I held the blade a bit too long on the grinder, it burned the metal. After a couple of tries, I did a creditable job.

By the second class five of the guys had dropped out. The course was too easy for them. After practicing with such basic tools as a plane, chisel, and saw, we moved on to make a miter box, which is a three-sided rectangle with slots cut in it as guides for angled cuts, and a square frame made of two-by-fours. We also had a couple of written tests, and I studied as hard as I ever did for nineteenth-century American literature or Chaucer. We marked our own tests, and my grades ran from 50 percent to 90 percent. The course gave us a little taste of carpentering, but it was clear that if anyone aspired to becoming a general carpenter, he or she would have to lay out a lot more money and time.

The adjustment committee did the best it could. The committee members faced a demanding, often confused clientele and limited resources. They organized dozens of courses in conjunction with unions and local schools that hundreds of Scarborough people attended. Many of the courses were intended as introductions to a particular field; more extensive training would have to be the responsibility of the individual. Compared to what many workplaces offered, we were lucky to get that much. Under Canada's unemployment-insurance system, you could still collect benefits while going to school; normally you had to be actively looking for work. So it was conceivable that people could train while living on their unemployment checks, if the unemployment check allowed ends to meet. The adjustment committee also put up notices about jobs available at other industrial workplaces and within GM.

In the midst of all this worrying, Lance had good news. His wife had had a baby girl, Lana Erin, and Trim 2 chipped in for a card and gift. Upon his return from a few days' paternity leave, he passed around the proud-papa photos, and said he loved it when the baby would duck her face behind her tiny hand, as if waving the world away.

The long arm of Detroit reached out toward us as a couple of executives from GM Truck and Bus toured the plant. The day before their visit Lance and a couple of white shirts were inspecting my window-building machine, which leaked zinc-oxide grease and looked as if it hadn't been cleaned in years. When the Truck and Bus bunch walked by the next day, the window-building station had been cleaned up some-what—a large piece of cardboard sat under the bucket of white grease.

About a week later Don Dornan communicated with us via a notice headlined QUALITY IMPROVEMENT:

"We have been working hard at the plant to continue our quality improvement on our vans. It is essential that we continue to strive for better and better quality so that our customers are the most satisfied customers in the full-size van market." The notice went on to say that we had been visited by Mr. Gus Bragg, Vice President and Group Director of Operations for North American Truck Platforms, and Mr. Gordon Zachary, Director of Reliability and Quality Network/Synchronous Process for North American Truck Platforms. (How did they fit all that on name tags?)

"Both Gus Bragg and Gordon Zachary commented favorably about our quality improvement efforts and encouraged us to continue on our path of improvement," Dornan wrote. It didn't say that we were actually making better vans, just that we were giving it the old college try. Nevertheless, Dornan graciously thanked us for our efforts so far and asked for our "continued support to ensure that each and every vehicle that we build is built with the end customer in mind." Just before that, a notice had been put up scheduling three Saturday shifts due to start-up difficulties.

Union plant chairperson Red Rolland played dueling memos with personnel director John Short. An apoplectic four-page screed from Rol-land excoriated the company for dragging its heels on production of Individual Benefit Entitlement Notifications, always referred to as IBENs and pronounced "EYE-bens." People were starting to wonder what their options were at plant closing, and each of us was to get an IBEN setting them out. A committeeman characterized it as a pissing match: "That's what it's like: 'You're an asshole!' 'You're a bigger asshole!' " he said.

The message board gave us the news one day that the previous day's build number of 394 was the first day of the new model year that we had met our production target, and therefore coffee, tea, and drinks were free until first break. The COVE, however, was 5.2. The vultures de-scended on the cafeterias, some carting off two and three milks or juices each. It was good to know you could depend on something.

# T H E   T R I A L

Although the reviews were in and the show was due to close, one final melodrama remained to be played out: a nasty spat between a member of Local 303 and Red Rolland that went to a rarely used dispute-settlement forum—an internal union trial. The subject of the fight spoke to the core of Red Rolland's character and how he viewed his power and the people he represented.

So far I hadn't seen much of the inner workings of Local 303. For the first six months of my tenure I was just trying to get to know my co-workers. I also was more interested in discovering how the plant closing affected the average worker, rather than delving into union politics. Like its counterpart, the UAW, the CAW was a big union, and in some respects CAW president Bob White was as far from the average GM worker as GM Canada president George Peapples.

However, I began to learn a few things about Local 303 that piqued my interest. While the CAW was considered more left-wing than the UAW (it had split from the parent union in 1984 when it refused to go along with contract concessions at a time when the auto companies were hurting), Local 303 sported a reputation as one of the most militant locals in the CAW. A significant portion of the leadership was British, Irish, or Scottish, veterans of Labour Party class wars. Management was forever Them; the working class would always be Us.

The van plant was by far the largest employer covered by Local 303. The top union official at each employer carried the title of plant

■

chairperson. Rolland had a lot of clout within the local and the CAW; in fact, he led the CAW committee that was to negotiate the next contract with GM.

Chain-smoking, hefty, bearded, Rolland was a brilliant, perpetually outraged radical from Newfoundland who seldom failed to stir up emotions. He was a dedicated socialist and had an awesome capacity for facts and figures. He also possessed amazing recall, which made him an arrogantly charming raconteur. He could also be defensive, temperamental, and crude. Rolland fascinated me, and I thought I would attend some portion of the trial to see if any of it told me something essential about Local 303 and the van plant's union leader.

In February a notice went up on the bulletin boards that there was to be a special meeting of the membership of Local 303. Its sole purpose, the notice said, would be to choose a committee to conduct an internal union trial of plant chairperson Red Rolland. A Scarborough worker named Patty Thibodeau had brought five charges against Rolland, and according to the CAW constitution, Red had to stand trial.

I wasn't sure what was behind this altercation, but it seemed to be shaping up as good theater, so I went to the union meeting, which was held on a frosty Sunday afternoon. The local's hall was a drab little building on a busy suburban thoroughfare that held a large meeting room, a downstairs bar/lounge, a couple of smaller meeting rooms, a banquet hall, and several offices. As I signed in, I picked up an agenda and a sheet of paper that listed Thibodeau's five charges:

1. I charge brother Rolland did act in a manner unbecoming a Union member under the CAW Constitution, Article 26, page 79.
2. That brother Rolland's actions are in direct violation of the CAW/Canada ethical practices code of the CAW Constitution, page 159.
3. That he did act as legal counsel for one union member against another in a criminal court of law and that brother Rolland's

actions (acting as legal counsel for one member over another) where [sic] a direct retaliation for my critisizm [sic] of the representation I recieved [sic] in regards [sic] to incident related on page 2.3.4.

4. That he did use his elected union position of Chairperson of the G.M. unit, in an attempt to coerce the withdrawal of said criminal charges.

5. That this action took place prior to the scheduled court date for the hearing of said charges and while he was acting legal counsel for the now convicted member.

Rolland acted as "legal counsel" for somebody? In a criminal court? Since when was he a lawyer? What was the crime? This looked more and more interesting.

The agenda sheet said that the union procedure for choosing the trial committee was to put the names of those who attended the special meeting in a box. Nineteen names would be drawn from the box. Any who couldn't serve could ask that their names be removed, at which point other names would be selected. From the final nineteen names, the complainant and the defendant could request that five names be removed. This would leave nine names. The first seven drawn from the box would be the committee, with the remaining two as alternates.

About fifty people attended, including Chris and Gerhard Schmidt, both of whom I greeted warmly. Walt Hanrahan, vice chairperson of Local 303, a handsome man in his fifties with an iron-gray mustache who was as calm as Rolland was volatile, presided over the special meeting.

"When I call out your name, indicate whether you can or can't serve on the trial committee and if you can't, why not," he said.

"Pete Carson."

A bony, thirtyish man of medium height with a drooping mustache and hair that was cut short in front but left long in back, said, "I'll stand."

"Gerhard Schmidt."

■

"I cannot serve."

"Why not, Gerhard?"

"I am painting my house."

Smiles greeted this reason.

"Earl Hughes."

A tall man in his fifties, with ruddy cheeks, sandy hair, and blue eyes, said, "I'll serve."

"Sally De Santis."

"Yes, I can serve," I heard myself saying. I had no good reason to say no, but did I have a good reason to say yes? Oh yes, definitely yes. There was no way I was going to stay away from this kind of trouble. Apart from a momentary apprehension (What am I getting into?), I could barely restrain my curiosity over the inner workings of a union dispute. If it involved Rolland, there were sure to be fireworks. The only questions were, What color and how high? Also, darn it, I was a real member of Local 303 by this time and I wanted to know what had caused another member to bring charges against my representative, the man who had negotiated the closing agreement for the plant.

Hanrahan continued reading names until he had nineteen willing to serve. Now on to the discards. He read the nineteen names again. Rolland, who was conferring in the back of the room with a shop steward I recognized named Charles McQuaid, would bark, "He's gone," or "He's outta here," when a name came up that he wanted tossed out. Someone who was representing Patty Thibodeau also objected to five names. No one seemed to have a problem with me, so I stayed in.

Hanrahan asked the trial committee to stay behind and adjourned the meeting, and people began to drift out. McQuaid, whom I'd met briefly in the plant, walked past me, said a short hello, then added, "You're the only one . . . nobody can figure out which side you're on."

Gradually nine people—eight men and me—gathered at the long table where Hanrahan had been running the meeting. The man who identified himself as Earl Hughes seemed to know what we should do next, as he said we should all sit down and elect a committee chair and

vice chair. A tall black man with sleepy eyes—our only black member—
nominated Earl for chair. No one else was interested in being nominated, so he was in.

"Who would like to be nominated for vice chair?" Earl asked, looking
around the table.

Guess who spoke up, congenitally unable to keep out of the fray?
"Well, I've been a foreman on two juries, one in civil court and one in
criminal court," I said.

"Okay, anyone else want to be nominated for vice chair?" asked Earl.
No one did, so I was in.

The black man was named Sandor Legrand. He had a close-cut
beard and mustache, and his voice carried a hint of a Caribbean accent.
I'd already spotted Pete Carson. George Painter, who always wore a wool
plaid jacket, was a middle-aged man with a quiet manner, gray mustache, and swept-back gray hair. Angus MacAusland sported a sizable
gut, florid cheeks, and a distinct Scottish burr. Paul Cahill was a middle-
aged man with a quiet demeanor, white hair, and glasses, the kind of
man who looked as if he owned an easy chair with a little magazine
holder on the side for the TV Guide and a crossword-puzzle book. When
we made a list of our phone numbers and work departments, Earl and
Paul listed pager numbers instead of departments, which indicated that
they worked within the union. Earl had been appointed by Rolland to be
alternate committeeperson in the body shop last July to fill a vacancy. I
didn't know what Paul did. Our two alternates both worked in the plant
as stacker drivers.

We received a three-page statement written by Patty Thibodeau,
setting out the sequence of events that had brought us to this point.

It began by saying she had had "an altercation with another brother
at my workstation, which resulted in me being shoved." The statement
went on to say that someone named Sanjay Patel (the committeeman, I
assumed) was called, and Thibodeau told him she wanted the "brother,"
who was named Dixon Green, charged with assault. Patel said he
couldn't do that, and the next day he informed Thibodeau that he'd

gotten a "deal" on discipline for the incident: two weeks on record with three days served.

She accepted the terms of the discipline, because she thought she'd be fired if she didn't, then discovered she couldn't file a grievance after the fact. She told Red Rolland that she felt she shouldn't have been penalized for the shoving incident.

Green had been disciplined, too, and Rolland spoke to management about getting a better deal for Thibodeau and Green. (The deal-making was standard practice and a constant dance between company and union. The company would discipline somebody, and the union would go to bat for the worker and try to get the penalty reduced.)

Rolland got a better deal for Thibodeau: one week on record and three days served. Thibodeau wanted the discipline removed completely and told Rolland he was "misrepresenting" her. She filed a criminal charge of assault against Green and then went on to relate that Rolland and Patel appeared in court on Green's behalf, with Rolland saying that he was acting as Green's agent. Green countersued her for assault also.

Her statement said that Green was found guilty of assault and the countersuit dropped. Rolland's appearance in court on Green's behalf "blatantly" and "viciously" discriminated against her, since he had discussed the case with her first in the plant, as her union representative. She also wrote that she believed it was her "human right to come to work and not have to worry about getting shoved, let alone worry about getting disciplined for it too."

Hmmm, I thought. Doesn't seem fair that Rolland represented one union member in court in a case against another member, especially when he'd obtained information from the other member in connection with his job as plant chairperson. But the tone of the statement, while angry, was also defensive and aggrieved. What had led up to this famous shove? I wondered.

Earl distributed copies of the CAW constitution and emphasized the importance of carrying out our responsibilities according to the method outlined in the constitution for conducting union trials. We also got a booklet on union trials and decided to tape-record the proceedings rather than produce a written transcript. The trial would be open to the membership. Even better, we were getting time off work for this. GM stopped paying us for the hours we spent on trial business, but the union made up the difference.

Several days later Earl and I set a meeting with Rolland's and Thibodeau's representatives to get an idea of the number of witnesses and documents they planned to introduce. We gathered in a front-office meeting room in the plant one afternoon before the start of the afternoon shift. Charles McQuaid arrived as Rolland's representative, and a fellow named Joe Carella turned up for Patty Thibodeau. Carella had black hair and eyebrows, a black mustache, and chipmunky cheeks, and he seemed to walk about in a perpetual huff. He was not very tall, wore cowboy boots, and had a bit of a stomach, but he was also solidly muscled, which gave him a heavy walk. There was a touch of Joe Pesci in *My Cousin Vinny*.

Earl called the meeting to order. No sooner had he reviewed the purpose of the meeting than Carella interrupted him.

"I object." He began slowly, portentously, frequently looking down at some papers, then shuffling them. "We have not had enough time to prepare our case." He wanted to postpone the date of the trial by a week and complained that no one had put in for "union leaves" for himself and Thibodeau, to allow them time off work to be at the trial. McQuaid said he'd arranged his own time off and so should Carella. McQuaid, who was apparently smarter and definitely better prepared than Carella, could hardly contain his annoyance. "We are opposed to putting off the trial. It is about, in Sister Thibodeau's case, building a case on the constitution," McQuaid pointed out.

Carella, rolling his head and looking at us with a "let's be reasonable" expression, complained, "I'm doing some catch-up here. The last thing we want is a kangaroo court."

"This is a political situation," McQuaid insisted, adding that union elections were scheduled to take place three weeks later. An interesting

■

point, I thought, but perhaps not relevant to the issues to be considered at the trial.

Carella had had ten days to prepare. Earl and I conferred privately and decided to go ahead with the trial two days later, since we felt that Carella had had plenty of time to get ready and we were running smack into the union election. Earl announced this to an unhappy Carella and a satisfied McQuaid.

We opened the trial in the union hall. The seven of us took our seats at a long table at one end of the hall. Red Rolland and Charles McQuaid sat at a table perpendicular to ours on our right, Carella at a table placed in a similar fashion to our left. And there, sitting next to him, was Patty Thibodeau, a slim blonde with long, crinkly hair, a tough expression, and great cheekbones. Barney Gillis, a pompous union stalwart, acted as sergeant-at-arms. (Were we expecting trouble?) We had fifteen spectators.

The moment Earl called the meeting to order, Carella jumped to his feet and objected to the date of the trial. McQuaid would have none of it, accused Thibodeau of not knowing whether she had a case, and moved for the dismissal of all charges.

This motion stopped us dead in our tracks, and we adjourned to a small meeting room to consider it. We weren't sure that we had the power to dismiss the charges. The union constitution said that once the charges are filed, a trial must be held. Sandor Legrand, in what would become a pattern, babbled endlessly on the question of the timeliness of the charges. We took a vote and decided, 4–3, to continue with the trial.

When we returned to the trial room, Earl took a firm hand. He told the two sides that the trial would proceed thus: opening statements, direct questioning and cross-examination of Thibodeau and Rolland, committee questions.

"We will proceed, and we do so under protest," Carella intoned. I feared that Sandor Legrand might want to adjourn to consider what "under protest" meant, but all was quiet.

By the time we finally got under way, we had six spectators. Carella then launched into his statement.

First he read the five charges, then continued, "The charges brought forward by Sister Thibodeau are serious in nature. I have never seen the like. A chairperson in a position of trust uses his position to go to a criminal court to present a case of one brother over one sister. One would think that outside GM you would let the court of law take care of it. It is hard to believe the chairperson would use information he's gathered through his position as plant chairperson to make a case for the brother he represented. Brother Rolland is a distinguished member of our local union. We believe he has erred in his judgment."

Carella actually made some sense, and it sounded as if Thibodeau really did have a case. McQuaid then got his turn, accusing Thibodeau of "attempting to destroy fifteen years of service by Brother Rolland." McQuaid said that a guilty verdict would be catastrophic for Rolland but would have little or no effect on Thibodeau's life in or out of work, as she was not contesting an election. He said that the charges were outside the collective-bargaining relationship, acknowledged that Rolland had acted as Green's agent, but said it was reasonable that in his role of chairperson that he would do so.

I chewed over McQuaid's points. The first one didn't impress me much. If Rolland had done something seriously wrong, then it was he who was destroying fifteen years of service, not Thibodeau. Whether or not he was running in an election had nothing to do with the charges before us, as far as I was concerned. As for the charges being outside the collective-bargaining relationship, that might be worth exploring. He immediately conceded charges three and four, so there was no arguing over whether those are accurate, I thought.

It was a measure of Rolland's power that even the accusers were deferring to his position a bit ("a distinguished member of our local union"), but I thought it made them sound reasonable. His defender, of course, was taking full advantage, trying to brush Thibodeau off like an

annoying little gnat. As the only woman on the committee, I was inclined to take Thibodeau's charges quite seriously to counter the attitudes men have used for years to brush women off—she's a bitch, she's
crazy.

Earl said that he was prepared to accept a statement from the ac-
cuser, and Thibodeau got up and walked to a chair that had been placed
as a witness stand between the defense and plaintiff desks. She looked
terminally pissed off and briefly repeated part of the sequence of events
that had taken place in the plant.

"It has been accused that I am a political smear. I am not a political
smear. I'm not here to get him [Rolland] thrown out. I think he should
go to election. He made a mistake. People think he is a very smart man,
but he went out of his way to misrepresent me."

Under questioning by Carella, she said she had never met Rolland
before.

"I don't even vote. I've never dealt with a union representative except for the case with Brother Green. I didn't even have a year in at that
time," she said, trying to show that she wasn't bringing this case because
she had a previous problem with Rolland or the union.

McQuaid asked Thibodeau to cite how Rolland's behavior violated
article 26, page 79 of the CAW constitution as she described it as conduct unbecoming a union member.

"I think showing up in court was conduct unbecoming a union
member—knowing my side and taking the other side," she retorted.

I saw where McQuaid was going. He referred us to page two of the
CAW trial guide, which stated that the charges must set forth the exact
nature of the alleged offense. In a comment, the guide said "a broad,
general charge, such as 'conduct unbecoming a member of the union' is
not sufficient." That was exactly what Thibodeau's first charge was. I
understood her outrage, but it looked as if she hadn't prepared her case
properly.

On the second charge McQuaid again said that she had failed to make a detailed charge. He moved on to the third charge. "There is no section of the constitution cited." Thibodeau saw where he was going and didn't like it one bit. "These are very serious charges. They shouldn't be let go because of a technicality. Can you cite a section of the constitution that says one union member cannot go to court and act on behalf of another member?" McQuaid made similar points on charges four and five.

When we reconvened on Monday, Carella looked refreshed by the weekend. He had a list of witnesses he intended to call and a list of documents he intended to introduce. Then he dropped a bombshell. "On Wednesday, March third, Brother MacAusland was forced to postpone shop-committee elections from March eleventh due to questionable behavior. We request that Brother MacAusland be relieved of his duties and be replaced by one of the alternates."

McQuaid said that MacAusland was not under any charges and that it would be the responsibility of a membership meeting to relieve him of any duties. Carella said he had "questions on his integrity and character." I was mystified, but on we went, and Thibodeau returned to the stand.

McQuaid asked whether there had been bad feelings between her and Green. Yes, she said, there had been personality problems, and he'd been asked to stay out of her work area. McQuaid reviewed the incident with her and the union's handling of it. McQuaid asked Thibodeau if a criminal court is "outside the collective-bargaining arrangement." She agreed, but pointed out that Rolland had identified himself in court as chairman of the General Motors unit of Local 303.

Then it was the committee's turn to question Thibodeau. I was intrigued by the persistence with which this woman had pursued this matter. She had a child and a full-time job. Surely she had better things to do than go through endless legal hassles. She'd charged Rolland before a provincial board, then taken the matter to the union, all for an incident that by this time was almost a year old. She'd said she didn't

■

want to see Rolland kicked out of his job. I had one question for her: "You've gone through a lot for this. Why?"

She referred back to Green. "There was conflict between Mr. Green and myself. He would spit on the floor. He would try and help me on my job. I said, 'Don't help me with my job.' He was told to stay out of my area."

Sandor piped up, "You were totally annoyed by this man?"

"Yes," she replied.

"What do you hope to gain?" Sandor asked, and Thibodeau went straight to the heart of the matter:

"That I'm right. That I was wronged," adding that she didn't think the union representatives' hands were tied, and if they'd done their best for her, the court case would never have happened.

Although it sounded as if Ms. Thibodeau had a prickly side to her personality, she was angry at a guy who wouldn't leave her alone, at a couple of guys who, as she saw it, had failed her, and a union led by a whole bunch of guys who were closing ranks. I thought that she might be taking a relatively minor incident a bit too far, but was justifiably angry about Rolland's behavior in court.

Next up on the witness stand was committeeman Sanjay Patel. He'd been a committeeman for four years and was obviously intelligent. "They both had a problem" was his succinct beginning. Dixon had complained about Patty before the shoving incident, saying she had gone into his workstation. Patel had sat down with both of them and told them to stay away from each other.

As for the fateful shove, the company felt that both workers were in the wrong, kind of like the military, I guess, where if two soldiers are caught fighting, it doesn't matter who started it, both are in trouble. Dixon had been working ahead, and Thibodeau had blocked his path, so he pushed her. "The company said it was Dixon's fault he pushed her, but she was wrong, too. They felt she provoked him," he said. The company had wanted to fire them both, Patel said, but he'd suggested a verbal warning. That was rejected immediately, so he bargained the dis-

cipline down to the two weeks on record, three days served. He related
all this without animosity toward anyone, but with a coolly competent
manner.

The next day Carella was in a snarly mood, lapsing into paranoid
bitching about the fact that one of our alternates was operating a tape.
"We proceed under protest," he again declaimed. Earl lost his temper,
yelling at him to "stop talking and recognize the authority of this
chair."

The whole thing deteriorated into a shouting match between Carella
and Earl, so we recessed to give everyone a chance to cool off. When we
returned, I read a statement on behalf of myself and the other five
members of the committee, apart from the chair, that we supported
Earl's handling of the trial procedure and reminded counsel for the
plaintiff that we had the authority to have him removed.

This seemed to calm Carella down, maybe because he sensed that
attacking the very people judging his case was not a shrewd move. Earl
asked if he'd concluded his case, and Carella answered that he hadn't,
but didn't seem to have anything further. At this point the lights went
out in the union hall, which left some people both metaphorically and
physically in the dark.

When the power returned an hour later, McQuaid called Dixon
Green to the stand. The shover was a thin man of medium height who
had a squinty, nervously shy manner. Earl swore him in. He was barely
audible. He testified that Rolland had refused to represent him when
Green first approached him, but he'd asked him again because "I hadn't
the means to get a lawyer." After making a few phone calls, Rolland had
agreed to represent him.

Carella entered the transcript of Rolland's court appearance on behalf of Dixon Green. Some of it made pretty amusing reading. The
judge thought it was highly unusual that Rolland, as plant union
chairperson, was defending one member against another. Thibodeau's
lawyer thought it was fairly weird that Rolland had cross-examined a
witness to the incident using notes that Rolland had prepared himself,

and the judge had refused to let Rolland cross-examine on the basis of the document.

Rolland was up next, wearing a testy expression and toting an ashtray. He testified that he'd been plant chairperson eight of the last ten years. He also said that Dixon Green had begged him to be his representative in court. He started to swing into a speech several times, only to be shushed by Earl. Then Carella got his whacks in, but Rolland maintained that he'd been defending Green, not harming Thibodeau. Rolland also said he'd received an opinion from the CAW legal department that he could proceed.

After lunch the committee took its turn. I asked Rolland whether after getting the CAW legal department's opinion he felt that there still might be a problem representing Dixon Green. He answered that he still felt there might be a problem. "Why did you go ahead, then?" I asked. Basically, his answer showed, he felt sorry for the old guy. Green was sixty-two, he had worked as a car jockey before GM, and he didn't have money for a lawyer. He said Karen Stinson had told him Patty was charging Green to get him to spend money on a lawyer. Possibly against his better judgment, he went ahead and represented him.

Angus and Sandor belabored some points with Rolland. George had no questions, for which I was profoundly grateful. Rolland's appearance ended the trial. Now it was up to us.

At this point I figured that Pete Carson—who I learned was a friend of Thibodeau's—would vote for conviction. Earl and Sandor—both union officials—would probably vote for acquittal, because they doubted she'd proved that Rolland's actions violated the constitution. Angus, Paul, and George would probably be swayed by the strongest arguments. I was inclined to find him innocent on all but charge two. I did think it was unethical for him to have done what he did, but I wouldn't necessarily recommend a penalty, since Thibodeau herself had said she was not trying to get him removed from office.

Pete showed up next day in the same clothes he'd been in the day before, and on lunch break he told me that he'd sat up all night in a doughnut shop (smoking and drinking coffee, no doubt), reading the material and trying to understand it.

"Well, I feel basically lost right now," he admitted before we came to order. Although he detested Rolland, he was really agonizing over how he could do the right thing, once he figured out what that was. I felt for him; he was trying so hard.

The deliberations took all day. A two-thirds vote was necessary to convict on any of the charges. At 3 P.M. we began voting, and at three-fifteen we were done. I voted not guilty on charges one and five—one, because the section of the constitution cited really wasn't addressed by the charge, and five, because it really wasn't a charge. I voted guilty on charge two, since I thought that what he'd done was indeed unethical, and guilty on three and four because Rolland's own defense had conceded those.

We counted the votes on the five charges:

|          | GUILTY | NOT GUILTY |
|----------|--------|------------|
| CHARGE 1 | 1      | 6          |
| CHARGE 2 | 3      | 4          |
| CHARGE 3 | 3      | 4          |
| CHARGE 4 | 3      | 4          |
| CHARGE 5 | 2      | 5          |

I was stunned at the not-guilty vote on charges three and four—to which the defense had admitted! The thinking seemed to be that the plaintiff didn't cite sections of the constitution, and if it was not guilty on one and two, then it must be not guilty on three, four, and five.

The room was quiet with a current of unease that I couldn't quite identify. I asked if everyone wanted to see the trial report. Pete lit another cigarette and spat out, "I don't care what youse do now. This is a farce." He pushed his chair back from the table. "This is a joke. Everybody agrees there was something wrong, but it's 'not guilty.' I know what this says. The union process is a joke."

We all looked a little uncomfortable, but Earl jumped to his feet, absolutely livid, his neck red, his eyes flashing at Pete.

"No! Wait just a minute!" he cried, his hand banging the table. "I started at GM working in a dirty, filthy grinding booth. The union gave me opportunities for training. I had opportunities through the union! You cannot condemn the union movement!" His passion was such that I saw him, a young man, imprisoned in that grimy booth, choking on metal dust, with the union reaching in a giant hand to help him out.

At that instant I realized what had happened for the past two weeks, why Earl was so careful about adhering to the CAW constitution, about discussing whether the charges were proper. I realized that he never would have voted guilty, no matter what his personal feelings were about Red Rolland, no matter who was in that position, because an attack on the plant chairperson—even by another member—was an attack on the union, and the union lay deep in Earl's soul.

I was surprised that George had voted not guilty, but even if he had gone to the other side, we wouldn't have had a two-thirds vote. Two people—Pete and Paul—had had their minds made up for guilty, and three people—Earl, Sandor, and Angus—were inclined toward not guilty. Sandor and Angus had held various posts within Local 303. With three from the beginning, there was no hope of a conviction.

Pete was right in one respect. The process for choosing the trial committee was flawed. By choosing a committee only from people who attended a special meeting, you got only people interested in the trial, with the result that the committee could be stacked if one side or the other stuffed the meeting with partisans. After the trial was over, I discovered that Paul Cahill was Patty Thibodeau's uncle. Pete Carson worked near her and was a friend. Perhaps a better way, as in society at large, would be to send notices to members picked at random, then see if they could serve on a jury and keep picking at random until a committee was formed.

I had gotten involved in the trial to learn something about Red Rolland, but at the end I knew what I'd known before. He was two men—one dedicated to the cause of workers and one egomaniac. What I'd learned about Local 303 was that, within the bounds of legality, the leadership would manipulate any process it could to remain in power. That didn't seem too unusual; it happens at any organization anywhere. No, my real lesson had come from Earl Hughes, who showed me the pure emotion and human face of deeply committed unionism. My cynicism and impatience with union politics faded after Earl inadvertently reminded me that unions existed to bring justice and hope to the powerless.

Barely a week after the trial ended, it was union election time. There was an air of unreality to the whole exercise, since the plant had only three more months to live, but short time or no, terms were ending, and we needed a plant chairperson, shop stewards, benefit reps, and people to fill such mysterious jobs as "trustee" and "guide."

Red Rolland, of course, was up for reelection, and why not? He'd been acquitted. The plant quickly became festooned with a dizzying array of colored sheets of paper that assaulted the eye from the second you crossed the threshold.

A yellow sheet: "Re-elect SANJAY PATEL/ Committeeperson/ Zone 7"

Sanjay informed us brothers and sisters that he'd worked in the plant for eighteen years. "Unfortunately, despite the limited amount of time left for our plant, management has recently stepped up its efforts to discipline workers at every opportunity," Sanjay claimed. This, of course, created "a situation where experienced representation is absolutely necessary."

A blue sheet proclaimed Doreen Cooper's candidacy for trustee, a

■

job I couldn't quite figure out. After listing the union positions she'd held, she wrote, "I HAVE A DREAM . . . that, at this time of travesty, We will collectively 'thumb our noses' at the corporate agenda of Union-Busting, and go 'out in a Blaze' of record-breaking numbers at the polls in a show of DEFIANT SOLIDARITY!" Okay, so it wasn't Martin Luther King, but it had a certain verve.

Ron Fennessey, president of Local 303, distributed a flier titled MY RESUME which included the declaration "No one can say that I was never there when required," a statement that needed to be read a couple of times.

One day, as I was lounging with the TR9 crew, listening to the bitching about union politics, I said, "Maybe I'll run for committeeperson." I knew something about such a job; I had been shop steward at AP Radio in New York, and served on a union committee that formulated our contract demands. I wanted to get involved in another facet of life in the plant, and, as usual, I couldn't resist the desire to put something in motion and see what happened. Stretch thought it was a great idea, so I ambled to the union office and put my name in among the nominations.

I started my campaign in a desultory fashion. Bruce the Rock Star asked what was in it for him if he voted for me. "Nah, you've got it backward. If you *don't* vote for me, I'll hit you upside the head," I replied. He saw the light instantly, and I decided then and there that he was to be my campaign chairman. "AVOID PHYSICAL PAIN. VOTE FOR SALLY" was one campaign slogan we kicked around.

Bummer said he would vote for me if I bought him a beer. This kind of naked vote-buying received enthusiastic support in some quarters (booze and/or sexual favors were the bribes of choice), but I informed one and all that I would be running a clean campaign. As I was waiting for a hearing test late one day, a woman who was in the medical office waiting room asked, "Are you the only woman running?" We both thought a minute and recalled that another woman was running for employment-equity counselor. "I'll vote for you," she said. Maybe I can corral the knee-jerk female vote, I thought.

I kidded primer Jack Morgan that I was considering buying votes with booze, "but for those in recovery, lots of black coffee."

"I'll take a blow job."

Ah, Jack.

Maria urged me to distribute campaign literature, saying people were asking her about my candidacy, and I got serious about what had started almost as a lark. I thought about the complaints my colleagues had about their committeeman and how I could address them. At lunch I crossed the plant to the union office and typed up this statement:

VOTE FOR SALLY DE SANTIS

COMMITTEE PERSON ZONE 2

ASK YOURSELF: IS IT TIME FOR A CHANGE?

I'm an AR in Trim 2, A shift, and I'm asking for your vote on March 18 for the position of committee person in Zone 2, Trim and Hardware departments.

Here's what I will do as committee person:

- Vigorously defend workers in disputes with management concerning unjust discipline or dismissals.
- Monitor enforcement of the contract as it relates to our rights and working conditions.
- Represent the concerns of people on the floor within our union. This is important. People have a lot of questions now and will have more as things wind down. I'll take your questions to our union's leadership and get answers.
- Be visible and available every day in the plant to keep people up to date, answer questions and discuss issues.

ASK YOURSELF: IS IT TIME FOR A CHANGE?

■

I showed Rob my campaign statement, he beetled off to use a company copier somewhere, and came back with a stack of a hundred sheets.

He read the last paragraph and chuckled.

"Look at this here, politicians lyin' to us already. Available! Visible! You'll be home with the beeper on, watching *All My Children,* and bitch when it goes off and you have to answer the phone."

"Rob, now, that kind of cynical attitude is terrible. I mean every word here."

"Hah!"

As I was doing some trucks, my campaign manager plastered the TR9 workstation with about a dozen fliers, until it looked like some sort of weird float in a white-paper parade. Lance came by and quipped, "I can't wait for our first confrontation."

"Yeah, me neither!" I snapped as Stretch chanted "Sal-lee! Sal-lee!" behind me.

A day later I decided I'd better do a tour of my district, so to speak. Lance gave me some time off, and I wandered down the line with some fliers to chat with anybody who would listen and ask them to vote for me. It wasn't easy to talk to most people while they were working and not much easier to approach them on break, interrupting reading, eating, chatting, card games, etc. Generally people looked at me with a "who the hell is bothering me now?" attitude, but I wasn't actually told to get lost. I walked up to one group of three women, all of whom wore crew cuts, but their reception—cool but polite—didn't tell me whether I could count on any knee-jerk female vote there.

The pro– and anti–Red Rolland factions kicked into high gear. The group that had gone to Oshawa, been laid off, and returned to Scarborough circulated a two-page letter praising Rolland for going to bat for them. Rolland was opposed by a fellow named Drew Alcorn. An anonymous, undated letter addressed to "Brothers and Sisters" claimed that the Oshawa group's letter made "a number of damaging and libelous statements concerning brother Drew Alcorn."

It concluded hysterically and ridiculously, "This is an example of the leadership brother Rolland has been providing our members for the past three years, a web of lies and deceit are his trademark. The truth it seems has no place in brother Rolland's vocabulary, he will lie, cheat and do anything in his power to remain chairperson, you must decide if that is the kind of leadership you truly want and need at this most critical time for our membership."

Politics in the union world seemed to be just as ugly and filled with extreme personal attacks as the worst Tamany Hall mud fights. I saw Rolland sitting by himself in the cafeteria, smoking, of course, and sat down for a few minutes. The man seemed to live in a perpetual state of stress that, I thought, didn't bode well for his general health. Despite my opinion about the actions that had led to the trial, I admired his guts and tenacity and would never question his sincere devotion to the union and the causes of working people.

"Red, how are you doing?"

Never one for idle chitchat, Red launched into a diatribe against Carella and allowed as how he was going to hire a lawyer who was a "killer" in the libel and slander field to go after Carella.

"Oh, Red, let it drop," I responded, but this advice whistled into thin air.

"If I lose as chair, I'm resigning from the adjustment committee" was his surprising comment.

"Why, Red? You could do some good there."

"I'm nobody's whipping boy," he said.

In the midst of the dueling fliers, some exasperated line slave posted a campaign notice reading "For Experience at the Master Bargaining Table: Shep Jaboozey" that featured a dim photo of a black man, possibly smoking a huge joint, and the text "Hired Nov. 85, Fired Dec. 85, Re-hired Feb. 93." Discussions generally fell into three camps: for Rolland, against him, and who-gives-a-damn. As I voted, I heard a blond guy in coveralls remark, "It's all crooked anyway. See who goes home with the ballot box." As it turned out, I was the George McGovern of union politics, winning twenty-three votes to Dave Whipper's ninety. Whipper was familiar and had supporters in the departments; I was an unknown quantity.

Rolland was handily reelected. Although he often alienated his own members, he'd gone head-to-head with GM and wrung a generous severance plan for his workers. But it looked as if the Scarborough Van Plant was the end of the line for Red, too. He had back problems, so he obviously wasn't returning to production work, but his lack of diplomatic skills meant he'd never rise higher in the union either. "I've burned bridges before me and after me," he told me. It looked as if he was going to take some buyout money and move back to Newfoundland with his family.

■

# G O I N G ,   G O I N G  . . .

S ome of those who had opposed Red Rolland lost union work and were busted back to the line. Red controlled a certain number of appointed jobs and could request time off from work, or not, for the people in those jobs. Red also presided over a grumpy, sparsely attended union meeting in the bar/lounge of Local 303's hall when Earl presented our trial report. Patty Thibodeau was there, as was Pete Carson. Rolland was denounced from the floor and bellowed that he had recourse under Ontario's libel and slander laws. The election irregularity cited by Carella referred to a mistake Angus MacAusland had made: He'd opened the nomination boxes a day before nominations closed, so the election had to be postponed a week. I never learned why he did that, whether it was a genuine mistake or whether he was attempting to play fast and loose with the nominations, but it looked suspicious. When it came to elections, the place was worse than a den of Chicago ward heelers.

As for me, I was back to floating. Once we had so many people that I was sold in bondage to the motor line, halfway across the plant. The motor-line supervisor had phoned our office to see if we had extra bodies, but when I got there, he didn't seem to have much for me to do. He glanced around the area, then motioned to another man. "Nello, get Sally here to help you out. Sally, help Nello clean up the department."

The supervisor disappeared into his office, and Nello said, "I guess you can sweep up. Takes a couple of hours at the most." He showed me where the broom closet was for the department and went off. I got out a long-handled push broom and rummaged for a dustpan, but the best I could do was a big piece of cardboard.

I decided to start at the lunch area, so I wouldn't have to bother anyone at first. After I swept the floor dirt into a little pile, I awkwardly bent down to use the big broom to push the dirt onto the piece of cardboard, then get it to a garbage can without losing most of it. Then I moved on to the work areas. After a couple of sweeps, I quickly discovered the floor dust and grit swirled up around my face as I bent over to collect it, and I went back to the closet for a mask. I said, "Excuse me" to the first person in whose work area I was sweeping, but I needn't have bothered. He barely glanced at me as I steered my broom. I was the sweeper, the janitor. I was lower than low, nearly invisible. Doesn't seem as if pride would take a worse beating being a sweeper than being an unskilled laborer, but it did. I felt I had hit rock bottom. Tie me to a treadmill heaving regulators for fourteen hours, but dear God, don't make me clean up the dirt around people's feet.

I was janitor for only a day, and shortly thereafter found myself sitting at the left-side-regulator workbench, reading the paper. As I was glancing at a cartoon that contained a financial graph with a line heading straight down, Cam ambled by. He always managed to amble in those Frankenstein welding boots with the thick soles, steel toes and tongues. I said hi. He stopped to see what I was reading. It had been some eight months since we'd gone out, and I'd had a series of unsatisfying dates since. I pointed to the cartoon with a rueful smile.

"That's how my social life is going right now."

He looked at it, smiled back, nodded, seemed to turn something over in his mind, then asked, "Think you'd be interested in going out with a boring guy like me?"

That's a dumb line, I thought, but my momentary annoyance was quickly topped by the realization that the man was asking me out. Obviously people from Prince Edward Island did not make decisions in haste. I allowed as how I might be persuaded to go out and, later Cam asked if I would go to dinner with him next Saturday night at a nearby restaurant named, somewhat bizarrely, Boy on a Dolphin.

Boy on a Dolphin was just a couple of blocks from the plant, in a strip mall that also contained an Ontario courthouse. The interior decor ran to plaster statues and gold rococo trim. It was also, at 7 P.M. on a Saturday night, almost totally empty. The maître d' seated us at a table with a banquette and handed us a huge menu, complete with red vinyl cover and tassel. I saw the prices and nearly gasped. Just a neighborhood restaurant, but the entrées ran eighteen to thirty dollars for steak and seafood dishes that didn't seem to justify it. They had a seafood buffet that night for, I think, thirty dollars, and we both decided to go for that. We made our way to the buffet in the eerie silence of the restaurant, our voices reactively dropping to whispers, as if in a cathedral.

The food was delicious, but the conversation was a little slow getting started. I learned that Cam had worked in Scarborough for about ten years, in just about every department in the plant. He was the polar opposite of most of the autoworkers I'd met, who were content to groove in their little routines day after day—same buddies, same lunch site, same job, same card game. Not Cam. He'd put in for a couple of department transfers in the last few years, because he knew that with his seniority, good jobs would open up as people kept shifting around. He'd started in Trim, but had a couple of episodes out on workers' compensation (pinched nerve, sore back), so he would often get shipped out to another department when he returned and was assigned light duty for a spell. He'd also worked in the body shop, the axle line, the motor line, and final repair. He might have known more about the inner workings of the plant than manager Don Dornan.

After dinner I drove him home, since he didn't have a car. As I pulled up to a house just a block from the plant (he rented the basement apartment), he asked diffidently if I'd like to come in.

"No, thank you," I replied briskly but—I hoped—nicely, "but I had a good time tonight, and I'd like to do it again."

He nodded and I thought, We'll see what happens this time.

■

Cam didn't disappear this time and began stopping by our coffeepot a couple of times a day and contriving to walk past a couple more times. Since he'd transferred over to the motor line by this time, halfway across the plant, this was a little bit out of his way. He could as easily have gone up to the main cafeteria for coffee.

I didn't realize that it was becoming apparent that the tall, sandy-haired man was hanging around me until Maria and José teased me about it a little, along the lines of "What's with this guy that seems to be coming around to see Sally all the time?"

About a week after our dinner, he called. I invited him to dinner at my place. Upon arrival he asked whether he could help out with the preparation. I hesitated, not wanting to impose, then pointed out some potatoes that needed peeling.

"I guess you might be pretty well acquainted with those," I said, referring to the fact that in addition to seafood and tourism, potatoes are the third economic mainstay of PEI.

"I have seen a couple of them before," he replied, taking the peeler and the spuds and sitting down in front of a bucket. The homely brown tubers jogged his memories of his earliest working days.

"At the age of five I would pick the potatoes up out of the field after the harvester turned over the earth. When I was a teenager, I sewed up the potato bags—seventy-five-, hundred-, hundred-and-fifteen-pound bags. You'd grab the ears of the bag and sew it up with this big needle. Then you'd lift the bag off the grader. When I was fourteen, I loaded boats with potato bags for overseas. It was a hard job. One pallet held twenty-five bags of potatoes, and you had to grab the bags and fill up the pallet. Another time I worked in a potato warehouse. The potatoes were packed in boxes, and you had to hammer down the last couple of boards. My hands were so bloody [from the rough boards and missing with the hammer]"—he laughed, remembering it—"the women didn't want to work with me."

He was the second-youngest of eleven children and had spent his early years on a farm in western Prince Edward Island. Of his ten surviving siblings, seven had trod an extremely well-worn path from the East Coast to rich, busy Ontario. For decades the economies of the four Atlantic provinces—PEI, Newfoundland, Nova Scotia, and New Brunswick—had depended upon seasonal activities such as fishing and farming and the boom-and-bust industries of mining and forestry.

That upbringing had produced a stoic man in Cam. He was slow to speak but thoughtful, and he seemed to possess a rocklike temperament, a mental ability to roll with punches that probably echoed his karate falls. By the end of our evening we knew we wanted to see each other again.

I was back on right-side remotes when a young woman with great brown expressive eyes and long brown hair came around taking pictures. We fell into conversation. She had a soft but compelling manner of speaking. Something about the way she swung her hair as she turned and raised her camera unearthed memories of hash pipes and bead curtains, and I thought, If this had been the sixties, she would have been a hippie. Her name was Gayle Hurmuses, and we had a mutual acquaintance, by odd coincidence—someone who didn't work in the plant. A dedicated socialist, Gayle also liked physical labor and had come to work at General Motors several years before, partly in order to radicalize the proletariat.

Gayle's introduction to the van-plant cosmos had not been gentle. She'd started in Respot, and while some of the men helped her get up to speed on the welding jobs, others, as she said later, "expressed doubt that a little girl like me would ever be able to perform the jobs assigned." She triumphed, though, day in and day out. After nine years she went off on comp with wrist and back problems and was studying photography. She'd gotten some money from the union (for materials only, not for her time) to document the plant and its workers and was working with a consultant, David Sobel, on a history of Local 303.

Sobel had carved out a most interesting job for himself. He actually

made a living as a freelance historian. I had never heard of anyone with
the job title "historian" who wasn't attached to a university or museum or
some other research institution. A leftist who nevertheless drove a Japanese car, Sobel did work for unions and was co-writing a book about the
century-old Inglis plant on the Toronto waterfront, which had shut down
a few years before. Gayle told me that he needed people to interview
Scarborough workers for the local's history. I phoned him, we met in his
office and hit it off well, but when he turned up at the plant one morning, he saw a different me.

I was still on right-side remotes. It was the first day of the two-week
run on day shift. I had awakened at five-thirty that morning. It was hot.
My head was still fuzzy even after a thermos of coffee. The parts weren't
cooperating. My body wasn't cooperating. Since six-thirty I had been
arranging parts, opening boxes between the jobs, trying carefully to work
ahead to get two minutes to sit down on the stool bolted to my workbench and look at the newspaper. Sobel arrived around eight-thirty.

At that point he was not a friend I was glad to see; he was a prickly
interruption, a finger flicking the house of cards I had built about myself
that morning, and my mind was enraged.

"Fuck off, asshole! Can't you see I am *trying* to read the paper for
two seconds. Can't you see that my legs are telling me I *have* to sit down,
but that in two minutes I will *have* to get up again, pick up these parts,
and plod through the next job? Get *out* of here, fool!"

Naturally I did not give voice to these thoughts, but I believe I
greeted Sobel rather abruptly and likewise said hello to his friend. This
was borne out later when Sobel remarked that he was a bit shocked by
the look on my face that morning. How easily the line made beasts of us.
Fatigue, heat, noise, dirt, repetitive manual labor did not combine to
produce perky human beings. In my case especially they created a snap-
pish individual who bit poor Cam's head off so badly one day that it was
a wonder he later came near enough to the department for me to apolo-
gize. I understood why some men stared at the floor and some women
went off by themselves on breaks. The job had changed me in ways I

liked--I was tougher physically and mentally—and in ways I didn't like. I wanted to be angry. I reveled in my anger, only to feel ashamed of it when I'd had a chance to rest.

Without letting Sobel know too much about my background, I volunteered to interview people about their working lives in the van plant for the Local 303 history. Sobel had access to employment records and gave me a list of people who'd worked in Scarborough the longest. He said he could use as many interviews as I wanted to do, so I said I would also talk to people in Trim 2. This opportunity was serendipitous: Not only would I have the chance to find out what the closing meant to people who had spent three or four decades in the plant, but I had an excuse to ask my co-workers deeper questions than I could have on a lunch break.

I started with an elderly man who wasn't working at the plant anymore, who knew the most about the beginning: Aaron L. Cord. He was the midwife who had brought the van plant into the world as vice president of finance for GM Canada in the early 1950s. He showed me pictures of the area and reminisced about how he'd obtained the land for about a million dollars.

I gained valuable information about the van plant's start-up and was charmed when Cord told me how much he loved "the romance of the automobile industry," but was disappointed to discover he wasn't particularly nostalgic about the demise of the plant he'd had a hand in building, or about the company. "They gave me an oil painting on retirement," he mused; "then we sold it."

Maybe the plant meant more to someone who'd been there at the beginning and who was still working there, I thought, so I made my way to the front office to talk to Agnita Diamond, a woman with soft arms, short blond hair, glasses, and a small mouth. She worked as secretary for the head of the material-control department and had a brisk, efficient manner.

She had started on St. Patrick's Day 1947 and made $127.50 a month. She had attended business school and was living at home. She remem-

■

bered an auction of "the big steel presses" when the refrigerators moved
out and auto parts moved in. I did the math as she was talking, and I
realized I was speaking to someone who'd worked for the company for
forty-six years. That was more than half an average lifetime, and for
Agnita the company had filled much more than half her life. "I never
married. There was somebody, in 1949. He was Catholic. I was Protestant. We went our separate ways. I've never been out of work a day. I've
never been laid off," she said.

She believed she would be able to stay on as caretaking staff for a
year after the closing; then she'd be sixty-five and would retire, she said.
Though she was ready to retire anyway, Agnita wasn't happy to see such
a large part of her life meet its end in such a fashion, and I found the
emotion I was seeking. "It's going to be sad to see it go down," she said,
"because I watched it go up. I've enjoyed working with the hourly people. Sometimes I preferred them to the salaried people. They treat me
with respect. I feel sorry for the people out on the floor, for the people
who don't have seniority, husband and wife both work here, the children
of these parents."

As we talked, I noticed a sheet of paper tacked up near Agnita's
desk. It was a list of the times Scarborough had gone down due to
mechanical problems, and it gave production figures for Scarborough
and for Flint. It looked as if Flint was up to speed and the cold hand was
squeezing Scarborough just a little tighter. As we wound up our conversation, Agnita recalled that she'd been ready to quit in the first two
weeks because she wasn't getting along with a co-worker, but her father
had persuaded her to give it a fair chance. "I've been here ever since,"
she mused. "Who'd have thought I'd have stayed this long?"

I returned to our department to discover that Barry Harvey had
excavated an old record player, set a short piece of hose in a base of
putty on the turntable and attached a little white flag reading FLINT to
the end of the hose. He'd plugged in the record player (what a master
scavenger this man was; where the heck did he find that in an auto
plant?) at the repair station, and the white flag was going round and

round in a frenzy of surrender as I walked by. Back at the line, I started my interviews with Murray, aka Spaz.

He'd been laid off from GE in 1978 and heard GM was hiring, but he described a van plant that was foreign to me. "The term we heard always was 'The line stops for nobody.' If you were a little late coming back from lunch, they were stricter then. There was no eating, no newspapers, no working ahead, no Makita guns, no wandering around."

Neal joined us at the lunch tables, picking up the theme. "If you did anything within the [first] ninety days—go to the nurse, miss two jobs in a row—you were gone. If you were caught with your safety glasses off, you were fired on the spot. There were no picnic areas then." How had things come to change so much? "The union gained a little bit and a little bit," Neal related. Also, I thought, I came in at the end of all this, and with just eighteen months to go, management was tolerating a good deal of slack.

Neal said he'd started in 1977 on headlights in Trim 3, and "scary" was how he described his first impression of the line. "Three weeks after I started, my son was born. The foreman told me on the line." As for working conditions, " 'ergonomics' wasn't in the dictionary then."

"My knees were like hamburger," Murray chimed in. "The [company] doctor told me to go back to work. 'Does your mother wash floors?' he said." (In other words, lots of other people's knees hurt, too, so quit whining.)

I asked Murray if he had any firmer plans once the plant was closed. "Look for a full-time job," he cracked. "Maybe try for preferential hire with GM," he added more seriously.

Neal was weighing the various alphabet-soup options: VTEP, UIC, SUB, IMP, IBEN. In other words, should he take a buyout—Voluntary Termination of Employment Plan—and leave GM? Or should he go on Unemployment Insurance Compensation for a year, then, if he was still laid off, get a bit less on Supplemental Unemployment Benefits for a year, then, if he was still laid off, get a bit less than that on the Income Maintenance Program for another year? And when would he be seeing

■

an Individual Benefit Entitlement Notification so he could try and figure out all this stuff?

Back in Trim 2 I sat down with Laverne, whose husband also worked in the plant. He was from Trinidad, too. She'd started at GM in 1982 on the motor line. "I saw the motors coming toward me and I thought it would never end. I hated this place. It was the first time I worked in a factory environment, and it was a shock. I had worked for an insurance company, but it was not as well paid," she said.

"What are you going to do after this place closes, Laverne?"

"I trained as a medical secretary. I have my high-school diploma. I am going to do nursing; that is what I originally came to this country to do, and look where I ended up," said Laverne.

I sat down with Cam at one of Trim 1's lunch tables. He definitely didn't want the plant to close. "I want another ten years. I've got bills to pay and places to go and kids to raise. (He contributed to the support of his stepdaughter, Kellie, as well as his daughter, Melody.) He reminisced about the many departments he'd worked in—body shop, trim, motor line, chassis. "I guess I'm well rounded. Or maybe well used."

Ivan told the classic immigrant's tale. He came to Canada in 1973 from Belgrade, avoiding the United States "because I didn't want to go to Vietnam," and speaking hardly a word of English. Like the fictional Hyman Kaplan, with whom Ivan had more than a little in common, he went to night school for three months. (Canada offered a certain amount of free language training for immigrants.) He was working at a Volkswagen facility across the street from GM. "Many times I fell asleep at school, I was so tired."

But he persevered, trying to overcome the inevitable embarrassments of learning a language. "People make fun of you. My English is not good and never will be. But I never complain if someone correct me. I remember, so they don't make fun of me. So that's how I learn the English."

He got married a year after he came to Canada and had two children, a boy and a girl. He started at GM in 1977, in Respot 2, hanging rear doors, and developed a bad back after a year—no surprise. But he related that after his first three months at GM, "I got a prize for quality. Set of glasses. It makes me very proud." He managed to transfer to Trim and so, for the past thirteen years, had been installing taillights.

José Venancio grew up in Manila speaking Tagalog and a little Spanish. He came to Canada in 1983 and started at GM in 1989. His philosophical attitude really nailed the essence of fitting into a new land. "As an immigrant, you see people speak a different language, the way people socialize, the food they eat. It just takes adjustment. Everywhere there is discrimination, depending on your status in the community, whether you are poor or rich. Some people don't understand, don't realize you have a different background," he said.

He genuinely liked working at GM. "People talk about GM, they are impressed when you say you work there. The products we produce are part of our everyday living, so everywhere you go you see them. I'm proud to work at GM. I have dreams when I come here, to make a good living." José was uncertain about the future—"maybe Oshawa"—but was sure about one thing. "I'm happy to be here, but it didn't last long. It was too short a stay."

I tried to interview Travis, but he was too drunk. I managed to track down Stan, one of the initial group of ten I was in, and he said he was getting into a bricklaying business. The recession was easing off, and construction was coming back. The business had had fifty orders in the last couple of months, he said, smiling. People in our group, with our tiny seniority, had better be lining up different options, because we were going to be well down on the preferential-hire list.

I saw Chas the musician working overtime in the body shop and chased over to talk to him. He said he'd been working there eight years, but he was in a dark mood. "When I look back, it's a big gap. I'm tired, dejected, broke. I went out with six women in that time, spent all my money." I wanted to take his picture, but he wouldn't let me. "No one needs to know I work here. It could hurt my career [as a musician]," he said. Nevertheless, I took a photo of him from the back, his long, wild hair falling forward as he leaned over to meet the next job sliding into his workstation.

I was eager to interview Rob, the soul of Trim 2. He seemed to have a lot of experience in the plant, and I figured he would have some colorful stories to tell. He was sitting at the lunch table when I approached him.

"Rob, I'm interviewing people for a history of Local 303, and I want to talk to you."

He waved me off. "There is no history of GM anymore. Not for me."

I kept on. "How long have you worked at GM?"

"I've been at GM eighteen years. Now, get away from me."

"Did you start at GM when you first came to Ontario?"

"I worked at Lynch Foods first. I got lost here my first day. I thought I would retire here. I made a lot of good friends here, maybe keep in touch with some people."

"Think you'll apply for Oshawa?"

"I guess. Don't have too much education."

"Did you finish high school?"

And then Rob said something that shocked me. He looked at me, and his look was opaque.

"What's high school?"

He didn't mean that literally. Of course he knew what high school was; he'd just never gone. The man had an eighth-grade education. I guess I was so startled because I associated that level of schooling with my grandfather's generation, certainly not mine, especially since school-leaving laws made it illegal to quit school before fifteen or sixteen, depending upon the jurisdiction. And work-permit laws in New York State meant you couldn't even get working papers before age fifteen. Legally or not, Rob had left school in rural Newfoundland at the age of fourteen and gone to work. When I later visited PEI with Cam, I saw how that was quite possible. A boy, or a girl for that matter, could help out on a farm or on a fishing boat or at any number of other enterprises—an auto-repair shop, a boatyard, a lumberyard—working for cash until he was of legal age to work. Rob wouldn't talk to me anymore, so I took my meager notes and left, hoping for the best for him.

After my second Christmas in the plant, for which I organized a downhome buffet—thirty different potluck dishes brought by forty people—and swore I would never do such a thing again, we turned the corner into the new year, and the reality of the closing seemed to bring the hammer down on a number of people.

Elmer, one of our stacker drivers, a fiftyish man with iron-gray hair and a quiet, keep-to-himself manner, had either a stroke or a heart attack. This notice was posted:

"Shortly before Christmas, Elmer Wilcox from material control became extremely ill at work. He has been hospitalized in the intensive care unit and is on a life support system. Elmer's only means of communication is by blinking his eyes, as he is totally paralyzed. In the near future, Elmer's family will be faced with serious decisions. They are also facing an extreme financial dilemma. Workers will be accepting donations at the plant entrances on Friday, February 5th before the start of the shifts. Your generous donations will be very much appreciated."

One weekend Jason McInnis killed himself. He was a heavyset, wide-eyed-looking blond guy who worked either in paint shop or in maintenance, the stories varied. A blown-up copy of a newspaper obit notice was taped on the cafeteria door:

"McInnis, Jason M. (Jay)—Suddenly on Saturday, January 9, 1993. Jason McInnis beloved son of Audrey (nee Gowan) and the late Richard. Dear brother of Troy and Linda and her husband Sidney Carrigan. Lovingly remembered by his niece Andrea. Friends may call at the Giffen-Mack 'Danforth Chapel', 2570 Danforth Ave. (at the Main Street subway) 2–4 and 7–9 p.m. Monday. Service and committal in the chapel on Tuesday afternoon at 2 o'clock. Cremation to follow."

■

Murray said Jason had come in on Saturday, threatened his supervisor with a gun, then jumped in front of a subway train. "One suicide and four heart attacks since Christmas," said Murray. "It's starting already."

Later I saw Ed.

"Did you know this Jason McInnis?"

"Sure. Used to work for me."

"So far today I've heard three versions of how he offed himself."

"Well, I heard he shot himself, or jumped in front of a train. I also heard he threatened his supervisor on Friday by phone and was fired. He had problems. Substance abuse was his main problem."

"There was no mention of a wife and children in the obituary."

"Nope."

I didn't know Jason McInnis at all. So why did I go to the funeral home that evening? I worked with him, in a manner of speaking. He was a fellow member of a huge and dysfunctional family. He'd brought his own story to an end, but he was 1/2,700th of the van-plant story. And the plant closing wasn't just twenty-seven hundred stories, it was hundreds more—the spouses, children, parents of the workers; the suppliers far from the plant; and the small-business owners close to the plant. Jason McInnis had had a family: a mother named Audrey; a brother called Troy; a sister, Linda; and a niece, Andrea. I couldn't help them—indeed, I barely knew what to say to them—but I went to see them.

The funeral home was on a major commercial street not far from where I lived, across from a small shopping mall and high-rise apartment building. The room where the McInnises were receiving was small. There were two other families receiving in rooms on the same hall, and there were lots more people there for them than for the McInnises. The casket was resting at one end of the room, closed, with a picture of Jason on top. Several floral wreaths and funeral bouquets stood near the bier. An elderly white-haired woman, clutching a tissue, was standing looking at the casket, along with a younger woman and two young men, both in black suits. The older woman was in a light-blue suit. A couch and several chairs were ranged at the other end of the room. I entered along with two men and a woman who had arrived at the same time. They looked vaguely familiar; I'd seen them at work. I signed the book and went over to the two men.

"I'm Sally. I work at Scarborough, and I came to pay my respects."

"I'm Troy. Thank you very much. It's been a great help to us to see how many friends he had in Scarborough. Jason was feeling very alone in the past few days."

I wasn't sure what Troy meant, whether he was referring to a personal situation in Jason's life or to the plant. "Well, it's a stressful time at work. Was he feeling it?"

"Yes. It's very hard for everybody at GM. St. Catharines closing, too. He worked there for seventeen years, worked all over the plant. Did you work with Jason?"

"I didn't know him well. I just wanted to stop by to pay my respects."

"Thank you very much for coming."

As we spoke, the white-haired woman, who had sat down on the couch with the younger woman, wept quietly. The younger woman put her arm around the older lady. I left, feeling as if I'd been holding my breath for hours, passing a couple of guys in the hall whom I recognized from work. I didn't know why Jason McInnis had chosen his self-destructive path, but I certainly felt sorry for him, although I felt sorrier for his family. I suppose if his workplace hadn't closed, something else might have tipped him over, but some of the blame for an ended life had to be laid at the van plant's door.

In the midst of depressing events I received the good word that Mother and Dad would be coming to Toronto for a week. Since I'd moved to Canada, they'd been up several times, greatly enjoying the city for the usual reasons (it was so clean, it was so pleasant) and expressing that opinion to one and all, as Americans are wont to do.

"I want you to see where I work," I told them, and they humored me, although I had the impression that an auto-assembly plant wouldn't have automatically been slotted above opera, ballet, and dining out on their list of Toronto treats. One reason they always drove was that Mother packed as if she were making a transatlantic crossing in first class. (Another reason was that once it had taken twenty-four hours for Mother to get back to New York from Quebec City due to nasty weather, and she was convinced that flying in Canada meant enduring such an ordeal every time, no matter the season.) She took four or five jackets and coats, one for each ten-degree change in temperature, not to mention, in addition to suitcases, one of those square cases for makeup, toiletries, and hair curlers. And, of course, a roomy tote bag for several books, the Sunday *New York Times,* and the inevitable ten pounds of reading material (brochures, books, magazines, booklets) she would pick up along the way.

They always broke up the ten-hour drive from New York in Rochester or Syracuse, so they arrived in Scarborough at about 2 P.M. I had booked some time off the line toward the end of the day shift and met them at the main guard booth. Mom was wearing a pink jacket and casual slacks, and Dad looked spiffy as usual in a tan windbreaker and tweed driving cap. They seemed to brighten up the gray guard station with their animated chatter, and I was able to sign them in quickly.

It was break time as we entered the double doors by Respot 2, so there was no deafening noise to smack you between the ears. We walked along, and I earnestly explained what would be happening to the vans, now stationary, in the departments we passed. Barry Harvey drove by in an electric runabout and stopped.

"These your folks, Sally? Hop on, I'll give you a ride," he said. Mom and Dad clambered into the double seat that faced backward, and I sat next to Barry as he trundled us down to Trim 2. My parents, perched on the back, looked about with interest, and carried themselves as if they were being transported by sedan chair through nineteenth-century New Delhi.

We disembarked at Trim 2. I introduced Mom to Maria, and although Mom undiplomatically let slip that I'd told her Maria had breast cancer ("I had a scare along those lines myself"), they got along smoothly. The Wop happened to pass by, consumed with curiosity, and I introduced Dad (to Paul Lemorello, not the Wop). Mom and Maria talked about their kids, and Dad chatted in Italian with the Wop, both just as if they'd known these people all their lives. Maurice, Ivan, Bonnie, and Glen gathered around, and I introduced them all. Dad spoke French with Maurice. Lance, of course, had to come by to get a look at my parents, and I introduced them. "Good to meet you, sir," said Lance to my father. After about twenty minutes conversation was petering out and it was almost the end of break time, so we took our leave.

As the months wound down, tragedy and farce shared equal time onstage. One day Barry told me, "Buttonhead"—his favorite name for Lance—"is outta here."

"What are you talking about?"

Barry then related that Lance was being transferred out due to the Incident of the Putty Penis, which actually had nothing to do with Lance. Seems someone on our shift had a little too much time on his hands and fashioned a penis from the strips of black putty we used to waterproof the screw holes in the sidemarkers. When it came time to go home, this person neglected to break down or throw out his work, so it was sitting on the workbench for the person on the next shift. Who happened to be a woman. Who didn't think the object on her workbench was very funny. Who kicked up an almighty fuss. It wasn't aimed at her; it was just an accident, I heard, but I could see why she might be upset. Management believed that it was unfunny enough to send Lance to Trim 3, the Trim 3 supervisor to Trim 2 on A shift, and the B-shift supervisor to us.

Our new supervisor was a man named Ben Burke, nicknamed the Undertaker. That was a little unfair, because Ben was a very good-natured guy. It was just that he had a long face, droopy mustache, and gray hair that also drooped a bit. His face could easily look long and sad.

He was a contract player, like Lorne O'Halloran, so he was a bit mellower about the job than Lance, who wanted to hang on as a supervisor with GM. Ben had come in knowing he'd be going out.

We hourly workers received our official layoff notices in the mail, but the supervisors had to sign theirs. I asked Lance what he was thinking when he got the notice.

"I wasn't going to sign it. Karen says, 'Come on, sign it.' I was going to sign Alfred E. Neuman. It's just a piece of paper. Part of the bureaucracy. This says that as of May I don't have a job. Guy says to me today, 'The plant's not going to close.' 'Oh, why is that?' He says, 'I prayed.'"

"So the Lord is going to save the plant?"

"Yeah, right."

"Have you done your résumé?"

"No, not yet. I've been busy."

"Well, do it."

"Yeah, yeah. I know."

His wife had let him have it the day before. "I was coming home and burying myself in golf. She was right. I just wanted to get away from GM. I'm trying to deal with losing my job, and I didn't tell her enough."

He saw no future with the company. "I don't have any letters after my name. They said, 'Well, you could be summer help.' I'm thirty-four fuckin' years old. I don't want to be summer help! And I won't go back to the line."

Finally I told him who I was, what I'd done—the university degrees, the journalism jobs, the whole thing.

His reaction was more muted than I thought it would be, but I realized that he saw me as a friend, not as a spy.

"I'm not surprised. And now you're turning a screw?"

"I'm hoping to write all this up in a book."

His eyebrows rose. "Hmm. Well, I suppose we have some measure of infamy."

# FIFTEEN

# ENDINGS

The Message God was at it again: "Nobody really knows enough to be a pessimist." Then, a few days later, "It is hard to make predictions, especially about the future." This, a couple of months before shutdown, went beyond ludicrous to egregiously insulting.

Ben Burke came around early one shift with a large box, handing out fluorescent lime-green caps made of some light synthetic fabric with GM SCARBOROUGH on the front. They were prizes for achieving an average COVE number of 4.8 the previous week. Maria, Rafe, and I didn't put them on, since they were so ugly. But most folks grabbed them, and some wore them. Ivan put his on, grinned, and yelled, "Solly!" and I went over, curved the brim a bit, and adjusted it a bit lower down on his forehead so he didn't look like Crazy Googenham on the old *Jackie Gleason Show*.

As we were chuckling over this, I noticed that Travis had ripped his cap to shreds, crossed the aisle, and tossed it at—not exactly in—the garbage can. I moseyed over.

"Travis, you're not crazy about the design of this hat."

"It's not the design!" he rasped, eyes wild. "They're kicking us out of a job, and they give us a fuckin' forty-nine-cent hat! And people are laughin' and jokin' about it! Take the hat, hold it out in the street, and ask people for a handout."

Stretch handed Travis his hat, and Travis attempted to rip it apart

with his bare hands. Apparently he had only one bare-handed hat assault in him, so I handed him my box-cutter knife. "Thank you,
Shally," he slurred, slashed the cap to death, and tossed it in the
aisle.

"Stupid hats!"

About fifteen hats found their way to Travis throughout the night
and met the same fate. There were bits of murdered lime-green hat all
over the floor. In Trim 1 some were hanged in effigy and set on fire above
the line. This did not go over terribly well with what management there
was around the plant that night, and supervisors were seen picking up
the remnants and tossing them.

Later Ben Burke came along while I was sitting between jobs.

"Those hats aren't very popular," I said.

"Yeah, but do they have to destroy them? They could give them to
their kids or something." There really is a gulf between management and
worker, I thought. He just doesn't understand how offensive that gesture
was. The animals struck back, Ben.

Ivan thought it was silly and that he had more right to be angry than
Travis, but he wasn't making such a commotion. "Travis, he is single. I
have a mortgage. I have family."

I didn't offer my hat for sacrifice; I didn't really know why. I guess I
did want something to remember the place by. Lee Argus said, "Keep it
as a memento. Then you can take it out, look at it, and say, 'Boy am I
glad I don't work at that place anymore.' "

We got some good news, courtesy of the *Van Express* newsletter:

TO ALL SCARBOROUGH VAN PLANT EMPLOYEES:
CONGRATULATIONS—YOU DID IT!
WEEK ENDING MARCH 21, 1993
4.3 defects/vehicle
204 vehicles/shift
There will be a draw at 7:30 Thursday morning at the Quality

Meeting. REMEMBER! To be a winner you need PERFECT
attendance. Winner and prize will be announced on Thursday.
KEEP UP THE GOOD WORK!
(signed)
Reg Pike

Reg, another forty-year veteran, had taken over as plant manager
after Don Dornan was transferred out to another plant. Don was a young
up-and-comer within GM. Reg's job was simply to keep the old ship on
course to the scrapyard, then head off into GM pensionland. The draw
enabled employees who had shown up for work every day to qualify for
prizes such as a camcorder, provided the plant achieved quality ratings
of fewer than five defects per vehicle for the week.

Bummer and I snorted at this latest memo and figured Reg and
company would be dreaming up ever wilder schemes in the dying weeks
to keep the place running and the product intact. "Camcorders for everybody!" "Free meals till shutdown!" "Dancing girls in the aisles!" "Male
strippers!"

We weren't far off. Management subsequently announced that one
of the last vans to be produced would be raffled off to the workers—as if
all twenty-seven hundred of us would be panting to win that van and
wouldn't be tempted to take out our frustrations on a side panel. Ever-
escalating rumors of vandalism made the rounds, some stoked by those
who enjoyed spreading stories and watching how far they flew. According to one, someone had pumped six bullets into a van in the paint shop,
but that was a fairy tale. Someone actually had, however, taken a cigarette lighter to the manifest on a couple of vans and fried the paint on
the doors. Bonnie said she'd seen the wrecked paint. Oddly, the most
serious instance of vandalism at that time came at the Oshawa plant. A
couple of guys were arrested for throwing sand, coins, and sugar in the
paint on sixty-two Chevy Luminas, causing a complete production-line
shutdown for a day. It was the subject of much talk ("you wait, we'll see

that here"), but no one I knew in Scarborough seemed to know why it had happened, and I never saw the reason reported in the papers.

Along with dark mutterings about sabotage, there was the inevitable "someone's going to come in with a gun" talk. Murray was convinced it was going to happen.

"Fred Melvin. That's the guy I'm scared of. If anyone's going to pull a gun out, it's going to be him."

Ed chimed in, "Yeah, we all better watch our backs."

As Flint began to take over our production, we saw fewer and fewer power trucks and more chop vans, which Flint wasn't making yet. It was as if the vans were gradually disappearing, like the Cheshire Cat. First the back of the truck goes, then the roof, then the sides. . . .

Someone wrote up a notice reading "PROTEST YOUR I.B.E.N.'S WED. APRIL 7, 1993 AT 1:30 P.M. SHOW YOUR DISSATISFACTION WITH YOUR I.B.E.N. PACKAGES AND JOIN IN THE RALLY ON EGLINGTON [sic]AVE. IN FRONT OF G.M. THERE'S STRENGTH IN NUMBERS TOGETHER WE CAN FIND OUT THE FACTS. BRING YOUR OWN SIGN!" Jody noted that this was a cash-strapped demonstration—the organizers couldn't even provide the signs.

Next morning a notice on CAW Local 303 letterhead was posted at the entrance:

CAW Local 303 Membership, G.M. Unit

Please be advised that the leaflet circulating around the General Motors Plant calling for a demonstration on the IBEN's for Wednesday April 7th, 1993 at 1:30 p.m. DOES NOT have the support or approval of CAW Local 303 Executive Board and/or the General Motors Shop Committee, Local 303. Official demonstrations are presently being discussed by the Local Union Leadership which will soon be released.

In Solidarity,

Ron Fennessey

President,

On behalf of Local 303, Executive Board

Curious to see whether this wildcat demo would attract many people, at one-thirty I walked to the front gate, behind a couple of other small groups, one including Marnie. We all seemed to be striding purposefully toward the great outside. Wow, I thought, This is drawing some people. I had passed lots of people on break, sitting at their workstations, sleeping in a truck, etc., and figured apathy reigned. Maybe not. Maybe we were about to rise up in a last, spontaneous, grassroots gesture, shaking our fists at company, union, and fate.

I was a few steps behind Marnie as she peeked out the window and said, "Oh, there's no one there. They were supposed to be demonstrating." I headed out the door—it was a cool, bright, early-spring day—and wandered to the front of the plant. Nobody marching on Eglinton. Returning to the side gate, I saw a small crowd of men, mostly in coveralls, gathered in a parking area close to the plant. I headed over. They were not protesting. They were shaking no fists. They were looking over a brand-new, tomato-red Chevrolet Camaro, right out of Ste. Thérèse. Next to it rested a Cadillac Seville, also getting the once-over from the boys. I hung out in the sunshine awhile, chatting about the cars, then headed inside.

I ducked into the personnel office and checked out the applications for cleanup work after the plant closed. We'd heard that GM was going to clear out all the equipment, but try to sell the building and the land. There were 160 utility-maintenance jobs, one receiver (non-expense stores), two expense-stores jobs, whatever those were, and one battery attendant. Job descriptions were posted. The utility-maintenance people would basically tear the inside out. Pay rate was $19.49 per hour. I was perusing the form when a middle-aged man walking into the plant next to me said, "You don't want those jobs. Those are going to be dirty jobs. They have to drain the paint tanks, and they'll be working with all kinds of toxic substances."

"Well, I don't have much seniority anyway, so I don't think I'll get one." I decided to fill out a form to see whether low-seniority people would be offered one of those jobs. I also wanted to get an inside look at the tear-out.

In the last week of April they posted 1.1 hours of overtime for each night shift, Monday through Thursday, which meant we would be working until 2:06 A.M. The idea was to build enough so we ended the week of May 2, and we didn't have to go into the next week by a day or so, or we would get paid for the entire week. A stacker driver named Joe said he'd heard if we didn't make the numbers, they would schedule Saturday, May 8.

"If we all call in sick that day, they'll have to work Monday," he said. Sounded like a good idea to me.

Maria and I were working out the coffee supplies for the next week, and she said we'd need them for two weeks. "Well, no, really, it's just a week and a day or so," I reminded her.

"Oh, my, it just hit me. It's going to be such a big adjustment. It's really ending," she said, with a look of stunned wonder.

"You know what's really nuts, Maria? I just spent four hundred dollars on a radio/cassette player for my car, and I'm not going to have a job in a few weeks," I said, shaking my head.

"I know what you mean. I've been spending money, too. It's like putting off the inevitable," she replied.

Management posted a notice saying that there would be no charge for coffee for three days.

"What do you think of the free coffee?" I asked Travis.

"Big tickle," he rasped. "Tryin' to keep everybody quiet, and what'll it cost 'em? Three hundred dollars? After this place closes, I want 'em to bring me coffee at home every morning. Before this is over, we'll get a free meal, too, just you watch."

Bruce the Rock Star, who was standing nearby, raised his arms and shouted, "Yes! Gallons of free rotgut coffee! Thank you, GM!"

I collapsed in laughter.

Ed had sent out some résumés and was considering going to school for more intensive computer work during the summer. But few people had anything lined up. Murray said he'd heard of something in industrial glazing. Ivan had finished his forklift-driving course. Billy Davis said no one he knew had any idea what they were going to do. "People want to take their memories and go; get on with their lives," he said.

Jan Lennon, who was still plowing through her locksmithing course, asked me what I was going to do, and I answered, "Write a book."

She brightened. "It will be very successful."

"Well, maybe at least the people here would read it," I answered.

"Yes, just to see if their names are in it."

I was telling more and more people about the possibility of a book and something about my background as a writer. It was time to take off the mask, but who would be first to say the word "spy"? The answer was . . . nobody. The general reaction was "No kidding, you've been a writer? Cool!" Given that people came to work at GM from many different backgrounds, learning that your co-worker had been a writer just put another color in the rainbow. I also realized that these people were my friends now; we'd lived together for a year and a half, so I wasn't some suspicious stranger. Sandy, a blonde in Trim 1 who said she wanted to be a feminist lawyer, came up with some titles—*Accidental Auto Death* was one.

As the days wound down toward the end, I wrote in my journal, "I feel strange, too. Sometimes I despair of being able to tell this story, to do justice to this thing. The place is so big and there is so much going on—all I know is my little corner. I hope I don't betray these people. They deserve better. I feel more and more like a spy." All the days and weeks of keeping my journal, of taking notes in the margins of newspapers, on notepads slipped into my lunch bag, made me feel guilty. How could I write about people who didn't know I was recording their conversations, who confided in me? What if I got something wrong? Many, many times, I saw only pieces of lives, heard bits of talk. Could I make of these bits a mosaic of the Scarborough Van Plant?

The union did schedule an official rally for the Saturday afternoon before the closing date. According to *The Toronto Star*, it was designed

■

to "vent rage over closing of van plant." Maria wasn't too sure of the value of such an exercise.

"Getting people angry can be dangerous. Besides, it's too late. This would have made sense a year ago," she said. We both wondered how many people were going to show up. Our last week was on nights, and Travis threw a party before work. Maria and I went over to his apartment, about a five-minute drive from the plant. The Newfie contingent was there—Rob, Roy (a trainer from Trim 1), Augie the Codfather, and of course Travis himself. His apartment reflected his Newfoundland heritage. Near the bar (well, would you expect Travis Allman's apartment not to have a bar?) hung a large black-and-white photo of a tiny cove, girt with wooden shacks, docks, and boats.

"Hanlan's Cove, near St. John's," said Travis.

In the hall a black-and-white photo showed an elderly man sitting next to Fred Davis, host of a long-running TV quiz show called *Front Page Challenge*. "That's my grandfather," explained Travis proudly. "He soldered the wires when Marconi received the first radio transmission on Signal Hill." Wow, Travis Allman a part of history and technology.

Murray was there, as were Barry and Dan, a sandy-haired, mustached guy who didn't say much. Harley Dave, a biker from Trim 1, was there, too. We got some burgers going on the grill, located on Travis's balcony, and naturally the beer flowed like a river. Someone started a joint and passed it. Somebody handed me a camera, and I slunk around, snapping candids. Murray recommended I not shoot people when they were toking. I had two beers and a burger. Harley Dave took over the grill, and I went out to chat with him.

"Anything lined up, jobwise?" I asked.

He said he was thinking of taking the summer off first. "Then I might try to get something with the board of education, like janitor. They pay fifteen, sixteen dollars an hour. But I liked working at GM. I used to be a machinist. You had to be very precise, or it was garbage. I always took the job home, but at GM you don't have to think; just do your job and leave it there."

Just after four the party broke up, and we headed for work. Maria had had two beers and asked me to drive. I felt a little high, but not loaded by any means. We arrived five minutes before the line was to start, most unusual. So did Rob, and we scrambled to cover jobs. Bad Bob, a truculent yet funny acquisition from Windsor, and I helped Travis, who was incapable of doing anything, much less a job. He turned toward a truck and stood there, swaying, unable to decide whether to step up into it or not. Rob sent him away, and he passed out at the lunch table in among the lockers. Ben came along. Trim 1 was desperate for people, but Rob said we didn't have anyone to spare.

We got our commemorative book, entitled *1901 Eglinton Avenue East,* a decent production with historical photos of the plant's phases, the last couple of barbecues, charity drives, and the group photos from every department. There was a picture of the mysterious John Short, personnel director, the dark presence whose signature was on all the personnel notices, who I'd imagined to be a fat, bald lifer. What a surprise it was to see a photo of a weedy guy who looked as if he was maybe thirty. A few people started asking their co-workers to sign the books, the way high-school students do with their yearbooks, and that spread like wildfire.

At second break Barry came by with his giant slingshot and a bag of water balloons. "Water-balloon party," he tossed over his shoulder. I thought they'd retired the great catapult. Murray and I followed to see what was up, and Barry and Monty Allen took positions in the aisle between Trim 1 and the body shop, facing down the line, and let fly. Their missile exploded on the floor about a hundred feet away with a satisfying *splat.* A small crowd of eight or nine spectators gathered to watch the nuclear test, but the place was remarkably quiet. Most important, there were no supervisors to be seen.

Murray had brought in a video camera and was taping the fun. And so it came to pass that there exists a filmed documentation of the next launch. Monty turned to his left a little and knelt down, holding the ends of the slingshot. Barry pulled the cradle back and let go. And a water balloon sped unerringly through the air straight toward the empty gate-line supervisor's office, shattering the window and spewing water and glass all over the desk, chair, and floor.

Almost immediately some of us, high on furtive, gleeful astonishment, found reasons to walk purposefully toward anywhere that wasn't the body shop. Nobody thought it was a bad idea to trash a supervisor's office. As far as I knew, no one was disciplined for it, and no one in authority knew that the whole thing had been captured on tape. The office was cleaned up, and several days later the window opening was boarded up. It looked like a sad little abandoned building.

If Barry and Monty found vent for their emotions in direct action, some chose the virtual reality of art. Primer Jack Morgan's drawings got wilder as the countdown began to the last day. One was a swirl of colors that included an eye and a breast in a maelstrom of angry motion. As I was changing my shoes at my locker after one shift, he showed me a dainty diamond ring.

"Here, you want this?"

"What are you talking about? Is that an engagement ring, Jack?"

"Yeah. I don't need it anymore. She moved out. I might as well move, too. Don't know why I need that big apartment anymore."

"Oh, Jack, I'm sorry. Maybe you can work it out."

On our last Friday-night shift I dragged Maria over to Gene's to check out the scene. I meant to stay only fifteen minutes, but Marc, the student who'd taken a year off school to make some money, showed up and sat down with us.

"How are things on the axle line?" I asked.

He started to laugh. "Well, my hands hurt so bad I can't pick up a pencil. I have got the most awful job. Trim Two doesn't have anything like this. This is ten times worse. You have to stand and stick your hands up into the axle and put some nuts on—like this." He demonstrated by sticking out his arms, making claws of his hands, and pointing the fingers backward at himself. "Then my chest keeps hitting the axle, so I've got a nice bruise on the right side of my chest. There isn't a spare minute. That's why I haven't been over to visit on breaks, because I'm just sitting there like this," and he stared into space for a second. We laughed at his comic, rueful descriptions, but my heart went out to him.

I got about three hours' sleep and slogged in at 6:30 A.M. to do TR9s for five and a half hours of overtime. It was a very easy schedule. Out of about 120 vans, I did maybe 15. My B-shift friends signed my book. Rob was also working the overtime, but he did the window-install job. Since he had ten times the seniority I had, he could have bumped me off TR9s and forced me to take the heavier job—heaving windows into every single truck. But he didn't, and at the end of the shift he was breathing hard.

At midday, on a gorgeous May day, sunny and mild, the CAW house band, Rank and File, began to play on a stage set up at the front of the plant on Eglinton Avenue. People began to arrive, many wearing black T-shirts the union had made up for the occasion, which read FIGHTING FOR OUR WORKING FUTURE. A young woman named Rose Anna Reid held a sign reading ROSEMARY AND ROBERT/ MOMMY'S HOME SOON FOR GOOD!

Red Rolland took the stage.

"This plant has produced about two billion dollars in net profits over the past ten years, and GM has spent thirty-five million dollars on it. That is an absolutely incredible return. The reward for the workers has been the boot, nothing but the GM boot. Three thousand workers will lose their jobs."

"Except you!" shouted a girl in the crowd. It was an amusing crack, but not really fair. Rolland, whatever his faults, had been constantly negotiating with GM to get better deals for Scarborough people. He wrote a touching note in Local 303's newsletter, which read in part: "You came from every province in this country, and from most of the countries on this planet. We are one! You have made this country a better place to live by your presence here."

CAW president Buzz Hargrove, who'd recently succeeded Bob

■

White, took the mike and went on about "the corporate agenda" and how the government in Ottawa didn't "have the guts to stand up to the American administration."

"Bullshit!" yelled a voice from the crowd, and another cried, "Too late!"

I saw Laverne, Stan, the Wop, Bruce the Rock Star, Jack Morgan in the crowd, which had swelled by now to about a thousand. I ran into Chris and Gerhard, who said they would probably retire. "Who will take us, at our age?" Chris asked.

Scarborough's representative to the provincial parliament, Anne Swarbrick, got a turn at the mike and said she was "filled with a mixture of emotions." She patted the government on the back for giving Local 303 ten thousand dollars for the history book and for giving grants to the adjustment committee, which, she said, had helped 40 percent of the people in the plant.

I learned later that about twenty-six hundred places had been filled in all those courses—some people had taken more than one course. In one respect we were lucky. Many a workplace has shut down abruptly, with no warning whatsoever to the workers, who show up one morning to find the gate padlocked. Because we labored for the world's biggest corporation and a union had negotiated benefits for decades, those who were able had time to work out some kind of plan for their lives.

Patty Thibodeau was at the demonstration, too. As Swarbrick said that we in Ontario "want to be the highest quality workers," Patty yelled, "Highest welfare!" An Indian man made a brief foray into traffic, shouting, "Lie down! Lie down!" but he sheepishly retreated as no one followed him. A drunk reeled past, screaming, "This plant is closing, and no one gives a shit!"

At about a quarter to three the band left, the speakers dispersed, and the crowd started to thin out. A few guys still walked around with signs on the sidewalk, but most folks and their families drifted toward the parking lot. It was still brilliantly sunny, a heartbreakingly beautiful day. Most of the signs were dropped on the grass, hither and yon, and the union people were beginning to gather them.

I walked along the front of the plant, starting on the east side. Well, this is it. It's really over, I thought, and I could not contain my emotions. It all started to fall in on me, all the last year and a half: the pain, drama, rage, kindnesses, laughter, nastiness, craziness, stupidity, noise, smell, grease, beer, dirt, beauty, and intrigue.

Bill Devine, a thin, gray-haired union official, passed by and stopped. "How do you think it went?" he asked.

I found it hard to choke out a couple of words. "Oh. Well, I think. It went well. Lot of people."

I nodded and moved on. A few horns honked. A couple of shouts from a guy with a black CAW LOCAL 303 T-shirt and a sign. I sat on the grass slope, facing the Scarborough Van Plant, and behind my sunglasses I just cried.

Stories about the plant's closing began to appear in the newspapers and on television and radio news, and I had the chance—always instructive for a journalist—to observe coverage of a news story in which I was directly participating. The stories naturally focused on the human cost of the shutdown, on the people who were having difficulties, with a few quotes from some people who were just as glad to bid good-bye to manual labor. Some stories also noted that we would be paid up to 90 percent of our take-home pay for one to three years, a point I felt was important, to counter the image that we'd all be begging by the side of the road next week.

The story that caused snorts of derision at the Trim-2 lunch table was one that quoted an "industrial relations expert" at York University, who intoned, "These are people who, while they deserve their money, are probably overpaid in relation to their job skills. They undoubtedly will have to learn to live on less for the rest of their life [sic]." Murray had the newspaper with him at lunch and read the professor's comments aloud, prompting Neal Callahan to spit, "You're not paid for job skills, you are paid for fuckin' suffering." The prof's ungrammatical remarks angered me, too. It wasn't the first time I'd heard myself and my friends referred to as "these people," as in "this is the best job/highest pay these people will ever have," as if all twenty-seven hundred of us were hopeless losers who once in our lives had the rare luck to trip and fall onto an auto-assembly line.

I also saw the union repeatedly blame free trade for the closing and slam GM for closing a profitable facility, which was to be expected, but they also claimed time and again, in the words of one article, that the plant boasted "superb quality." In another story Ron Fennessey said that the plant had "won several quality awards." I hadn't hallucinated all those quality problems, but no one covering this story without knowledge from the inside would have caught that. The union seemed to be trying to make GM look bad, knowing GM certainly couldn't admit there had been problems.

Maria came to stay with me for the last week, since she and Marnie had given up their apartment at the end of April. She slept on the fold-out futon in the living room, and we had long talks on the back porch, the lights of Toronto twinkling in the distance. She felt as if she didn't want to go home, because she'd have to take up her old Supermom role, but I suggested she could use her new sense of herself as a free person within her family.

Graffiti began to sprout all over the plant, referring to the end. Someone pasted a collage of newspaper headlines on the wall of our cafeteria. Most of them didn't refer to the van plant, but ran along the lines of IT'S THE END, SO LONG, WE'RE OUTTA HERE. Another message read THE END IS NEAR. OUR DAYS ARE NUMBERED. THE FUN IS OVER. GOOD LUCK TO EVERYONE. Several copies of the last schedule arrived in our cupboard. It contained 415 vans. On the last page there was usually a handwritten note, "END OF SCHEDULE." Not this one. This one read "THE END." On the top schedule in the pile, someone wrote, in pen, "GOODBYE AND GOOD LUCK TO EVERYONE." Cafeteria coffee was no longer free, so we ran our coffeepot. Supplies having been paid for out of previous profits, our coffee was free.

On the second-to-last day the last job started in Ladder 2 at about 8:30 A.M. As the van moved through the welding stations, workers gathered in the aisles to watch it go. I was off the line, so I was able to walk along the aisle, keeping pace with the metal box that held the end of our van-plant lives. All over the naked steel, body-shop people had written graffiti in black marker: THANK GOD IT'S OVER, THE FAT LADY HAS SUNG, THIS IS THE END OF THE LINE. And they had signed their names: Billy Davis, Sharon Barstow, Dave Roswell, Chuck Easton, and so on. It would all be painted over, of course.

A knot of supervisors followed the last job to make sure no one took a whack. As the welders completed their task, heavy white gloves flew into the air, burly men shook hands and said good-bye. They gathered at the offices for their last checks. As we continued to work on the moving line of vans, workers started to dismantle the ladder line. We could see our job site being destroyed even as we were playing out the string. "Look, they can't wait to get us out of here," said Léo.

On the last day we arrived to discover number 380 in the remote station. Thirty-eight jobs to go. B shift had left us massively behind. They had tossed TR9 harnesses and vents in the trucks. I wired one, and Bonnie and I went to do two others, which were in Trim 3 by the time we got to them.

"This is the happiest day of my life," Bonnie said defiantly as we marched down the line.

"Jeez, Bonnie, I hope you've had happier ones."

"Oh, I'm just kidding," she said, tossing her head. She and Nick didn't have a sentimental bone in their bodies.

After we did them, I walked down the line, and the last job was off the paint-shop ramp. I got my camera. It was white, power, number 418C. Inside, a black cardboard coffin bore a sign: R.I.P. SCARBORO VAN PLANT, 1974–1993, reflecting the dates of van manufacture. The knot of supervisors watched it go. Murray was videotaping. People were climbing into the van and having their pictures taken with the coffin.

About twenty carriages behind the last job, Bad Bob was sitting on one, riding the empty line. I sat next to him, and my foot dragged along the floor.

"I feel sad, man. I'm gonna cry," he said. He was genuinely upset.

"Yeah, this is worse than I thought," I said, feeling numb.

"I've been here three years—what's it like for the people who have been here a lot longer?" As we passed Fred Melvin's station, Bob called out, "Hey, Freddie, man, you mind if we're in your area?" This broke me up, but Fred shook his head, twitched and blinked, and mumbled, "Just those people working ahead." There we were, riding the empty carriers, and he was still wound up about people working ahead.

I dismounted in Trim 2, where, among the men, Bob and Stretch were showing their emotions the most.

"So, Kieran, what are you doing later today?"

"Committing suicide."

José's eyes were red. The others were a little bit better at hiding it. The last job was just up to Maria. She went through the familiar remote-installing motions, and that was it. She turned toward the workbench and took off her apron. Bonnie, Stretch, and Bruce posed on the front of the last job with the coffin, and I stood on a chop van and snapped their picture.

After that I was losing control. The world I'd inhabited for the past year and a half was collapsing, the friends I'd made were about to scatter, and my voyage of discovery was ending. We wandered around, saying our good-byes and chatting, shaking hands, hugging, promising to keep in touch.

José came up and said, "How's it going?" I couldn't talk, and he asked, "Hey, are you all right?" Tears rolled down my face and he said, "Aw, hey, come on," and held me. I didn't try to hide it. Maria was overcome and hurried to the washroom to pull herself together.

The last truck moved past our office. Ben Burke asked Rob to help disconnect the hoses, put the guns in a box, clean out the cabinet. Rob asked me to help gather hoses, but I continued to take pictures and drift.

Glen Jackman came up and hugged Maria and me. "I hoped to retire here." He sighed. I walked down Trim 3 to find Lance and caught him halfway to his office, patting one of his women workers on the shoulder. He saw my face and said, "Look, I've told all the women on my line that if they get emotional, they're put on notice."

I laughed. "Still an asshole, Lance." I put out my hand, but he wouldn't shake it. It was too final.

"I will see you later," he said.

The group gathered around the office.

The last truck was winding through Trim 3. Ben started calling out names on checks. Jody got hers, waved "Bye, everybody!" and left quickly. I cleaned out my locker—Jack Morgan's art, shoes, jacket. Jack was packing up his stuff, too, and gave me his latest creation: a black-velvet painting of the word LOVE in an elaborate setting of flowers, birds, and decoration. He had also painted, in sealer, a flower on the wall. I pointed out that the top petal looked like an upthrust finger, and he made it more so. Someone had also written JOE GARCIA IS A ASSHOLE on the same wall. Joe Garcia would join Darcy Meade in oblivion.

Maria and I walked out into brilliant sunshine. We stopped for coffee and muffins in the Coffee Time shop on the corner. I felt better after putting something into my stomach. We then headed for Travis's apartment. For the first time in my life I started drinking beer at nine in the morning.

Barry and Rob were there, and Rob swallowed about three beers in fifteen minutes and was instantly soused.

"I don't think it's hit a lot of people yet. Now it's just like a long weekend. You know when it's gonna hit me? Monday, and Tuesday, and Wednesday, and Thursday." He came back to the subject a couple of times, compulsively dealing with it.

Bonnie and Bruce arrived. We started making reunion plans for four

■

to six weeks from then. All were excited about the idea, and as I told
Rob, "It will help us, too, because we can get together and talk about it
and see how we're doing. Someone won't feel quite as alone."

Nick, Stretch, and Bummer arrived. By one o'clock Maria and I had
to get some more food into our stomachs, so we captured Bruce and
went to Gene's. The joint was jumping. A TV camera crew filmed guys
hugging. Patio tables were jammed—I saw Bad Bob. We three went in
and ordered hamburgers. I saw Gene and asked him, "Hey, man, what're
you gonna do?"

"Life, life, is life," he responded.

Marc sat down with us, slurred his words, and made little sense.
Exhausted, Maria and I went home. Our eyes hurt from crying.

The next day I woke at six, and my first waking image was the inside
of the plant. I felt I'd dreamed about it, but I couldn't recall any clear
dream pictures. Maria dreamed about it, too. Maria and I had coffee,
and she packed her car. I got dressed and said good-bye. We hugged for
a long time and choked up.

"Your friendship has meant a lot to me," I said in farewell.

"No more than yours has meant to me," she said. "Take care."

I crossed the street, got into my car. She honked as she drove off,
and I answered. God, this is awful, I thought.

I went back to the plant to see the last job come off the line. Barry
had said it would come off in the morning. When I got there and walked
through the familiar doors, I stopped for a second, listening. The *squeak-
squeak* bird of greeting had fallen silent. Barry had led me astray. The
last van had come off the line at about six the night before. Nothing was
left. Chassis carriers and carriages were empty, and construction guys
were blowtorching their way through the beams holding the conveyors
over by Trim.

I saw some of our former supervisors, including Ben Burke and
Karen Stinson, walking around with gloves on and felt a deep sense of
satisfaction. They were getting their hands dirty. About time!

I wandered up to the cafeteria and ran into Lance. We talked for a long time. A company in Stratford, Ontario, had offered him a job, but it was too far to drive and not the money he wanted, so he'd turned it down. That was very hopeful, an initial offer.

"Just the first one," Lance said. He was looking forward to working at a new company, learning new things, a cleaner environment.

"Are you just as glad that this happened?" I asked as we walked past Chassis 4.

"No." He shook his head. "This is a tragedy. I wanted to stay with GM." That morning he had reported to his old area, back in the bargaining unit, no longer a sergeant but a foot soldier. He was not wearing one of his supervisor shirts with the GM logo. We looked at the empty carriers overhead and a couple of bins that were still full of mufflers.

"This is where I used to work. This was my workstation, from here"—he motioned to a column on his left—"to there"—thirty feet over to the right.

"Are those things heavy?"

"Those aren't too bad. The ones with the converters were."

I leaned on a metal bin. "I don't know where I belong anymore, Lance."

"Oh, stop."

"No, really, I've lived in the white-collar world, and now I've experienced the blue-collar world. I don't know where I want to go." After a year and a half I truly felt cut adrift. I'd sold an article on the last week of the van plant's life to *The Globe and Mail,* but I certainly had no journalism jobs lined up. All I knew for sure was that I would be collecting unemployment insurance of $650 after tax every two weeks for a year—better than nothing, but 60 percent of what I'd been taking home for the past one and a half years. Since I had low seniority, I would get the Supplemental Unemployment Benefit, or top-up, only for about six weeks.

I supposed I would return to freelance writing, but there was much about the manufacturing environment that attracted me. I liked the active life, and I liked making things; the thought of returning to deskbound paper-shuffling sickened me. Where was my place, exactly?

Lance had no doubts. "Stick with white collar. There's no future here. This"—he motioned toward the empty plant—"happens all the time."

After Lance left, I wandered around some more. A maintenance man was standing by a doorway that led down a flight of stairs, and I asked where the stairs went. "Come on, I show you," he said.

We clunked down the metal staircase into a subterranean world I never knew existed under the floor of the plant. After leading me down a dim corridor, he showed me a big room that contained a giant pool of waste water. A huge conveyor belt carried some kind of black sludge into enormous bins at the other end of the room. The HELL—MAIN OFFICE graffiti had been on the wrong door; it should have been affixed to the entrance of this dark, lonely Hades.

"Nineteen years I work here," the maintenance man said. "Nineteen years I do nothing. Now I gotta do hard work."

Back upstairs I picked up preferential hire forms at the personnel office and put down Oshawa, Ste. Thérèse, and London. I was curious to see if someone with my low seniority would be called; it would allow me to judge the job situation at GM, and—who knew?—I might need some steady money. My year and a half was brought full circle when I saw the young woman from personnel who had given my original group of ten its job assignments. She, too, would be laid off as of the end of the summer.

I went back through the plant toward the exit that led to the hourly parking lot and ran into Big Dave and another maintenance guy near the body shop by Billy's old workstation. We looked around. Someone had hung two empty boots from the rafters with a sign reading THE LAST WORKER.

The maintenance guy with Dave had a final thought.

"Maybe they will put something else in this plant and call everyone back."

# EPILOGUE

Over the next long year they took apart the Scarborough Van Plant. I would pass by every so often and park outside the gate at the back, where the hourly parking lot used to be, where weeds quickly sprouted in the asphalt cracks and the white lines faded, bleached bones in the sun. On one occasion half of the missile-like stacks on the roof had been partly toppled, cannon aimed at the sky, poised to attack an invisible enemy. The plant was being ripped open like a lion's kill, and demolition had reached Trim 2. I could see the inside wall and the stairs leading up to the women's washroom. Back-hoes lurched through the great dead beast, clawing at the guts of our old working lives. Behind them the front-end loaders scooped up the rubble, depositing chunks of concrete over here, beams there, metal reinforcing rods over there. At the side of the plant our old wooden picnic tables were piled in a jumbled heap, bonfire fuel waiting for the weenies and marshmallows. One afternoon Cam and I sat in his van, surveying the scene. A load being dumped sent up a cloud of dust, momentarily soft-ening the edges like an Impressionist painting.

"There goes thirteen years of your working life," I said.

Cam mused, "Guess it was just a passing phase."

A month after the plant closed, I went to see Murray. I wanted him to make me a copy of the video he'd taped on the last couple of days at work. He lived in a town midway between Scarborough and Oshawa. We sat down at his kitchen table on a midweek morning, a time when most working people are at work.

The first week after we got laid off was the toughest, he said.

"I woke up at five A.M., rushing around, 'I'm going to be late,' and Julie says, 'What are you talking about? You don't have a job.' Then I just lost it one day, I think it was Thursday. I was sitting here at the table, and I started crying. 'I'm a failure,' and she said, 'It's not your fault; you're not a failure.' "

He'd put his name in for Oshawa. "I can't wait. I'm sick of this," he said.

A few months later I went to see the place that was now making "our" vans. I had friends in Windsor, a Canadian auto-plant town just across the border from Detroit, and I planned a trip to Flint, Michigan. I got the address of the plant that was now making our vans and set off on a one-hour drive from the border. I thought I might just walk into the plant at lunchtime, if the gates were open as they'd been at Scarborough, but then I thought it might be easier just to phone ahead and take a tour of the place. Yes, a friendly man informed me, there were tours; just check in at the main office.

I made the trip to Flint in my new Pontiac Grand Am (made in Lansing, Michigan). When I arrived at the huge factory, it was 11 A.M., the start of the lunch break. People were trickling through the gates, some heading for their vehicles doing the itchy-foot quickstep I knew so well and tearing automotive ass out toward the street and the local convenience-store beer cooler or watering hole, the infamous Mark's Lounge of Ben Hamper's book *Rivethead*.

The whole complex dated from before the fifties, and it looked as if GM didn't spruce up its offices more than once every forty years. I entered an unusual round lobby that was completely empty and was faced with a large desk on which sat a telephone. Behind the desk, steps led up to double doors. They were locked. I picked up the phone and dialed the extension of the man who was supposed to give tours, but got his voice mail.

Now what? I didn't know whom else to call, so I sat down on some benches along the curved walls. Then I walked up to the glass doors and peered in, but couldn't see anyone—just a hallway and heavy doors that probably led into the plant. I went back and sat down. I phoned again, got voice mail again. Two men came out of the double doors, down the steps, glanced at me, a bit curiously my imagination said (I was dressed in sweatshirt and jeans, autoworker clothes), and went out the front door. The double doors swung shut rather slowly behind them.

I had to wait only another fifteen minutes before another man came out, and as soon as he'd passed outside, I darted to the double doors and with a couple of inches to spare grabbed one before it shut. I pushed through the inner doors and—no *slam, bang, crash*. It was fairly quiet. I looked around quickly, trying to get my bearings. I was in a large, open space, the assembly line right in front of me. It wasn't as advanced as Oshawa, no AGVs gliding around the floor, just a regular ol' drag-chain assembly line, but the place looked a lot cleaner than Scarborough. Judging from the condition of the trucks, I was toward the end of the line. I began walking, not sure where I was going, just sure I didn't want to be seen wandering. I passed a couple of supervisors, but no one stopped me. They barely seemed to see me.

I set off down an aisle, passing people working on a motor line that looked just like ours. They've even got some of our racks! I thought, recognizing some furniture from Scarborough. The eating area was cleaner than ours, and it had molded plastic tables and chairs, not our taped and banged-up wooden tables and benches. A TV suspended over the eating area ran GM news on what looked like a closed-circuit channel. Retirees would be meeting in Lansing. Auto stocks were higher that day.

On the final line I stopped to talk to a woman who was checking the truck for missing parts by waving some kind of electronic wand over them—a function I didn't recall seeing in Scarborough.

"Hi. I'm visiting from Scarborough—the old van plant. They closed our plant to bring the vans here."

■

The woman nodded. She didn't seem terribly surprised that some-one would pop up next to her.

"Your plant was old. It was all old."

I introduced myself and asked what her name was. Margie Wallace, she said, and she'd been working at GM since 1972.

"What's it like to work here?" I asked.

"It's gotten better since I started. It's cleaner," she said.

Were people angry, I asked, when GM shut the Flint plant down a few years ago, before they announced the vans were coming to Flint? "We tried to make 'em better so we'd get something else," Margie re-plied, mentioning the concept of people working in teams at GM. For her these ideas had worked, since she obviously had a job again, but she didn't know why GM was putting the vans in Flint for just two years, then moving production to a plant in Missouri. I told her some Scarbor-ough people had taken buyouts and waved good-bye to GM, and she responded, "I wouldn't take no buyout."

I thanked her and continued on my journey, striding with a fixed, purposeful look on my face. I went up to a bathroom, and it was cleaner, too. They really had let Scarborough go in the last year and a half. Back down on the floor I passed by the front of the plant again, this time farther down, and saw a big display on the history of the Flint facility. It had opened in July 1947, making Chevrolet cars and trucks.

Maybe our first family car was built here, I wondered, looking at a photo of the 1958 assembly line holding cars that looked a lot like the 1956 Chevy that was the first family car I remembered. I was jotting down all this information on a little notepad I'd brought, and no one bothered me. I set off again, toward the beginning of the line, and found the body shop. It was, of course, cleaner and quieter than Scarborough. My God, we'd worked in a slum. At the door-hang station, a young man was sitting on a stool, reading a newspaper, his head resting on his hand. I went over to him. He raised tired eyes and said his name was Ted. The plant was working flat out: six days a week, ten hours a day.

"The metal guys work from three-thirty A.M. to six-thirty P.M.," he said.

"So you have lots of overtime money and are too dead to enjoy it?" I asked. He nodded and gave a short laugh. I wasn't surprised to read some months later that a wildcat strike had erupted over excessive over-time.

I didn't see any of my old jobs, and I didn't want to get lost. I felt a little shocked to see our vans moving on another line, the big steel cans I'd known so intimately for a year and a half, the hundreds of sidemarkers I'd held in my hands, the thousands of windows I'd hefted. Those trucks belonged to us. People I knew should be climbing all over them, not these strangers. As I headed for the exit, I passed the display. It said that Flint could make up to a hundred seventy thousand vans per year. Scarborough had maxed out at ninety thousand. How could I re-main indignant? The numbers were the coffin nails. Of course, if GM had figured out how to sell more vans, they could have built a whole new van plant in Scarborough, instead of consolidating capacity in Flint.

A few weeks later Maria and I organized our reunion picnic and a couple dozen people said they'd come, but on the day itself only Ivan and his family, Bummer, Bruce, Stretch, and Jan Lennon, with her husband, showed up. This, in addition to Maria and Tom and Cam and myself. Maria and I were disappointed, but we told each other that everyone was having a fine time, and the food was good, and didn't we have nice weather? I knew then that the Scarborough experience for me was definitely over and that I would not be seeing again most of the people I'd worked with for eighteen months. Like Army service, a com-mon cause had brought us together and created some intense experi-ences amid long stretches of tedium, but when it was over, we scattered. Many people maintained their van-plant friendships, but many more floated apart. That was one reason the shutdown was so upsetting— people who had been working side by side for years knew they probably wouldn't be that close again.

■

Cam was called to work in Oshawa at one of the car plants, and I went to meet him there one lunch hour. I ran into Bummer, who characterized Scarborough as "the old folks' home" compared to Oshawa, where the AGV system meant much less downtime. I also saw Ivan, who ended up in the body shop, his great fear, but the Oshawa body shop was not the jungle hell of the Scarborough body shop. Robots did the welding, and humans fed parts to the robots. No one got clawhand or white finger from gripping triggers on fifty-pound welding guns two hundred times a day. "Is not heavy, Solly, but is fast," Ivan said. Nevertheless, he'd gone out on comp for a few weeks with a twisted back.

Rob was called to Oshawa and found himself back on the line, working on radiators in the truck plant. "You get thirty to thirty-five seconds to do your job, and if you don't do it in that time, the lights flash. They'll come down on you about that," he said.

Neal Callahan was called to the truck plant to install bumpers—up to sixty-eight per hour. "I'm back on the line with a bang, and my brain is fried. I don't think I knew what production work was before this. Jesus, my hands . . ." They worked an eight-hour day, with two ten-minute breaks and twenty minutes for lunch. How does a meal fit into twenty minutes? "Well, you learn to eat fast," he said.

Skinny Bruce the Rock Star bolted tires onto Luminas—one every thirty seconds. "I really screwed up my hands. They were swollen, and I couldn't play," he said.

Barry Harvey was working in Oshawa. "I started doing engine harnesses, and going home in the car I was crying. I said, 'This isn't human.'" Jack Morgan had been working near him. "I say hello to him, and he's behind," Barry said.

I ran into Laverne as I waited to cross the street with the stream of people coming off shift. The Ontario government was rejigging its health-care budget, closing hospitals it considered redundant, and lots of nurses were out of work. She hadn't been able to find anything in nursing, so there she was on the line in Oshawa.

Nick, Bonnie, and Travis transferred to the GM plant in London,

Ontario, about 120 miles west of Toronto, which made locomotives and armored personnel carriers. Although Bonnie had vowed to leave GM behind, she said she hadn't been able to find anything, though she was continuing studies in geriatric work. Lots of Scarborough people were out there, Bonnie said. It was beyond commuting distance, which meant uprooting lives, renting or selling houses and moving with the work. Maria worked in London for a while, then retired to spend summers at the cottage, visit the boys, and travel with Tom to Las Vegas and Florida.

Billy Davis left GM, glad to be done with factory work, and went to work in the maintenance department of a local TV station. Ed Donohue got a computer-programming job at the Hospital for Sick Children in Toronto and blossomed in a new career. Lance and his wife had another baby, and he got a supervisor job in an auto-parts plant.

Working at GM produced a marvelous and completely unexpected bonus: Cam Peters and I were married in May 1995. Five months after our plant closed, General Motors called him to work in Oshawa, then laid him off after twelve weeks. In 1994 he was called to work in London and was laid off in March 1996. After two years with no recall, he took a buyout and has started his own courier business.

One year after the plant closed, I accepted a job as a reporter with *The Wall Street Journal.* Eight months later I was still on GM's list, and I was called to work in Oshawa. I had to walk a few steps down the road not taken, to see where I would have gone had I been a real autoworker. I took a day off and reported at seven o'clock on a rainy morning to the personnel office, where one other person arrived for an assignment—Jan Lennon. We greeted each other with delight and bumbled our way through the huge complex to one of the car plants. As usual, the supervisors hadn't known we were coming, and it took a while to get us sorted out. I was assigned to learn a job that involved pulling seat belts through the seats and installing a bolt under the seat. I wasn't completely out of shape. The gun nestled in my hand, a familiar weapon, but I was sore and breathing hard after a hundred cars. Even then I didn't feel panic. "I'm not too strong at this job yet," I told the man who was training me.

The job was timed at fifty-five seconds. If we were too slow, a light flashed and a buzzer sounded. Jan and I met for a drink after work. She'd been working in a locksmithing shop when she got the call from GM. It had paid half of what she could make in the car plants, and she had a daughter to marry off in a year.

I'd been up since 5 A.M. and remembered this kind of fatigue. I said good-bye to GM for good that day, knowing that if I were to work at something other than journalism, it wouldn't be production labor. Once was enough. Besides, it was hard to grow old in those jobs. In the ensuing months, looking back on it all, I was surprised at how the experience affected me. I had thought I would simply observe and report, not become part of the story. I found that I could endure a physical and mental test. When I think I can't go any further now, I can. I'm a little tougher, not quite as nice anymore. I've gained a wealth of insight into human labor. I need to hold my temper in check when a white-collar friend asks, as happened recently, "Do those people really earn their money?"

I'm talking to the CEOs and the public relations people again, but the stories I really like to do involve, as always, people and their communities: an Inuit who's an Internet service provider in the Arctic, a bookbinder who creates masterpieces from leather and gold leaf in a shed in the Ontario countryside, a ferry worker watching his job disappear as a bridge to Prince Edward Island rises over the waves. I try not to treat people as less worthy of my attention if they don't have a title before their names. I know the name of many a CEO's secretary. I greet Ramón and Yasmeen as they take orders in the sandwich shop downstairs in the skyscraper. Before I worked at GM I wouldn't necessarily have learned their names. When I look out the window of an office building, I know more than I did before about that factory on the lake shore. For the rest of my life, nobody will be able to tell me I don't know what hard work really is. I've returned to my old, air-conditioned existence, but not with a sense of relief. I'm still restless, still curious about other lives, other work.